Wildlife Gardening
for Everyone and Everything

Second Edition

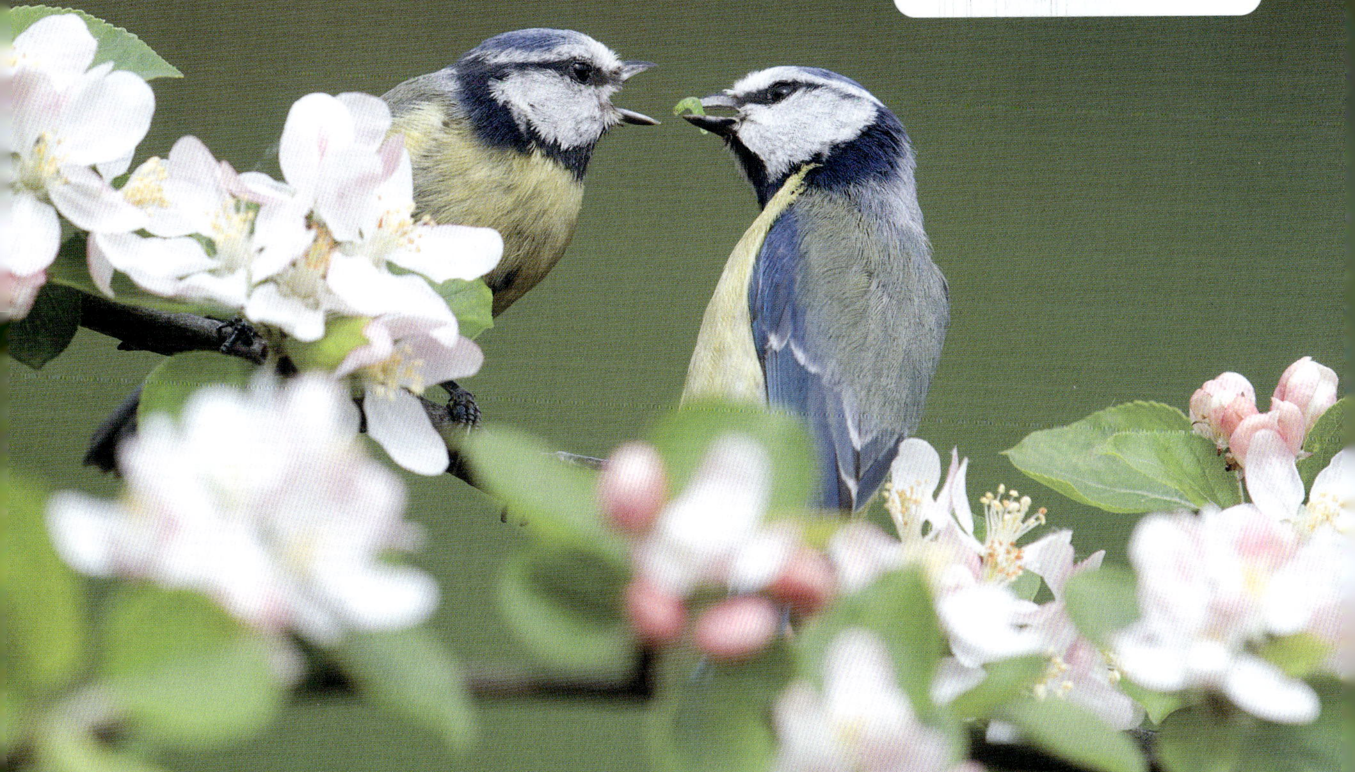

KATE BRADBURY

BLOOMSBURY WILDLIFE
LONDON · OXFORD · NEW YORK · NEW DELHI · SYDNEY

BLOOMSBURY WILDLIFE
Bloomsbury Publishing Plc
50 Bedford Square, London, WC1B 3DP, UK
Bloomsbury Publishing Ireland Limited,
29 Earlsfort Terrace, Dublin 2, D02 AY28, Ireland

BLOOMSBURY, BLOOMSBURY WILDLIFE and the Diana logo are trademarks of
Bloomsbury Publishing Plc

First published in the United Kingdom 2026

Copyright © Kate Bradbury, 2018, 2026

Kate Bradbury has asserted her right under the Copyright, Designs and Patents Act, 1988, to be identified as Author of this work

For legal purposes the Photo Credits on p.192 constitute an extension of this copyright page

All rights reserved. No part of this publication may be: i) reproduced or transmitted in any form, electronic or mechanical, including photocopying, recording or by means of any information storage or retrieval system without prior permission in writing from the publishers; or ii) used or reproduced in any way for the training, development or operation of artificial intelligence (AI) technologies, including generative AI technologies. The rights holders expressly reserve this publication from the text and data mining exception as per Article 4(3) of the Digital Single Market Directive (EU) 2019/790

Bloomsbury Publishing Plc does not have any control over, or responsibility for, any third-party websites referred to or in this book. All internet addresses given in this book were correct at the time of going to press. The author and publisher regret any inconvenience caused if addresses have changed or sites have ceased to exist, but can accept no responsibility for any such changes

A catalogue record for this book is available from the British Library

Library of Congress Cataloguing-in-Publication data has been applied for

ISBN: PB:978-1-3994-2267-3; ePDF: 978-1-3994-2265-9; ePub: 978-1-3994-2266-6

2 4 6 8 10 9 7 5 3 1

Designed by Rod Teasdale
Printed and bound in Dubai by Oriental Press

To find out more about our authors and books visit www.bloomsbury.com and sign up for our newsletters
For product safety related questions contact productsafety@bloomsbury.com

Royal Horticultural Society
Publisher Helen Griffin
Editor Simon Maughan
Head of Editorial Tom Howard
Consultant Helen Bostock

The Wildlife Trusts
Head of Communications Joanna Richards
Content Officer Thomas Hibbert
Digital Fundraising and Communications Officer Jamey Douglas

Contents

Why should we garden with nature in mind?   4

The principles of wildlife gardening   9

Wildlife gardening for...
- Pollinators   25
- Bees   35
- Butterflies and moths   62
- Wasps   75
- Beetles   84
- True flies   92
- True bugs   100
- Other minibeasts   108
- Birds   116
- Amphibians and reptiles   135
- Mammals   147
- Fungi   179

Climate change   182

Identifying and recording wildlife   185

Glossary   188
Resources   188
Acknowledgements   189
Index   190
Photograph credits   192

Why should we garden with nature in mind?

The United Kingdom is one of the most nature-depleted countries in the world. According to the last State of Nature report, nearly one in six UK species is at risk of extinction, and overall, species populations have declined by an average of 19 per cent since 1970.

On average, invertebrates are found in 13 per cent fewer locations in the UK than they were in 1970. As a result, some insect groups are suffering steep declines. Pollinators like bees, hoverflies and moths have decreased by an average of 18 per cent, while predatory species like ladybirds and certain beetles have dropped by 34 per cent. Over the same time, more than half of our native flowering plants, mosses, liverworts and hornworts have vanished from areas where they once thrived.

On land and in freshwater, these losses are primarily driven by industrial-scale agriculture and the greenhouse gases we've emitted since the Industrial Revolution. At sea and along our coasts, overfishing, climate change and development are the main culprits.

But decline is not inevitable. By changing how we manage land, we can create space for nature to recover and thrive alongside us. This means adopting more nature-friendly farming practices and restoring vital habitats like peat bogs, meadows and forests. It also means respecting – and in some cases reinstating – natural processes that help mitigate climate change, for example beavers helping to prevent floods, and bison enriching the soil with carbon.

Ultimately, we need to rewild – not just our landscapes, but our relationship with nature. We don't need to return to a more primitive way of life, but we do need to give space back to nature, reconnect fragmented landscapes and tread more lightly on the planet we all share. And if we choose to work with nature, we can restore ecosystems, draw down carbon and secure a healthier future for everyone. This process can begin at home, in our own gardens.

◂ My friend Helen's garden in Hove in Sussex. Sparrow nest boxes, pollinator-friendly borders and still space for her young family to play.

What is rewilding?

▲ Wildlife gardens comprise a variety of different habitats for a range of species.

Rewilding is an approach to conservation that seeks to restore natural ecosystems by allowing them to function with minimal human interference, returning to ancient, natural ways of managing the land. Up until a few hundred to about 1,000 years ago, large herbivores such as wild boar, deer, horses and aurochs (wild cattle) roamed freely in the British Isles, alongside lynx and wolves that helped regulate their numbers. These animals played a crucial role in shaping landscapes – trampling and rootling the ground, disturbing the soil, browsing plant growth and fertilising the soil, which, in turn, supported a vast web of plants, insects and fungi. Everything existed in equilibrium.

Since then, human activity, such as hunting, deforestation, development and industrial farming, has wiped out or confined many of these animals, leading to habitat loss, degraded ecosystems and unchecked deer populations that damage woodlands. Rewilding seeks to reverse this by reintroducing key species and letting nature take the lead. A well-known example of rewilding in the UK is at Knepp Wildland in Sussex, where free-roaming longhorn cattle (similar to aurochs), Tamworth pigs (similar to wild boar) and Exmoor ponies (similar to tarpans, extinct wild horses) rub shoulders with wild deer. Together, they mimic the role of their ancient ancestors, creating a rich mosaic of habitats where wildlife flourishes.

Rewilding isn't just for vast landscapes – it can also influence how we garden. That doesn't mean hanging up our boots and letting nature take its course. It means working with nature by mimicking the roles of free-roaming animals via mindful pruning (grazing), weeding (browsing) and digging (rootling). Even small changes – like leaving some seedheads when removing others, allowing deadwood to accumulate or letting some grass grow long – can create thriving microhabitats for garden wildlife.

It's often said that gardens replicate the woodland edge with its complex habitats of trees, shrubs and herbaceous plants, grass and perhaps a water body. To further mirror this habitat, you can let piles of plant material accumulate in corners or use logs and branches as part of a natural border. You can drill holes in your fence posts, erect a bee hotel to replicate the work of wood-boring beetles, or let grass grow long to mimic a woodland glade.

Rewilding isn't about gardening less, it's about working with nature, not against it. Most gardeners who want to help wildlife are already using 'rewilding' practices to increase our garden biodiversity, we just might use different language now. Off to prune the roses? Surely you mean you're heading out for a quick browse?

How can gardening for wildlife help?

In the UK, gardens account for less than two per cent of the total land mass. Sounds insignificant, doesn't it? Especially when compared to the 70 per cent of UK land mass that's occupied by farmland. Yet the total area of gardens in the UK is estimated to be 433,000 ha (4,330 km²) – around a fifth the size of Wales and equivalent to nearly three times the size of all of our National Nature Reserves put together. Think of all the homes for wildlife we could make in that much space.

And, since 87 per cent of UK households have a garden, gardens are our easiest route back to nature. We don't need to travel or pay an entrance fee to reach the spaces outside our back door, or the nature in them, and we don't need fancy clothes or kit to enjoy them. Often, we can simply sit in the comfort of our homes and observe nature right outside our windows. I think that's really powerful.

Nature needs our help. If we garden with wildlife in mind and encourage nature back into our outdoor spaces, I believe more of us would connect to the natural world. More of us would then push for nature-friendly farming practices and buy organic food, and we'd think twice about taking part in activities we know harm the environment. We would have more empathy for, and feel more responsibility for, the species that live among us. This could mean we all look for more ways to protect species (swift bricks in new builds, anyone?). And this wouldn't just benefit nature – this would benefit our physical and mental health, too.

Our gardens may represent only a small fraction of the country's land mass, but they're anything but insignificant. They bring us cheek-by-jowl with foxes and hedgehogs, bees, birds and butterflies. They

▲ Even a paved garden can benefit wildlife if filled with plants.

provide a window into a world that is suffering but that we can help recover. In our gardens we can provide food, shelter and water for a number of different species that can then repopulate the wider landscape. By connecting them to each other and the local environment, we can make our gardens part of the wilder space, we can extend their reach into the fields and the forests around us. The RHS estimates there are 30 million gardens in the UK. That's 30 million opportunities to help nature, 30 million opportunities to fight back against ecological vandalism and a lack of care in the wider countryside. Wildlife gardening isn't just a nice thing to do, it's also important and life-affirming. It brings us closer to the natural world and awakens us to all of the things that need fixing. Above all, wildlife gardening makes us happy; it brings us joy and distracts us from the day-to-day. It lowers blood pressure and reduces stress. What's not to like?

What's new in this edition?

This book is for everyone who wants to help nature, whether they have a garden, allotment, patio, balcony or windowsill. Like the first edition, this book includes information about garden wildlife, advice on how to attract it and identification (ID) parades to help you identify the species that visit. But, with several more years' worth of knowledge, some advice has changed.

The wonderful thing about science is that it's constantly evolving to make us more knowledgeable and therefore help us to make better decisions. We now know that, as well as mealworms, sunflower hearts and peanuts are bad for hedgehogs, due to a poor calcium-phosphorus ratio that can lead to bone breakages. Thanks to the work of John Little, we know a lot more about creating sand-based habitats for solitary mining bees. We also know that bird feeding isn't quite what it was cracked up to be – in fact, much to my own sadness as that of others, I argue that we should consider no longer feeding birds in our gardens (see pages 122-23 for details).

You'll also find new sections on climate change, fungi and recording wildlife in your garden. There's also more now on pesticides and peat, along with new ideas and perspectives for those who want to attract as many species as possible. What will the coming years bring? Hopefully more wildlife.

Until then, happy wildlife gardening.

The principles of wildlife gardening

To bring more nature into your garden, you'll need to fulfil the same three basic needs for as many species as possible, by providing them with food, shelter and water. There's not much difference in your needs and those of the hedgehogs that roam your garden at night. We need somewhere safe to sleep, rest, raise young and shelter from a particularly heavy burst of rain, and we need food to eat and water for drinking and bathing.

Food, shelter and water come in a variety of guises to meet the needs of the species they support. Food could be a flower or a berry, some dead wood or other decaying matter. It could be another species in the food web, like a tadpole, mosquito, moth or aphid. It could be leaves and grass. Shelter can be a log pile or compost heap, a dense hedge or a pond. Water is water – what varies is how it's delivered. In a bird bath? In a pond? As droplets on grass stems? The more species you cater for in your garden and the greater the variety of opportunities it provides for them, the more wildlife will visit your garden – it's that simple.

Some wildlife gardens can be messy, but they don't have to be. They can be full of native trees and shrubs, but they don't have to be. Like all gardens, wildlife gardens can be anything you want. You don't need to compromise to create a wildlife garden but the more you do, the better the results for nature. If you have a bit of mess here and there, overwintering invertebrates or birds looking for grubs to eat will take advantage of that mess. Native shrubs and trees provide food and habitat for more species than non-native species, so if you have a small garden, bear in mind that native species will meet the needs of your local wildlife more and better than non-natives can.

Your garden can still work for you, too, and if you use this book to help you create as much food, water and shelter as you can in the space you have available, you'll have a busy wildlife garden in no time.

Food

Virtually everything in your garden is food for something starting with the bacteria and fungi in the soil, all the way up to mammals and birds. However, plants form the ecological foundation of our gardens.

As a general rule, the greater variety of plants we can grow in our gardens, the more wildlife species we will attract. Yet the species of plants you choose are also very important.

Grow food plants

We know that flowers provide nectar and pollen for bees and other pollinators, but less is written about the needs of foliage feeders – the caterpillars and other species that graze on the leaves and stems of herbaceous plants, trees and shrubs. Most of these do so little damage to plants that you wouldn't even notice their presence. The majority of the known caterpillar food plants are native to the British Isles and these are the ones I list in this book. They can be incorporated in your garden in many ways:

- A native wildlife hedge
- A single shrub, such as hawthorn, planted at the back of a border
- A wildflower meadow, which also includes native grasses
- A lawn allowed to grow long where clover, dandelions and vetches can thrive
- A container planted with primroses, foxgloves and dandelions

See the Resources section on page 189 for caterpillar food plant lists compiled by the wildlife charity **Butterfly Conservation**.

Nectar and pollen

Flowering plants provide nectar and pollen for bees and other pollinators. Aim to grow a diverse range of flowering plants for as long as you can manage – in your borders, on the roof of your shed, in pots, in cracks in the walls … anywhere you have space! Here are a few suggestions:

- Spring flowers such as winter heather, crocus and primroses for emerging bumblebee queens
- Simple, open flowers, where you can see the centre of the flower (avoid double flowers like this dahlia)
- Late-flowering blooms such as sedums and *Verbena bonariensis*, which help insects feed up before overwintering or migrating south
- Leguminous plants, such as beans, peas and vetches, which typically have better quality pollen than other plants
- Flowering trees, for abundant nectar and pollen in a small area

See Resources on page 189 for the RHS Plants for Pollinators lists.

Berries, seeds and nuts

Growing as many fruiting shrubs and trees as possible will provide birds with the food they need to sustain them in winter, while invertebrates are overwintering. This provides a more reliable and sustainable source of food than, say, supplementary bird food, which studies suggest is becoming increasingly problematic (see page 122 for details). Many berries are loaded with antioxidants, which are thought to help migrating species deal with the physical stresses of migration – many species will feast on berries, hips and crab apples before embarking on their long journey. Plants include rowan, hawthorn, ivy, holly, crab apple, shrub and climbing roses, and guelder rose. Most berries are either red or black, and it's thought the darker berries offer birds the best source of antioxidants.

Leaving seed-bearing plants and trees such as sunflower, teasel, birch, alder and hyssop may attract a wide range of birds and small mammals, while growing hazel and other nut-bearing species will ensure the local mice and voles (and therefore the species that eat them) are well catered for. You'll be amazed how many different plants will attract birds if you leave their seedheads standing. We all know teasels and sunflowers provide seeds for birds, but buddleia, phlomis, ornamental grasses and lavender seeds are also on the menu. Looking back to the garden as a mimic of the woodland edge, leaving plants intact through to spring will provide a natural, sustainable source of food for a host of different birds and small mammals, just as nature intended.

For more on plants for birds, see page 120.

Water

Water is essential to garden wildlife, from the birds and mammals that need to drink and bathe, to the amphibians and invertebrates that use water for breeding. If your garden is large enough, you may even encourage species, such as grass snakes and grey herons, to use your pond to hunt for prey. Whatever size your garden, patio or allotment, it's easy to provide water, for example:

- A birdbath. Leave a stone in it, as honeybees may also use it for drinking and will need a prop to rest on.
- A container pond. Build a pile of stones outside the pond to make a 'frog ladder' if you need to.

◂ A male blackbird takes a dip in the shallows of a garden pond.

▴ Garden ponds are perfect habitat for baby common frogs, like this one hiding among the pond weed.

- A small, shallow pond. Shallows are where most species live, including tadpoles and aquatic insect larvae. If you only have room for a small pond, then make it no deeper than 45cm with a marginal depth of just 5–10cm. This will also enable birds to bathe and hedgehogs to get in and out easily.
- A large pond with a maximum depth of around 60cm to 1m, graduating to a large, shallow shelf for all the above reasons. A large pond may attract toads, larger species of dragonfly or even ducks.
- A bog garden, which can be built around a pond, on its own in a border or even created in a large container.

Shelter

In a nutshell, shelter is simply space where wildlife can safely breed, sleep, overwinter or avoid inclement weather. It can be anything from a little gap between two fence panels or a collection of plant pots piled up next to your shed, to an overgrown hedge or large tree. Almost every part of your garden can provide shelter for some creature or other; the key is to provide more shelter for as many different species as possible, and to respect the wildlife that's taking shelter at any one time. So choosing not to empty your compost bin when slow-worms might be breeding, trim hedges in bird-nesting season or strim grass when hedgehogs might be sleeping is all part and parcel of the choices we make as wildlife gardeners. We create habitats (shelter), and we maintain them in the interests of the wildlife we want to attract.

Virtually every garden can be improved on in this area – all of us can create more shelter. If you have a bare wall or fence, grow a climber or two up it, so birds might nest or insects might bask or feed. Let areas of your lawn grow a bit longer to provide shelter for beetles, pile leaves into a corner, or throw sticks and prunings behind a shrub – see over the page for more ideas. Look at your garden through the eyes of a frog or bird or bee – where would you take shelter if you were them? Ask yourself: what would the woodland edge do? Could you make changes to make your garden mimic more natural habitats and bring more wildlife in? Of course you could!

Hedge

A mixed hedge will attract anything from voles, mice and hedgehogs to birds and insects. It will act as a 'shelter belt', providing a wind-free spot where insects can congregate (and where bats can come

▲ Hedges provide birds with a safe place to build their nests and raise their chicks.

and eat them). Birds will dive into a hedge for safety; hedgehogs will breed or hibernate in the leaf litter that builds up beneath a hedge; caterpillars will eat the leaves – and birds will eat the caterpillars; bees will visit the flowers, fertilising them to help them become fruit or nuts; and then birds and small mammals will come to eat the fruit and nuts. A hedge is an ecosystem in its own right; it's a habitat for many and varied creatures, for a number of different reasons. A hedge makes the perfect shelter.

Where space allows, plant a native hedge including plants such as hawthorn, beech, spindle, hazel, holly, field maple and buckthorn. Thread climbers such as honeysuckle, dog rose and clematis through the hedge and you add interest and wildlife value. Allowing leaf litter to pile up beneath it will create five-star accommodation for hedgehogs.

Compost heap

By finding room for a compost heap, we are creating shelter for a huge range of wildlife. The accumulation of plant and kitchen waste feeds bacteria, yeasts and fungi. These will attract detritivores (animals that feed on dead and decaying material), such as worms, millipedes and woodlice, and the creatures that eat them. If you're lucky, you may attract nesting bumblebees, hedgehogs, grass snakes and slow-worms. Frogs and toads may spend winter here. There's a chance you might attract a rat, but if you act quickly you can sort this out before it becomes a problem (see page 169).

All compost heaps attract wildlife, but a large, open heap is easiest for wildlife to access. Contain it in a slatted wooden box or assemble one using pallets, and the birds, bees, hedgehogs and slow-worms will be able to enter and exit easily. Plastic bins tend to attract less wildlife but warm up more quickly and, as such, attract different species. On my allotment I have five compost heaps – two contained in bays made using pallets and three in bespoke plastic compost bins. The pallet heaps attract voles, amphibians, birds and beetles, while the plastic bins are full of breeding slow-worms. You may even attract grass snakes to your compost bin.

Decomposing plants

While composting plants creates fantastic shelter for wildlife, *not* composting them can be just as beneficial. Simply leaving ornamental borders to rot down naturally can provide lots of nooks and crannies for creatures such as beetles, caterpillars, tiny flies and ladybirds, which you will find anywhere from inside seed heads to tucked down in hollow plant stems. You could also employ the 'chop and drop' strategy, whereby you simply cut plants back but leave their foliage to die down around the plant, or chuck it roughly to the back of the border. This is a more natural process than collecting 'waste' and taking it to the compost heap, and benefits the soil and the species that use it.

◂ Seed heads provide food for birds and shelter for insects.

▾ This 'dead hedge' provides shelter for a variety of species such as small mammals, insects and birds.

Leaf, log and twig piles

Habitat piles made of leaves, logs and twigs or prunings recreate conditions found in woodland and therefore provide shelter for a wide range of species, including hedgehogs and amphibians, and the invertebrates they eat. In particular, dead wood is an amazing habitat for a huge number of species, including some types of beetle which rely on this for breeding. Simply choose a quiet corner where you can create a pile and leave it undisturbed for several years. If making a log pile, remember that some species need wood that is fully or partially buried in the ground, others need sun or shade, and some, such as the wasp beetle (*Clytus arietis*), need dead wood at height. So, if you have the space, try to provide as much variety as possible. This means starting your dead wood pile below ground so that some is completely buried and some is partially buried, while there's plenty left on the surface. Fixing some to a trellis or laid safely on a flat roof caters to other species. Having dead wood in both sun and shade will attract different types of solitary bee and beetle, along with other species such as small mammals, reptiles and amphibians.

Dead wood can take many forms, but common examples include a log pile, dead hedge (either low to the ground or piled high), and logs randomly placed in a border, which provide visual interest in winter but are obscured by plants in summer. As in life, different species of dead wood attract different species of invertebrate, so try to add a range of tree and shrub types to your wood pile. In my neighbourhood there is often tree work taking place, where trees are pollarded or (sadly) chopped down. If I'm in the right place at the right time I will ask for a log or two – most tree surgeons and neighbours will happily oblige. As such, my woodpile is as varied as the woodland edge itself, with logs and branches of elder, willow, hawthorn, oak, apple, walnut, birch and cherry. I love seeing the different wood and bark types in my pile and observing the different fungi that colonise each species. Making a cage using chicken wire can help contain a leaf pile if you need it (just make sure you leave a hole 12–15cm in diameter for hedgehogs and amphibians to enter and exit easily). Top it up as and when you need to.

▲ A mixed native hedge is the perfect habitat for anything from hedgehogs to moths, bats and birds.

Long grass and meadows

If left unmown, your lawn can become a wonderful wildlife habitat, and everything from bees and butterflies to birds and small mammals will quickly move in to take advantage of it. You needn't abandon the look of your whole lawn – a patch in an out-of-the-way corner or space around a tree will do admirably. If you have room, you could go the whole hog and plant a hay meadow. See page 67 for details.

Don't be too tidy

Your garden doesn't have to be messy to attract wildlife, but remember that messy doesn't have to mean 'unkempt'. Even small concessions can benefit wildlife, from the birds that feed from unpruned seed heads to the toads eating invertebrates among leaf litter in the borders. But don't panic – tidy gardens can still cater for wildlife. Some inconspicuous small changes include:

- Leaving piles of plant pots behind your shed, to shelter spiders and other invertebrates
- Cutting back your hedge less often to provide more cover for birds and possibly allow overwintering butterfly eggs to develop
- Leaving ornamental borders to shrink into themselves in autumn and winter, rather than cutting everything back, to provide overwintering sites for insects
- Mowing your lawn less often to let clover and trefoils flower for bees

All of the above will help to create shelter for wildlife. Without shelter, you don't have a wildlife garden. Shelter also includes bespoke habitats you create specifically for certain species – the bird boxes you put up to attract tits, the hedgehog hibernaculum, the bee hotel. There's a huge range of such items to make and buy to provide shelter for wildlife – the key to success is to install these once you've improved your garden habitats.

Create wildlife corridors

Many wildlife species have greater habitat needs than you can provide in your garden. Indeed, your garden is part of a wider network of knitted-together habitats, rather than a standalone territory. It is therefore vital that you allow wildlife into your garden in the first place.

Fences and walls are not particularly helpful to wildlife, especially hedgehogs, which are sometimes forced to make a long journey out onto the road and back in again simply to access the garden next door. A 15cm hole at the bottom of the fence on either side of your garden is all that's needed. Encourage your neighbours to do the same and you will have a whole network of linked gardens so that hedgehogs and other animals never need to travel on the road again.

▼ Hedgehog highways are vital to ensure hedgehogs can travel safely between gardens.

Avoid using pesticides

'Pesticide' is an umbrella term used to describe insecticides, fungicides and herbicides, designed to tackle 'problem' insects, plants and fungi. They can have a wider impact on wildlife, and there's a growing body of evidence that suggests pesticides are extremely harmful to species that aren't the intended target – even vertebrates like us.

Neonics and glyphosate

Neonicotinoids, or neonics for short, have been the subject of much debate over the last decade. Neonics are systemic agricultural insecticides that farmers sometimes use to treat seeds. The insecticides are absorbed after seedlings germinate so that any 'pests' that nibble on treated plants die. Unfortunately, pollinators that collect pollen or nectar from plants treated with neonics can also be harmed. Research conducted by Dave Goulson, professor at University of Sussex and ambassador of The Wildlife Trusts, found that bumblebees collected 'sub-lethal' doses of neonics when they visited plants that had been treated, but because the bumblebees took pollen and nectar back to their nest to feed the grubs, these initial doses quickly built up to a significant dosage. The study found that when bumblebee nests were exposed to neonics, they grew more slowly than nests that hadn't been exposed. And, in affected nests, the production of daughter queens (the next year's reproductive females) was reduced by 85 per cent. Other studies found that even small doses of neonics negatively impact bumblebees' ability to collect pollen and lay eggs and affect honeybees' ability to navigate back to their hives.

In 2018, neonics were banned for use in agriculture across Europe and the UK, but they are still available for home gardeners to use. At the time of writing, anyone can buy a bug spray and poison their garden and those that live in it. This means your bug spray, your rose guard and your vine weevil root wash contain neonics, unless stated organic or soap-based on the label. Look at the ingredients on the back of the bottle and you will likely find imidacloprid, thiamethoxam or clothianidin – all neonics – listed.

Glyphosate is the most commonly used weed killer worldwide and, although its use is becoming increasingly controversial, it is currently still available for use in agriculture and gardens in the UK. Its effect on wildlife is still being researched, but studies so far have found that glyphosate can leach into water, potentially polluting groundwater, rivers or lakes. It's been shown to be harmful to fungi that live near plant roots and can also increase the severity or re-emergence of

crop diseases, potentially by changing the balance between beneficial and harmful microbes in the soil. Some studies also found that glyphosate had a negative impact on the reproduction, movement and activity of earthworms.

Choose carefully when buying plants

Another study, by Professor Dave Goulson at the University of Sussex, found that plants sold at garden centres, DIY stores and supermarkets contained a mixture of fungicides and insecticides. Many of these plants were labelled as 'bee-friendly' yet their labels failed to mention they also had pesticides present in the compost, roots, plant stems and flowers. In the study, 76 per cent of plants tested contained at least one insecticide, and 38 per cent contained two or more insecticides. One flowering heather – a favourite nectar plant for bumblebees – contained five different insecticides and five different fungicides.

Alternatives to pesticides

Remove unwanted visitors by hand
You can use your hose to wash off large clusters of aphids. But do bear in mind that the ladybirds, hoverflies and lacewings that eat them may already have started doing so, and that you may be washing these predators off your plants, too. Conducting nightly patrols can help reduce numbers of slugs and snails.

Encourage insect predators
Encourage more insects such as hoverflies, ladybirds and lacewings into your garden. Ladybirds and lacewings should just turn up anywhere aphids are present, but hoverflies can be encouraged by planting open flowers such as daisies and umbellifers (see page 95).

Use biological methods of control
You can buy nematodes to kill slugs, vine weevils, chafer larvae and leatherjackets. You can also buy native ladybirds, parasitic flies, wasps and other insects to control insects in problem spots such as greenhouses.

Buy resistant cultivars
Some plants are more resistant to insect attack and diseases than others. This is particularly true of roses and some vegetable cultivars.

Remove diseased material
By picking up fallen leaves and fruits of infected plants you can limit the chances of reinfection the following season. Avoid composting the infected material as this could reinfect your garden when returned as a mulch. Burn it or dispose of it in your green waste bin instead.

Weed by hand
Annuals can be removed by hoeing, hand-pulling or hand-weeding with a fork. Perennials can be dug out, including as much root as possible. You can also use a flame or heat gun to scorch unwanted plants growing between paving slabs and on driveways (remove insects first).

Mulch soil
Mulching with home-made compost, leaf mould, bark or wood chips can smother unwanted plants. However, bear in mind that compost may contain unexpected seeds. Compost and leaf mould also benefits wildlife, increasing worm and other invertebrate activity.

▲ Try removing unwanted plants by hand to avoid harming or killing garden wildlife with chemicals.

▶ Spot-on flea treatments for dogs and cats could introduce pesticides into your garden.

◀ Lacewings, like this common green lacewing (*Chrysoperla carnea*), feed on aphids.

Since this report was published in 2017, some retailers have asked their suppliers to stop using pesticides but there's a long way to go until all retailers follow suit. If you're in doubt, always ask a member of staff before buying a plant. If retailers can't confirm whether their suppliers still use neonics or any other pesticides, don't buy plants from them. When gardeners let retailers know they want to make informed choices before they buy garden products from their stores, it sends a clear message to retailers that consumers want more information about products before they'll purchase them.

Toxic chemicals in pet treatments

While not directly related to gardens, research conducted by Sussex University has exposed the dangers to wildlife of treating pets with flea and tick treatments. The chemicals (often also neonicotinoids) are frequently applied to pets and livestock in the form of shampoos, spot-treatments and sprays. These chemicals leach into the soil from farms, eventually ending up in rivers. They also wash off dogs that play in water bodies and wash off our hands down the sink and into waterways. The research found the toxic insecticide fipronil in 99 per cent of samples from 20 rivers.

So far, gardens haven't been studied, but if you regularly apply flea treatment to your pet, it would follow that these insecticides are present in your garden, and perhaps your pond.

Even more research (again, from Sussex University but funded by the charity Songbird Survival) has found that birds using pet fur to

line their nests are exposing pesticides to their chicks, and – not surprisingly – this is leading to an increased mortality rate of chicks.

Researchers collected 103 nests from blue tits and great tits, which were lined with fur, and detected 17 out of the 20 insecticides screened. All nests contained fipronil, and 89 per cent contained imidacloprid. Both have been banned for agricultural use in the EU for several years. The study found a higher incidence of unhatched eggs or dead chicks in nests with higher levels of insecticides.

Pesticides and the future

The Wildlife Trusts is campaigning for wider adoption of insect-friendly farming practices, increased regulation of pesticides and a reduction in their use. It will take a long time for new regulations to become policy which means it will be many years before we observe significant reductions in pesticide use. But, as wildlife gardeners, we can act now. If we want to provide habitats for more, not less, wildlife, we have to ditch all insecticides, fungicides and weed killers from our gardens so the wildlife on our doorstep can live safely. What's more, we should grow as much food ourselves as we can and do so organically and with nature in mind. We should also buy organic food wherever possible, as this has also been grown – at scale – without pesticides and sends a clear message that there is a demand for organic food production, a reduction in pesticide use and therefore more wildlife.

Don't use peat

Peat is formed when anaerobic, often acidic and waterlogged conditions prevent plant material from decomposing properly. Peat bogs make fantastic wetland habitats for a huge range of wildlife species, including wading birds, rare butterflies and dragonflies. What's more, peatlands:

- store carbon – over three billion tonnes of CO_2 are already stored in UK peatlands and, if repaired, they could remove a further three million tonnes of CO_2 from the atmosphere every year;
- store water and help reduce flooding – restoration of upland bogs could prevent flooding of lowland towns and cities.

Peat grows at a rate of just 1mm per year. Unfortunately, due to its lightweight and water-retentive properties, it's the perfect medium for some horticultural use, and 80 per cent of British peat bogs are in a poor condition because they've been drained for agriculture or forestry or damaged by extraction.

In 2020, alone, more than 2.29 million cubic metres of peat were dug up from overseas peatlands to be sold in the UK market (Wildlife Trusts 2022). As gardeners, we need to support restoration of British peat bogs but also stem the tide of peat extraction in other countries. In short, we need to stop using peat.

Alternatives to peat

There are increasing numbers of peat alternatives available commercially, including ericaceous mixes for growing acid-loving plants such as blueberries and rhododendrons. These compost mixes contain a range of ingredients such as coir (coconut fibre),

composted wood, composted green waste, locally available products such as leaf mould, wool and worm castes and some inorganic materials such as grit or sand. Gardeners also have much better options for soil improvers and organic mulches than peat, with bark, well-rotted farmyard manure and composted green waste being widely available. When buying compost:

- Don't just grab the cheapest bag of multipurpose and hope for the best – it will often contain peat. Always look for compost labelled 'peat-free'. Even bags labelled 'organic' may still contain peat.
- If your supermarket or garden centre doesn't sell peat-free compost, or has only one option, ask them to stock more.
- Shop online – there are some wonderful peat-free composts available.

Grow more plants

Plants provide habitats and food for wildlife (and for us). They help to cool urban environments. They give shade from the sun. They clean the air we and other animals breathe and every single plant absorbs carbon dioxide (CO_2). When we grow more plants in our gardens, we lower our risk of localised flooding and fire, because the roots hold on to water. More plants in a given area can also reduce local temperatures, thanks to the cooling effects of leaves and the shade they cast – this is especially useful in built-up urban areas. A hedge or dense mass of trees and shrubs can disperse and slow down strong winds, creating a shelter belt that can protect other plants during a storm and help insects to feed when it's windy. In addition to all those benefits, plants make us feel better. They lower our blood pressure and improve our mood, and simply being outside surrounded by plants is good for us.

Yet plants are disappearing on our watch. As part of its Greening Grey Britain campaign, RHS-backed studies found that areas of hard paving in gardens – on patios and front gardens paved over to provide parking spaces – are increasing. As gardeners mindful of biodiversity losses and climate change, our choices can make a difference. We can choose to grow more plants and minimise areas of hard surfacing in our outdoor spaces. Where our gardens have walls or fences, we can train climbing plants to grow up them. If our garden already has some hard surfacing, we can make it greener by growing plants in pots on it. Or we could remove some (or all) of the paving and replant a garden. I've done this twice. It's hard work but extremely rewarding!

And, when we make the positive choice to grow more plants and pave less of our gardens, we can

talk to our neighbours and explain what we're doing and why. Because the more plants we all grow in our garden, balcony, patio or windowsill, the better life is for all of us, for wildlife and for the planet.

Wildlife gardening for pollinators

When we think of pollinators, most of us imagine a bee. But scratch the surface and there's a world more besides, including butterflies and moths, beetles, flies, hoverflies and wasps, and in some countries birds, bats and even lizards. Pollinators come in all shapes and sizes, and have different pollination roles. Knowing a bit more about them will help us tailor the habitats in our gardens to better provide for them. In the next few pages I look at gardening for pollinators in general before focusing on bees, including a dedicated section on solitary bees and bee hotels, then butterflies, moths and hoverflies.

Why should we garden for pollinators?

Without bees, hoverflies and other insects, there would be no strawberries, apples, avocados, chocolate, cherries, olives, blueberries, carrots, grapes, pumpkins, pears, cotton, plums or peanuts. Reason enough to help them. But there are emotional reasons for gardening for pollinators and these are often ignored. To me, placing an economic value on an insect seems contrary to why we garden for pollinators (or certainly why I do). A world without bees and butterflies would threaten global food security, yes, but it would also be miserable. Pollinators pollinate our crop plants and wildflowers but they also lift our spirits. When I see a butterfly tumbling through my borders in summer, I don't think about food security. When I laugh at a bumblebee 'taking a bath' in a crocus or poppy, I don't think about the value of pollination services to the economy. I think how lucky I am to have seen them, how grateful I am that they came into my garden, how wonderful it is that there are so many

▲ The long flower buds of this catmint are perfect for this common carder bumblebee.

different pollinators out there that I know and love, and that I will dedicate my life to knowing and loving better. I can't be the only one to feel this way.

- An estimated 84 per cent of EU crops (valued at £12.6 billion) and 80 per cent of wildflowers rely on insect pollination.
- Around half of our bumblebee species are declining – seven have declined by more than 50 per cent in the last 25 years and three are already extinct.
- Two-thirds of our moths and 71 per cent of our butterflies are in long-term decline.
- Across Europe, 38 per cent of bee and hoverfly species are in decline.
- A study in Germany found that the abundance of flying insects across the country's nature reserves had plunged by 75 per cent over a 27-year period.

Another thing to remember is that, while statistics on pollinator declines are terrifying, most of our insects have short life cycles so there's potential for populations to increase as dramatically as they decreased. We could yet have clouds of butterflies visiting our buddleias again. We could yet find bumblebee nests at the bottom of every hedge, beneath every shed. We gardeners can't replace lost wild habitat or stop the widespread use of pesticides in agriculture, but we can mitigate losses and even reverse the fortunes of some of our bees, butterflies and pollinating beetles, flies and wasps, just through gardening. The more wildlife gardening we do, the more lives we save. (And by signing petitions to put pressure on governments to change laws on the use of pesticides in agriculture, we could make a difference outside our gardens too.)

Where to start?

In the British Isles we have around 270 species of bee and 2,500 species of butterfly and moth. On top of that, some of our 4,000 beetles, 7,000 flies and 9,000 wasps are pollinators. Each one has carved out a slightly different niche in the ecosystem. In gardening for them, we need to consider what they eat but also how and where they reproduce – many species can do so in our gardens. Learn the basics of the most common garden species and you become a better wildlife gardener because you know how to cater for them. Learn how to look after the rarer species and you could contribute to healthier local populations.

Gardening for pollinators is easy. Start by planting flowers, watch the bees, butterflies, moths and hoverflies come in, then look at how you can encourage them to breed in your garden. Some types of bumblebee nest in old mouse holes or beneath sheds; some solitary bees nest in the ground, in sand, bee hotels and even home-made cob bricks; hoverflies might lay eggs near aphid colonies on herbaceous plants, or in your pond; butterflies and moths usually require specific plants to lay eggs on, so you might pick a few and see what you can do. In my garden, every plant has a purpose for pollinators, be it flowers for nectar and pollen, leaves to help the pollinators create the next generation, or just something to lure in the aphids for hoverfly larvae to eat. I also create as many opportunities for pollinators as I can, from drilling holes in my fence panels to erecting bee hotels, making cob bricks and a bee bank, making a hoverfly lagoon and encouraging mice to nest in the garden, which attracts bumblebees. The more plants we grow, the better, but we can also create complete habitats for many species.

▲ Encouraging pollinators to your allotment can increase yields of crops such as courgettes and beans.

When to provide flowers for pollinators

Plant up a pollinator-friendly container

You will need:
- Large plant pot with a height and diameter of around 40cm
- Crocks
- Peat-free compost
- Selection of pollinator-friendly plants (I used *Salvia* x *sylvestris* 'Mainacht', *Geum* 'Mai Tai', *Geranium* 'Bertie Crûg' and *Heuchera villosa* 'Palace Purple')
- Water/watering can

You don't need a large garden, or a garden at all, to cater for pollinators. This simple project combines four plants with different flower shapes, which will provide nectar and pollen for a range of different species (see the plants for pollinators lists opposite for inspiration). As perennials, these plants will eventually outgrow this pot. If you have a garden then simply transplant them when they become too big, or take them out of the pot in spring and halve each one, using your fingers or a breadknife to pull the rootball apart. Replant the smaller portions of the plants back in the same pot and use the other portions to make another container display or give them to friends.

Steps...

1. Position the pot where you want it so you don't have to move it once it's been planted up. Add crocks to the bottom of the pot to help reduce soil loss from drainage holes, and fill two-thirds with compost.

2. Gently tap each plant from its pot and place on the surface of the compost. Place taller plants at the back, and those with more of a low-growing or trailing habit at the front.

3. Fill in compost around the plants and firm in well, checking there are no air pockets. Water thoroughly, until it runs out of the bottom of the pot. Add more compost if needed.

Climate change brings extreme weather and unpredictability. In the last decade, we have seen bumblebees emerge earlier from hibernation, with some species such as buff-tailed (*Bombus terrestris*) establishing winter colonies instead of hibernating. However, in the last few years, spring weather has been much wetter and colder than average, affecting nest survival (nest temperature needs to be around 30°C). Heavy rains can destroy spring flowers and also flood underground nests. We gardeners can help by growing more early spring flowers, particularly robust species like winter honeysuckle and winter heather, and keeping pots of crocus and other fragile blooms under the cover of a porch or even in a greenhouse with an open door or window. Try to have something in flower every day of the year – a drop of nectar will give pollinators the energy to return to overwintering or simply replace what they have lost from waking up at the wrong time of year. Growing flowers beyond summer is a much easier task in milder regions. But you can extend summer into autumn

Plants for pollinators by season

Winter to spring

Apples *Malus domestica*	Goat willow *Salix caprea*	Common lungwort *Pulmonaria officinalis*	Snowdrop *Galanthus nivalis*
Crocus	Grape hyacinth *Muscari armeniacum*	Primrose *Primula vulgaris*	Wallflowers *Erysimum*
Daphne	Hellebore *Helleborus*	*Rhododendron*	Winter aconite *Eranthis hyemalis*

Spring to summer

Allium	Globe thistles *Echinops*	Lavenders *Lavandula*	Red campion *Silene dioica*
Cardoon *Cynara cardunculus*	Hollyhock *Alcea rosea*	*Allium siculum*	Red clover *Trifolium pratense*
Catmint *Nepeta*	Honeywort *Cerinthe major 'Purpurascens'*	Oregano *Origanum vulgare*	Viper's bugloss *Echium vulgare*
Comfrey *Symphytum*	Hyssop *Hyssopus officinalis*	Ornamental thistles *Cirsium*	White clover *Trifolium repens*
Foxgloves *Digitalis*	Knapweeds *Centaurea*	Phacelia *Phacelia*	White dead-nettle *Lamium album*

Summer to autumn

Agastache	*Dahlia*	Japanese anemone *Anemone hupehensis*	*Salvia*
Bistort *Persicaria bistorta*	*Helenium*	Michaelmas daisies *Aster/ Symphyotrichum*	Shasta daisy *Leucanthemum × superbum*
Caryopteris	Ice plant *Hylotelephium spectabile*	*Rudbeckia*	Argentinian vervain *Verbena bonariensis*

Autumn to winter

Ivy *Hedera helix*	Winter clematis *Clematis cirrhosa*	Winter-flowering honeysuckle *Lonicera fragrantissima*	
Oregon grape *Mahonia aquifolium*	Winter-flowering heather *Erica carnea*		

by growing late-flowering plants such as ice plant, ivy, Michaelmas daisy, Argentinian vervain and perennial wallflowers. Bring spring to your garden as early as possible by planting spring bulbs such as snowdrops, winter aconite, crocus, mahonia, daphne, winter clematis, winter heather and winter honeysuckle. The last two are particularly robust and will continue to bloom through bouts of heavy rain, so are a good option in a changing climate. You should have no problems filling your garden with flowers in summer.

In the table above you'll find a rough guide to the sort of plants you should aim to grow across the year for bees and other pollinators. There are so many more to choose from – these are just suggestions.

Nectar, pollen and pollinators

Just as the honeybee gets more media coverage than wild bees and other types of pollinator, so nectar gets more publicity than pollen. And yet they are both important for the health of some pollinators. Nectar is essentially sugar water, and provides the energy to fly. Pollen provides protein. The amount of nectar and pollen on offer varies, depending on the flower, and the quality of pollen does too. Plants in the legume family (clover, peas, beans, etc.) have extremely high-quality pollen with large amounts of protein. The more pollen consumed by bees from plants in this family, the healthier, more robust and resistant to disease the bees are. So simply by mowing our lawns less often, we can grow more clover and therefore improve the health and well-being of our garden's bees. And we can pack our borders with a wide variety of leguminous plants, including vetches, peas and beans.

Flowers and pollinators have evolved together, sometimes in a very specialised way – there's no catch-all pollinator that could cover the world's pollinating needs. The bee or moth that pollinates honeysuckle isn't the same as the bee or moth that pollinates a tomato. Flower shapes differ widely and the 'mouthparts' of pollinators vary too. For example, the tubular flowers of honeysuckles may be more likely to be pollinated by longer-tongued bumblebees, whilst the open flowers of cow parsley can be visited by a wide range of pollinating insects. So the greater variety of flowering plants we grow in our gardens, the more pollinators we attract, and the better for everyone.

◂ Plants in the clover family are a fantastic source of pollen for a wide range of bees.

Mouthparts

Have you noticed that different types of pollinator visit flowers in different ways? Bees, moths and butterflies suck nectar through a straw-like proboscis, or tongue. Some species have a long tongue and others have a short tongue. You can sometimes guess how long an insect's tongue is by which type of flower it visits. Bear in mind that some short-tongued bees bite through the petals to 'rob' nectar from flowers with long tubes, such as broad beans.

Most flies, including hoverflies, have a sponge-like proboscis, which they use to dab pollen and nectar. They typically visit daisy-type flowers or umbellifers, where the nectar and pollen is easily available and laid out on a plate. (In my garden they can't get enough of the fennel.)

Most beetles have powerful jaws called mandibles, which they use to crush or cut food (or to defend against predators and rivals), but some flower-visiting beetles have also developed a proboscis. Wasps too have strong jaws for eating their insect prey, but they use these to drink as well.

▲ Beetles chew pollen with their mandibles.

▲ Hoverflies and other flies dab at flowers with their sponge-like proboscis.

▲ Bees and butterflies suck nectar through their straw-like proboscis.

Flower shapes

To cater for a diverse range of pollinator mouthparts, try to grow as many types of plant as possible. Here's a selection of common plant families to get you started.

Bellflower family (Campanulaceae)

Borage family (Boraginaceae)

Buttercup family (Ranunculaceae)

Cabbage family (Brassicaceae)

Carrot or parsley family (Apiaceae – formerly Umbelliferae)

Daisy family (Asteraceae)

Legume family (Caesalpiniaceae, Mimosaceae, Papilionaceae or Fabaceae – formerly Leguminosae)

Mint family (Lamiaceae)

Poppy family (Papaveraceae)

Rose family (Rosaceae)

Breeding habitats

Growing flowers for pollinators is only half the story. Just like all living species, pollinators need somewhere to rest and breed, but there's no catch-all shelter for them. Bees and wasps make nests and gather food to feed their young; butterflies and moths lay eggs on leaves, which their larvae then eat; beetles and flies lay eggs in a variety of situations – for example, some hoverflies and ladybirds lay eggs on aphid-infested plants and their larvae eat the aphids. While not everyone has the space for lots of breeding habitats, the more you can provide, the better.

Plants for Bugs

In 2009 the RHS launched Plants for Bugs, an ambitious experiment to find out more about native plants and how they relate to abundance and biodiversity. The project consisted of 36 plots (each 3x3m^2, the size of a typical garden border) on two sites, one at RHS Garden Wisley and the other on a nearby research field. Each bed was planted with a selection of plants from one of three geographical zones:

- UK (native)
- Northern hemisphere excluding the UK (near-native)
- Southern hemisphere (exotic)

All the plants were garden-worthy and matched in terms of garden habit and use. For the northern-hemisphere plant selection, the team chose similar plants or plants within the same family as those in the native beds, while plants chosen for the southern-hemisphere beds were unrelated to the native plants. For example, a climbing plant was used in each bed: the native honeysuckle (*Lonicera periclymenum*) in the UK beds was 'matched' by Chinese honeysuckle (*Lonicera tragophylla*) in the near-native beds, and the unrelated Chilean glory flower (*Eccremocarpus scaber*) was planted in the exotic beds.

Invertebrates were recorded from each bed every six weeks during the growing season, using pitfall traps, suction sampling and visual observation of flower-visiting insects (pollinators).

After four years, more than 80,000 invertebrates had been counted and 300 species identified. At the time of writing, three papers have been published – on pollinating insects, plant-dwelling invertebrates and ground-active invertebrates. More invertebrates were found in the native beds, but near-natives weren't that far behind, and interestingly all groups supported good numbers.

▲ A large white butterfly lays an egg on the underside of a leaf.

Best plants for pollinators: native or non-native species?

It's the age-old question in wildlife gardening. You might think the answer is obvious: native plants and insects have evolved together. They work together in relationships scientists have only started to scratch the surface of. We already know that most butterflies and moths are extremely fussy about the leaves they lay eggs on; many have very specific caterpillar food plants (see the Butterfly Conservation lists in Resources). We also know that some bees appear to have a preference for certain native flowers, and we continually discover more about this. No doubt there will be millions of other tiny relationships going on between native plants and native insects that largely go unnoticed by us. But relationships take place between non-native plants and native insects as well.

Any research that explores relationships between invertebrates and garden plants is extremely valuable for wildlife gardeners because it helps us make more informed decisions. If you have a small garden and you love wildlife, it makes sense to grow the plant that has been shown to cater for many invertebrates rather than just one or two, whether it's native or not.

▲ Caterpillars, such as this orange-tip butterfly, are a valuable source of food for baby birds.

For gardeners wanting to support pollinators, the RHS concluded:

- Planting a mix of flowering plants from different countries and regions is best.
- Priority should be given to plants native to the UK and northern hemisphere, although exotic plants native to the southern hemisphere can be used to extend the season for pollinators (e.g. *Fuchsia magellanica* var. *gracilis*).
- Regardless of plant origin, the more flowers a garden can offer throughout the year, the greater the number of bees, hoverflies and other pollinating insects it will attract and support.

To support plant-dwelling invertebrates, the RHS concluded:

- Plants native to the UK are best.
- Planting schemes largely from the northern hemisphere may support only marginally fewer invertebrates in some groups (including herbivores and some predators) than UK-native plant schemes.
- Plant schemes largely from the southern hemisphere (exotic) plants will still support a good number of invertebrates, albeit around 20 per cent fewer than UK native plants.
- Regardless of plant origin, the more densely a plant scheme is planted or allowed to grow, the more invertebrates of all kinds it will support. Spiders are the exception to this – the study found that spiders appear to benefit from more sparse planting.

For more information on the Plants for Bugs trial, visit the RHS website (see page 189).

Note: Analysis regarding specialist herbivores such as moth and butterfly caterpillars is so far inconclusive, so it's a good idea to grow known larval host plants for these.

Bees

The buzz of a bee in a flower is the quintessential sound of summer. There are approximately 270 bee species in the UK. Just one of them is the honeybee, around 25 are bumblebees, and the rest are known as solitary bees. Many come into gardens, and all of us, regardless of how big our outside space, can provide nectar and pollen plants for 20 or more different species. Some of us can provide nesting habitats for them too.

Bees fall into two categories: social and solitary. Social bees include bumblebees and honeybees. They live in large or small colonies dominated by an egg-laying queen, with workers (her daughters) gathering pollen and nectar to feed the larvae (grubs) back in the nest.

Bumblebee nests are usually annual, with the mated queen emerging from overwintering in spring, setting up a nest, and laying eggs throughout summer. In late summer she lays eggs that grow into males and new queens. These mate with other males and daughter queens from different nests, and then the males, original workers and old queen die. Only the mated daughter queens overwinter, ready to start the next generation the following spring.

▼ Poppies, such as the field poppy, provide a fantastic source of pollen for bumblebees.

The bumblebee life cycle

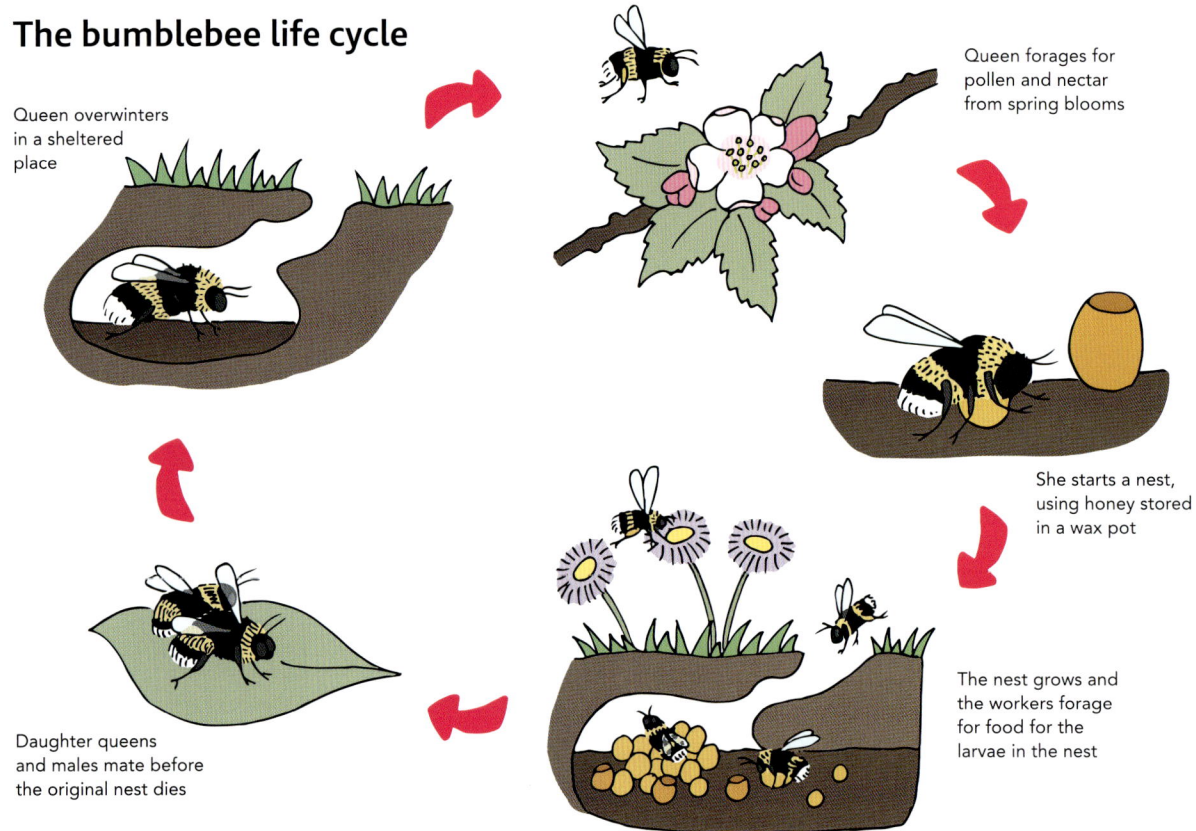

Queen overwinters in a sheltered place

Queen forages for pollen and nectar from spring blooms

She starts a nest, using honey stored in a wax pot

The nest grows and the workers forage for food for the larvae in the nest

Daughter queens and males mate before the original nest dies

Honeybees have a longer life cycle, with colonies reaching many thousands and lasting several years. The queen may be usurped by a new one raised in the nest or replaced by the beekeeper.

In contrast, solitary bees don't live in colonies and have a completely different life cycle. There are more than 200 species in the British Isles, and some of the more common solitary bees include mason bees and leafcutter bees, which readily use bee hotels as well as holes in dead wood or old plant stems. For more on solitary bees and bee hotels, see pages 43–45.

Whether social or solitary, wild or managed in a hive, all bees have a vital role to play and often do so within a very specific niche. Different bee species have evolved to benefit from certain habitats over others, and some pollinate certain plants over others. Also they are 'on the wing', i.e. flying, at different times of year – the first hairy-footed flower bee tells us spring is finally here, while the ivy bee, which flies in September, is the bee equivalent to the very last of the summer wine. Understanding the various roles and needs of as many bees as possible will equip us with everything we need to help them.

Gardening for bees

Gardening for bees means packing your borders and pots with as many nectar- and pollen-rich plants as you can squeeze in, and providing nesting opportunities where you can. It's well worth taking the time to learn to identify a few bee species (see pages 41–42 for starters) and to sit and watch bees visit flowers. You'll soon discover that certain bees have particular preferences, and that you can tailor your garden to suit them while experimenting with different flowers to see which other pollinators you can lure in.

The table below offers a few suggestions for bringing bees to your garden. For bee-friendly plants, see the RHS Plants for Pollinators lists (link on page 189).

Ideas for attracting bees

	Suitable for...				
	Small garden	Medium garden	Large garden	Allotment	Balcony/patio
Grow a range of flowering plants from spring to autumn, and try to have something in flower in winter too.	✓	✓	✓	✓	✓
Let an area of grass grow long, but also keep areas short to attract nesting solitary bees.	✓	✓	✓	✓	✗
Make a bee bank for mining bees, using fine sand.	✓	✓	✓	✓	✗
Build log, stick and leaf piles to encourage bumblebee queens to nest and/or hibernate.	✓	✓	✓	✓	✗
Make or buy a solitary bee hotel (see pages 54–61).	✓	✓	✓	✓	✓
Leave patches of bare earth in sunny borders for nesting solitary bees. Add a layer of fine sand to maximise nesting potential.	✓	✓	✓	✓	✗
Provide water for thirsty bees and other pollinators by including a pond with water lilies as landing pads, or a birdbath with stones.	✓	✓	✓	✓	Birdbath with stones
Make a cob brick for nesting hairy-footed flower bees (see page 43).	✓	✓	✓	✓	✗
Allow clover, selfheal, vetches and trefoils to grow in lawns.	✓	✓	✓	Pathways / grassy areas / borders	✗
Grow climbing plants, including ivy, single-flowered clematis and honeysuckle.	✓	✓	✓	✓	✓
Don't use pesticides (see pages 19–20).	✓	✓	✓	✓	✓
Leave a dish of mud, which red mason bees may use to seal their nests in dry springs.	✓	✓	✓	✓	✓
Grow roses with soft, matt leaves so that leafcutter bees can use them to make their nests.	✓	✓	✓	✓	✓
Grow as wide a range of flowering plants as possible.	✓	✓	✓	✓	✓

Which bees should I encourage to nest in my garden?

Provide nesting opportunities for bees and you're creating a complete habitat that will bring you hours of joy in the summer months.

Bumblebees

Of the 25 UK species, around 10 are likely to visit gardens. Some nest underground – in old mouse burrows, for example – while others nest above ground in leaf litter, your compost bin or long grass. The tree bumblebee (*Bombus hypnorum*) nests in trees, roof cavities or bird boxes.

Ideal for: Medium to large gardens

How to attract them: Build a compost heap or habitat pile using branches, twigs and other woody clippings, or leave a patch of long grass and leaf litter beneath hedges. Don't deter mice.

Honeybees

Typically raised in hives by a beekeeper but may nest in the wild, such as in the top of a tree or a cavity in a wall.

Ideal for: Large gardens close to other gardens, orchards or wildflower-rich countryside

How to attract them: Not really recommended except if you are a beekeeper. Honeybees swarm (look for a new nest) in June. Unless you have a huge, wild garden with a tree hollow or similar, it's probably best to call your local beekeeping association (see Resources on page 189) if you spot a swarm.

Solitary bees

These fall into two categories: ground-nesting and cavity-nesting. Ground-nesting bees typically need large areas of bare, sandy ground or a closely clipped lawn to nest in. Cavity-nesting bees use old beetle holes in dead wood, and holes in old mortar or hollow stems from the previous year's plants, but many will use bee hotels and almost any suitable-sized hole or cavity.

Ideal for: Balconies; small, medium and large gardens

How to attract them: Make or buy a bee hotel and fix it 1.5–2m off the ground, in the sunniest part of the garden. Keep part of your lawn closely clipped to provide opportunities for mining bees, or make sure there's bare ground in your borders. Maximise opportunity by making a bee bank and cob brick. See pages 43, 45 and 50–51 for more on solitary bees and nesting habitats.

Bedding plants for bumblebees

Bedding plants are often used by gardeners to fill gaps in borders or by councils in municipal planting schemes. Typically they've been bred to grow quickly, flower for as long as possible, and withstand summer drought. However, in the breeding process, many bedding plants have lost virtually all their pollen and nectar, or they have so many petals that the pollinators simply can't access the food beyond them. Despite being colourful and floriferous, bedding schemes containing plants such as begonias, busy lizzies, pelargoniums and petunias can often be a virtual desert for bees and other pollinators.

In 2017, researchers on the Blooms for Bees project at Coventry University conducted a trial of Mignon Series dahlias to find out if bumblebees visited them. Unlike many varieties of dahlia, Mignon dahlias are short-stemmed, making them a good alternative to traditional bedding plants. They bear single flowers with a rich source of nectar and pollen. Volunteers were sent seed and asked to grow three plants each of the white, red

▲ Mignon Series dahlias can provide bees with more food than traditional bedding plants.

and purple colour forms. Once the plants were in flower, participants were asked to conduct timed observations and photograph bumblebees on the blooms. Nearly 200 people took part and 10 species of bumblebee were recorded, although nearly 90 per cent of records were the buff-tailed bumblebee (*Bombus terrestris*), white-tailed bumblebee (*Bombus lucorum*) and common carder bumblebee (*Bombus pascuorum*).

The Blooms for Bees team themselves also grew the Mignon Series dahlias. As well as monitoring bumblebee visits, they measured the quantity of pollen and also the quantity and sugar concentration of nectar. They found no real

Be careful...

- when strimming or mowing the lawn, as you may destroy a ground-level bumblebee nest.
- when digging in winter, as you might dig up an overwintering bumblebee queen. Gently place her in a dry pile of leaves but don't rebury her.
- if your birdbath attracts honeybees, add a large stone or two that they can climb up, so they can drink safely without danger of drowning.
- when turning your compost heap in summer, as you could uncover (and harm) a bumblebee nest. Check for bee activity first.
- when digging areas used by ground-nesting solitary bees. Observe the ground first, especially in late spring.

difference between the colour forms, although some white-flowered blooms were recorded with extremely high levels of pollen and nectar.

Overall, while the Mignon dahlias were shown to bear pollen and nectar and attract bumblebees, some participants noted that fewer bumblebees foraged on them when other bee-friendly flowers, particularly lavender and cosmos, were in bloom nearby. However, the bright colours, dwarfing habit and long flowering period of Mignon Series dahlias make them suitable for growing as bedding plants, and they have been proved to be better performing than some traditional plants used in bedding schemes.

For more information on the Mignon Series dahlia trial and other trials, to get involved yourself or simply to brush up on your bumblebee ID skills, visit the Blooms for Bees website (see page 189).

Make a bumblebee nester

Of the 10 bumblebee species likely to come into your garden, most nest in old mouse holes, in compost heaps or beneath hedges and sheds. The common carder (*Bombus pascuorum*) typically nests above ground in grassy tussocks, while the tree bumblebee (*Bombus hypnorum*) seems to have a preference for bird boxes. They don't gather their own nesting material and so will only nest where a nesting site (such as an old mouse or bird's nest) is still intact.

This design mimics an old mouse or vole nest. Here, a hole is dug into the ground and nest material is placed in the centre.

Steps…
1. Dig a hole about half the size of a football. Add twigs to the bottom so the nesting material doesn't come into contact with the earth.

2. Place a generous amount of nest material in the centre and arrange it so it has a central dip. Carve a slight tunnel into the soil.

You will need:
- Garden trowel
- Twigs and sticks
- Nest material like dried grass and leaves, shredded paper or wood chips (I used the woollen insulation material that comes in the veg box)
- Slate tile

3. Cover with the slate tile, ensuring it protects the whole nest from rain. In spring a queen may find the tunnel in the soil, and investigate the nest.

With thanks to Dave Goulson for this design.

ID parade

Buff-tailed bumblebee
Bombus terrestris

Description: Our largest bumblebee, mostly black with a dark yellow band on the thorax and another central one on the abdomen, and either a completely buff tail or a white tail with a buff margin. Queens are enormous and are often seen flying very late or very early in the year. Workers vary in size and can be quite small. Males are smaller than the workers and have black facial hairs.
When to see it: February to November.
Nests: In holes underground, beneath sheds and in compost heaps.
Flowers visited: A huge variety.
Garden habitats: Compost heaps, areas of long grass, mouse burrows, flower borders.
Distribution: Widespread across Britain and Ireland, less common in Scotland.

Common carder bumblebee
Bombus pascuorum

Description: Medium-sized, gingery bumblebee, often quite scruffy-looking due to its ginger hairs bleaching easily in sun and the bald patch that can develop from visiting tubular flowers. Queens, workers and males all look alike, although queens are larger. Workers can be tiny, especially towards the end of the year.
When to see it: June to October.
Nests: Above ground in long grass that it combs, or 'cards', together; compost heaps.
Flowers visited: Its long tongue necessitates flowers with deep blooms, including foxglove (*Digitalis purpurea*) and honeysuckle (*Lonicera periclymenum*).
Garden habitats: Compost heaps, areas of long grass, in the flower border – particularly visiting flowers with long flower tubes.
Distribution: Common and widespread throughout Britain and Ireland.

Did you know?

- Bumblebees are the most efficient pollinators of tomatoes. They use a technique called 'buzz pollination', which vibrates the flower, dislodging the pollen. Other types of bee might visit tomato flowers, but only bumblebees use this efficient method.
- Studies by the Oxford Bee Company indicate that just one female red mason bee can pollinate as much apple blossom as 120–160 honeybees (see page 44). They estimate that only 500 red mason bees are needed to pollinate a hectare of apples, compared with 60,000–80,000 honeybees.
- Bumblebees can carry up to 50 per cent of their weight in pollen. They carry this on their hind legs in a series of comb-like hairs called a 'pollen basket'.

Garden bumblebee *Bombus hortorum*
Description: A large bumblebee with a very long tongue, which is often held outstretched as the bee approaches a flower. Black with a white tail, it has two yellow bands on the thorax and another one at the top of the abdomen.
When to see it: March to October.
Nests: Underground, but often only just below the surface; under sheds and in compost heaps.
Flowers visited: Its long tongue enables it to take nectar and pollen from flowers with deep blooms, including foxglove (*Digitalis purpurea*) and honeysuckle (*Lonicera periclymenum*). Pollen and nectar from these flowers is collected and fed to the larvae.
Garden habitats: Flower borders, particularly those planted with flowers with long flower tubes; compost bins.
Distribution: Common and widespread across Britain and Ireland, although less abundant than some other species.

Red-tailed bumblebee *Bombus lapidarius*
Description: Large, velvety black bumblebee with dark orange tail. Queens are enormous, workers (female) are larger than the males and look like the queen. Males have a yellow band across the thorax and yellow facial hairs.
When to see it: June to August.
Nests: Nests in holes underground, beneath sheds or sometimes in stone walls.
Flowers visited: With a medium-length tongue, adults visit a wide variety of flowers, but the species seems to have a preference for yellow flowers. The workers gather nectar and pollen for the larvae back in the nest.
Garden habitats: Flower borders, mouse holes, garden sheds.
Distribution: Widespread and common in Britain and Ireland, expanding its range northwards.

Honeybee *Apis mellifera*
Description: A medium-sized bee, widespread and common. Its abdomen ranges in colour from orange with black stripes to black.
When to see it: April to November.
Nests: In large colonies, usually managed by a beekeeper.
Flowers visited: With a small-to-medium tongue, adults are generalist feeders and visit a very wide range of flowers. The workers collect nectar and pollen to feed to the larvae back in the nest.
Garden habitats: Flower borders.
Distribution: Widespread and common throughout Britain and Ireland.

Solitary bees and bee hotels

Little was known about solitary bees a few years ago, but now, with increased awareness of the plight of bees and other pollinators, many of us own a bee hotel in which mason and leafcutter bees can raise their young.

In the next few pages I describe the solitary bees likely to use bee hotels, as well as other solitary species that don't use them, some of which nest in walls on the ground. Pages 45–47 are dedicated to leafcutter bees and the plants – particularly roses – they use to line their nests, so you can make more informed choices when gardening for them. I also look at bee hotels and the best types to make or buy (pages 54–61).

▲ To attract hairy-footed flower bees, a simple mix of topsoil, sand and straw can mimic a cob wall. Make a brick shape or fill a plant pot and lay on its side. Use a bamboo cane to make 10-12mm nest holes.

The solitary bee life cycle

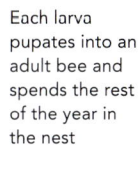

Each larva pupates into an adult bee and spends the rest of the year in the nest

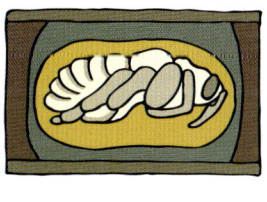

Males and females emerge from the nest where they were laid as an egg the previous year

Males and females mate

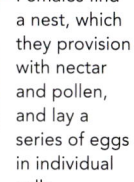

Females find a nest, which they provision with nectar and pollen, and lay a series of eggs in individual cells

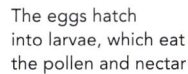

The eggs hatch into larvae, which eat the pollen and nectar

How to garden for solitary bees

Unlike bumblebees and honeybees, solitary bees don't live in a social family structure. There are no queens or workers, just males and females that mate before the male dies. The female lays eggs in individual nests and will never meet her young. These hatch from their eggs and eat a 'cake' of pollen and nectar left for them by their mother, then spend the best part of a year in the nest before emerging to mate and lay eggs of their own. Occasionally, some species of solitary bees nest in aggregations, giving the appearance of a social colony, but they're actually nesting individually.

There are several species of solitary bee likely to come into gardens. The red mason bee (*Osmia bicornis*) readily uses bee hotels. Medium-sized and rust-coloured, it is on the wing from April (when apple trees blossom) to around June. It's an excellent pollinator of apples and other fruit-tree crops, and is a brilliant species to attract if you grow your own fruit. It's said that one red mason bee can pollinate the same amount of apple blossom as 120 honeybees (see page 41) – watch them at work and you'll understand why – they collect pollen on a messy 'brush' on their abdomen instead of in neat 'baskets' like honeybees, and so distribute far more pollen as a result. Gardening for them involves growing flowers in spring, particularly apples and other fruit trees, and ensuring they have somewhere to nest (see bee hotels, page 54). In dry springs, watering your plants regularly and/or leaving a dish of mud can be helpful to them, as they won't have to travel as far to find the mud they need to seal their nests. Don't forget to leave a stone in the dish to ensure the bees have something to rest on.

Other species to look out for are the hairy-footed flower bee, an early spring species that looks a little

▲ The wonderful wool carder bee (*Anthidium manicatum*) is one of the most obvious solitary bees. Males 'guard' plants such as lamb's ear and have aerial battles with other males who come too close.

like a bumblebee and feeds on lungworts (*Pulmonaria*) and grape hyacinth (*Muscari armeniacum*). Ensuring there are plenty of early-spring flowers growing in full sun is a sure-fire way of encouraging them into the garden.

In summer, look out for the fiercely territorial wool carder bee, which patrols lamb's ear (*Stachys byzantina*) and foxglove (*Digitalis purpurea*) and has quite a high-pitched buzz. Males can be seen to attack other males, other species of bee and even butterflies that come too close to their 'patch'. They're very entertaining to watch. They occasionally use bee hotels; I have had them nest with me twice. As well as a good supply of lamb's ear, with which they make their nests, they also seem keen on bird's foot trefoil, so I always make sure I have plenty in flower for them.

Leafcutter bees

Leafcutters (*Megachile* species) get their name from the females' habit of cutting sections of leaves (and sometimes petals) to line their nest cells. About the same size as a honeybee, females are easy to spot because they have a patch of orange or golden hairs, called a pollen brush or scopa, on the underside of their abdomens. You might spot one flying around with this on show – almost as if she's sticking her bum out.

Seven species of leafcutter bee have been recorded in Britain, but of those only three are likely to come into gardens: patchwork leafcutter, brown-footed leafcutter, and Willughby's leafcutter. Patchwork and Willughby's are easy to identify.

Brown-footed leafcutter
Megachile versicolor
It is so similar to the patchwork leafcutter that it is very difficult to distinguish the two. Also nests in bee hotels as well as holes in wood, plant stems and in the ground. Common across the British Isles.

Patchwork leafcutter
Megachile centuncularis
Measures 9–12mm long. The forelegs of both sexes are black and the pollen brush of the female is orange-red. One of the leafcutters most likely to use bee hotels, it typically nests in holes in walls and dead wood. Common in England and Wales, but scarce in Scotland and Ireland.

Willughby's leafcutter
Megachile willughbiella
Slightly bigger than the patchwork leafcutter, at 10–15mm long. The forelegs of both sexes are black but the male has enlarged, cream-white tips which make him look like he's wearing gloves. The female's pollen brush is more of a pale gold colour than that of the patchwork leafcutter. Willughby's leafcutter nests in bee hotels as well as holes in rotten tree stumps, logs and posts; also under bark and in the soil. It's the one most likely to be found nesting in soil in plant pots in the greenhouse. It's common in Britain and Ireland.

▲ Brown-footed leafcutter – the brownish females have a more pointed abdomen than other species.

▲ Patchwork leafcutter – females are about the same size as a honeybee, with light brownish hair and bright orange pollen brush on the underside of the abdomen.

▲ Willughby's leafcutter – a larger species, with the females up to 18mm in length.

Gardening for leafcutters

Most leafcutters use a variety of leaves to line their nests, including birch, cercis, rose and wisteria. But for those of us with small gardens or with, say, only one gap for planting a rambling rose, it's useful to have a bit more detail on the specific nesting preferences of these (often quite fussy!) bees.

Roses are highly bred and have very different leaf textures. Leafcutters seem to prefer floppier-leaved varieties, such as cultivars of French rose (*Rosa gallica*). This makes sense – they roll them into a cigar-shaped nest, after all. In my garden, I grow the varieties 'Francis E. Lester' and 'Kew Gardens', which not only have floppy leaves but also single, open flowers, so they're used by a variety of pollinators as well as leafcutter bees. This is a huge win for a small garden, as one plant provides food and habitat for a wide range of species.

In the last version of this book, I asked other gardeners which rose varieties leafcutters used in their gardens, so those of us who wanted to help leafcutter bees could choose varieties proven to work. Before I knew it, I had a spreadsheet of more than 50 rose cultivars, plus a whole host of other plants that leafcutters had used for nesting. Many were familiar and already on lists given in books, but some were completely new to me – people told me they had leafcutters using buddleia and climbing beans as well as the flower petals of hollyhock, cosmos, ox-eye daisies and climbing hydrangea. In my garden I love watching leafcutters gathering flower petals, which make for really attractive 'cigar' nests.

What transpired was a huge list of plants suitable for growing in a wide range of situations, proving that leafcutter bees are a lot more individualistic than we thought they were, but also that really anyone can grow plants for them. You'll find the full list in the table opposite. It's by no means exhaustive and I'd love to hear from you if you can add to it. I really hope you find it useful. I hope you can attract leafcutters to nest in your garden. And I hope they bring you as much joy as they bring me.

◂ There's not much better than watching leafcutter bees at work.

Plants used by leafcutter bees to make their nests

Climbers

Virginia creeper *Parthenocissus quinquefolia*

Wisteria – Chinese wisteria *Wisteria sinensis* and white Japanese wisteria *Wisteria floribunda* 'Alba'

Climbing hydrangea *Hydrangea anomala* subsp. *petiolaris*

Herbaceous plants

Bridewort – *Spiraea salicifolia* and *Spiraea* x *billardii*

Climbing beans (Fabaceae family)

Common mallow *Malva sylvestris*

Enchanter's nightshade *Circaea lutetiana*

Evening primrose *Oenothera*

Fuchsia

Himalayan honeysuckle *Leycesteria formosa*

Hollyhock *Alcea rosea*

Purple loosestrife *Lythrum salicaria*

Rosebay willowherb *Chamaenerion angustifolium*

Wild strawberry *Fragaria vesca*

Shrubs and trees

Ash
Fraxinus excelsior

Beech
Fagus sylvatica

Buddleia
Buddleja

Cherry
Prunus

Crab apple
Malus sylvestris

Dogwood
Cornus alba 'Sibirica'

False robinia
Robinia pseudoacacia

Goat willow
Salix caprea

Hornbeam
Carpinus betulus

Japanese quince
Chaenomeles speciosa 'Moerloosei'

Judas tree
Cercis siliquastrum

Lilac
Syringa meyeri

Raspberry
Rubus idaeus

Redbud
Cercis canadensis

Red maple
Acer rubrum

Seven son flower tree
Heptacodium miconioides

Silver birch
Betula pendula

Snowberry
Symphoricarpos albus

Snowy mespilus
Amelanchier lamarckii

Stag's horn sumac
Rhus typhina

Vine maple
Acer circinatum

Rose (*Rosa*) species and cultivars

R. 'Amande Paternotte'

R. arvensis

R. blanda

R. chinensis 'Mutabilis'

R. 'Complicata'

R. 'The Dark Lady'

R. 'Drift Series' (great for small gardens and pots)

R. 'Duchess of Portland'

R. 'Fantin-Latour'

R. 'Francis E. Lester'

R. gallica 'Versicolor'

R. 'Gentle Hermione'

R. 'Gertrude Jekyll'

R. glauca

R. 'Golden Showers'

R. 'Harlow Carr'

R. 'Iceberg'

R. 'The Ingenious Mr Fairchild'

R. 'Jacques Cartier'

R. 'Jude the Obscure'

R. 'Lady Emma Hamilton'

R. 'L. D. Braithwaite'

R. 'Madame A. Meilland'

R. 'Madame Alfred Carrière'

R. 'Moonbeam'

R. 'Mortimer Sackler'

R. multiflora

R. palustris

R. 'Rambling Rector'

R. 'Roald Dahl'

R. 'Roseraie de l'Haÿ'

R. 'Tranquillity'

R. 'Westerland'

R. 'Wild Edric'

R. 'Zéphirine Drouhin'

R. 'Dupontii'

ID parade

Hairy-footed flower bee *Anthophora plumipes*
Description: A gorgeous, darting solitary bee that signals the beginning of spring. Looks a bit like a bumblebee, flies a bit like a hoverfly. Males are buff-coloured with a whitish face and females are all black with yellow or orange hind legs.
When to see it: March to June.
Nests: In cob walls, chimneys and occasionally the ground.
Flowers visited: Borage (*Borago officinalis*), daffodils (*Narcissus*), grape hyacinth (*Muscari armeniacum*), herb robert (*Geranium robertianum*), honeywort 'Purpurascens' (*Cerinthe major* 'Purpurascens'), ivy-leaved toadflax (*Cymbalaria muralis*), lungworts (*Pulmonaria*), primrose (*Primula vulgaris*).
Garden habitats: Flower borders, particularly where spring flowers are growing in full sun. Walls, chimneys and areas of bare soil.
Distribution: Widespread and common throughout much of England and south Wales, gradually spreading north. There have been unconfirmed records in Ireland.

Patchwork leafcutter bee *Megachile centuncularis*
Description: One of several similar species, this medium-sized bee is dark with scattered golden hairs. Females have an orange pollen brush, or scopa, on the underside of the abdomen, which they flick up, possibly as a signal to males that they have already mated.
When to see it: June to August.
Nests: Hollow plant stems, holes in wood, cavities in walls and occasionally in soil. Readily uses bee hotels. Uses leaves to seal its nest cells, particularly those of ash, birch, honeysuckle, horse chestnut, lilac and rose. Rose 'Francis E. Lester' appears to be a firm favourite.
Flowers visited: Adults visit a wide range of flowers, but seem to have a preference for blackberry (*Rubus fruticosus*) and thistles (*Cirsium*). The female gathers pollen and nectar, which she leaves in the nest for her young.
Garden habitats: Flower borders, walls or fences with holes in, bee hotels.
Distribution: Widespread in England and Wales but more common in the south. Less common in Scotland. Found in Ireland, although scarce in the north and west.

Red mason bee *Osmia bicornis*
Description: Rust-coloured solitary bee covered in dense, gingery hairs. Males are smaller than females with a white tuft of hair on the face.
When to see it: March to July.
Nests: Hollow plant stems, holes in dead wood made by beetles, cliffs, and crumbling mortar. Readily uses bee hotels. Uses mud to seal its nest cells.
Flowers visited: Adults visit apples (*Malus domestica*), pears (*Pyrus communis*), plum (*Prunus domestica*), raspberry (*Rubus idaeus*). Females collect nectar and pollen for the larvae in the nest.
Garden habitats: Flower borders, bee hotels and areas of damp soil.
Distribution: Widespread and common in Britain, but scarcer in the north of England and in Scotland. Only recently arrived in Ireland.

Wool carder bee *Anthidium manicatum*
Description: A large solitary bee that has a dark abdomen with a line of yellow spots on either side and two at the tip. It gets its name from the female's habit of combing (or 'carding') the fine hairs off leaves such as lamb's ear to line her nest. Highly territorial, the male fiercely guards his patch (usually a clump of flowers) against intruders. He has five spikes at the tip of his abdomen which he uses to fight off other males as well as larger bees and other insects.
When to see it: May to August.
Nests: Holes in dead wood, hollow stems, crevices in walls, beneath roof tiles. Will use bee hotels but appears to like them higher up – try erecting one in a south-facing position 3m off the ground. Uses the hairs of leaves from downy plants, such as lamb's ear to line its nest cells.
Flowers visited: A wide variety of flowers, including catmints (*Nepeta*), foxgloves (*Digitalis purpurea*), lamb's ear (*Stachys byzantina*) and lavenders (*Lavandula*). The female gathers pollen and nectar to leave in the nest for her young.
Garden habitats: Flower borders, particularly where there are lamb's ear and foxgloves; bee hotels.
Distribution: Widespread and common in much of southern England, scarcer in the north, Wales and Scotland. A recent colonist in Ireland.

Mining bees

Unlike cavity-nesting solitary bees, mining bees dig nesting burrows in the ground, typically in sandy soil. You might notice small volcano-like mounds of soil in your borders in spring, which are likely the work of the tawny mining bee (*Andrena fulva*), a beautiful russet-coloured bee that lays eggs in conspicuous underground chambers. Other mining bees are more discreet – buffish mining bees (*Andrena nigroaenea*) nest in my lawn beneath blades of grass, and I notice them only when I sit down and wait for them – if I didn't take time to look I wouldn't ever notice them. Some mining bees make a huge song and dance of nesting: the wonderful ivy bee nests in huge aggregations in September, with masses of bees buzzing around nest holes while looking for a mate and mating. Ivy bees are prone to forming a 'mating ball', where several males compete with each other for one female.

ID parade

Ivy bee *Colletes hederae*
Description: Similar looking to a honeybee, it has an orange-brown, hairy thorax, and black and yellow stripes on its abdomen.
When to see it: September to November.
Nests: In large aggregations in the ground.
Flowers visited: Mainly ivy.
Garden habitats: Garden lawns and borders.
Distribution: Southern England and Wales, plus the Channel Islands.

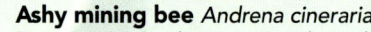

Tawny mining bee
Andrena fulva
Description: Russet-coloured and velvety, females are larger than males. Males have a distinguishing white tuft of hairs on the face.
When to see it: April to June.
Nests: Individually in sunny borders and lawns.
Flowers visited: Fruit tree flowers like apple and cherry.
Garden habitats: Sunny borders.
Distribution: Widespread in England and Wales, but rarer in Scotland.

Ashy mining bee *Andrena cineraria*
Description: Similar in size to a honeybee but coloured black and whitish grey. Females are larger than the males, with a glossy black abdomen, a light grey band of hairs at the top and bottom of the thorax, and a patch of grey-white hairs on the face. Males have similar markings, with less distinct bands of hair and whitish hairs along the thorax.
When to see it: April to July.
Nests: Bare patches of sandy soil in full sun.
Flowers visited: A variety of spring flowers, including willow, blackthorn and dandelions.
Garden habitats: Patchy lawns and bare soil in borders.
Distribution: Widespread throughout England and Wales.

Habitat for mining bees

In the wild, many solitary mining bees nest in coastal sand dunes, on south-facing banks such as railway banks, and at brownfield sites where sand and other aggregates form warm, sparsely vegetated habitats that attract a variety of nesting species. In gardens we are likely to have far less space than these natural and accidentally human-made habitats, but there's a lot we can do to replicate this type of habitat, even on a small scale. This involves adding sand to the garden, to create more opportunity and niche nesting habitat for ground-nesting species.

John Little, wildlife gardener and owner of the Grass Roof Company, has been experimenting with sand for many years. To date, he has increased the number of solitary mining bees in his garden in Essex by around 30 per cent since using sand.

Plasterer bee *Colletes daviesanus*

Description: One of several similar species, this one is widespread and likely to come into gardens. Gorgeous golden bee with a pale face and black-and-cream striped abdomen.
When to see it: May to September.
Nests: Dense aggregations in sunlit vertical surfaces, such as coastal sandstone cliffs, sand pits, roadside cuttings, cob walls and in soft mortar joints of brickwork.
Flowers visited: Adults visit a wide variety of flowers, including many from the daisy family, such as daisy (*Bellis perennis*), feverfew (*Tanacetum parthenium*) and yarrow (*Achillea*). Also thistles, including creeping thistle (*Cirsium arvense*). Females gather pollen and nectar, and leave them for the larvae in the nest.
Garden habitats: Flower borders, areas of bare, sandy soil.
Distribution: Widespread in England but scarce in Wales, Scotland and very rare in Ireland.

How to use sand in the garden

Create a bee bank
A bee bank mimics sand dune habitats found in coastal areas. John Little uses local Thanet sand, which is very fine, but if you can't get hold of this the next best thing is bricklayer's sand. Use it to make a large mound (no smaller than the volume of a wheelbarrow so it maintains a steady temperature, but you can go as large as you have space for) in a sunny, sheltered spot. Pack it down so it doesn't collapse when bees burrow into it, and create some steep sides that will heat up well in the sun. You can create an open mound or pack it into a wooden frame – then simply wait for the bees to arrive.

Add sand to borders or wildflower areas
Simply adding a layer of sand to planting areas helps to reduce fertility and vegetation, and increases local heat – perfect for sun-loving solitary bees. What's more, by top-dressing your soil with fine sand in a sunny, sheltered spot, you will improve growing opportunities for certain types of wildflower by reducing nutrient levels and increasing drainage. You will also attract solitary bees like the ivy bee, which can't seem to resist a good, sandy habitat.

Best flowers for specialist solitary bees

While many bees are generalist feeders, meaning they will visit a wide range of flowers, some are more specialist. This usually means they are unlikely to visit gardens, but you never know! If you live near a nature reserve, Site of Special Scientific Interest or you just fancy setting yourself a challenge, why not grow a selection of these flowers and see who turns up.

Campanulas attract the **bellflower blunthorn bee** (*Melitta haemorrhoidalis*), and the **small scissor bee** (*Chelostoma campanularum*). Varieties to try include common harebell (*Campanula rotundifolia*), clustered bellflower (*Campanula glomerata*) and nettle-leaved bellflower (*Campanula trachelium*).

Dandelions and similar looking relatives like cat's ear (*Hypochaeris radicata*), hawkbit (*Leontodon*), hawkweed (*Picris hieracioides*) and hawk's-beard (*Crepis*) attract lots of solitary bees, including **hawk's-beard mining bee** (*Andrena fulvago*).

Yellow loosestrife (*Lysimachia vulgaris*) – as well as taking pollen, the female **yellow-loosestrife bee** (*Macropis europaea*) takes floral oils from yellow loosestrife, which she uses to waterproof her nest.

Willows – willow catkins appear in spring when bees need pollen and nectar the most. Look for **Clarke's mining bee** (*Andrena clarkella*), the small and large **sallow mining bees** (*Andrena praecox* and *Andrena apicata*), the **northern mining bee** (*Andrena ruficrus*) and the early **colletes bee** (*Colletes cunicularius*). Varieties to choose include goat willow (*Salix caprea*) and grey willow (*Salix cinerea*), but in a small garden you may find the Kilmarnock willow (a compact, grafted willow) attracts a good number of species.

Scabiouses – the small scabious mining bee (*Andrena marginata*) and the large **scabious mining bee** (*Andrena hattorfiana*) are specialist scabious feeders. Varieties to choose include field scabious (*Knautia arvensis*), small scabious (*Scabiosa columbaria*) and devil's-bit scabious (*Succisa pratensis*).

Wild mignonette (*Reseda lutea*) attracts **yellow-face bees** (*Hylaeus species*).

White bryony (*Bryonia dioica*) may attract the **bryony mining bee** (*Andrena florea*) if you live in the south-east. This species collects pollen from bryony and looks similar to a honeybee.

Buttercups (*Ranunculus*) may attract the **large scissor bee** (*Chelostoma florisomne*). Males can be found resting in the centre of flowers during overcast weather.

Red bartsia (*Odontites verna*) or red rattle is a semi-parasite of grasses. It is often grown in conjunction with yellow rattle to reduce the competition of grasses with wildflowers in meadows. It also attracts the **red bartsia bee** (*Melitta tricincta*). If you live in the south-east of the UK near chalk downland, you might just lure this bee into your garden with its favourite plant.

The lowdown on bee hotels

Bee hotels are great fun. Designed to mimic the natural nesting habitat of leafcutter and mason bees, they can help increase local populations as well as offer a window into the remarkable world of solitary bee species. However, they can also do the opposite, and careful management is necessary to ensure your bee hotel doesn't end up doing more harm than good.

A bee hotel is simply a container filled with different-sized hollow tubes, such as cut lengths of bamboo. A female bee will select a tube, lay a single egg inside at the far end, and leave it with a little cake of nectar and pollen. Then she'll seal the cell and build another cell, laying another egg and provisioning it with nectar and pollen. She will keep doing this until the whole tube is filled. As such, a bee hotel will have several rows of eggs laid in single cells. Once hatched, the larvae will eat their store of pollen and nectar, pupate into an adult bee and then overwinter, ready to hatch out in spring and start the process again.

Bee hotels can be made using a variety of materials, including blocks of untreated wood with holes drilled in, bundles of bamboo canes, old plant stems or rolls of cardboard lined with paper, etc. They are readily available to buy or you can easily make your own – see below.

At the time of writing, I have been making and using bee hotels for 15 years. To date I have attracted six solitary bee species and two solitary wasps. I'm hoping to add to this number as I improve and learn more about the nesting requirements of individual species.

▲ You can decorate your bee hotel to suit your taste, as long as the nest holes within are clean and dry.

Things to bear in mind

- Some bee hotels are better than others.
- Bee hotels need to be dry, as damp conditions can bring on fungal diseases.
- They need to have the correct diameter of nest holes, since some species are remarkably fussy – as a general rule, aim for holes with different diameters between 2mm and 12mm (8–10mm is ideal for red mason bees, 7–8mm for blue mason bees and 10–12mm for leafcutters; tubes of 2–7mm may attract other types of bee). Most importantly, they need to be as unwelcoming to predators as any nest site in the wild. Sadly, many commercially available bee hotels are designed with holes too wide or insufficient protection against rain. Some use completely inappropriate materials, such as paper, which provides easy access to predators. Others include straw, wood chips and pine cones, which aren't used by solitary bees (what's more, the scales of pine cones move in response to changes in humidity, potentially squishing anything resting beneath one). There are good designs out there, but they can be few and far between.
- Bee hotels need to be managed. By simply erecting a bee hotel and leaving it in place, it's possible that it will encourage predators, parasites and diseases. Studies have shown that bee hotels can have high levels of parasitism and disease, and it is possible that this may actually decrease local solitary bee populations rather than increase them, although further research is required to determine the true effects. It's also thought that red mason bees prefer nesting in clean hotels. Studies are fairly recent and ongoing, but hopefully they will lead to the better

▲ Holes drilled in wood can replicate natural beetle holes, but need to be changed annually to avoid build-up of pests.

design of bee hotels in the future. The argument 'let nature take its course' doesn't really apply here, as bee hotels are artificial habitats. Please, if you put one up, look after your bees (see page 60).
- Bee hotels provide nesting sites for only a small number of solitary bee species. Other solitary species, such as the tawny mining bee (*Andrena fulva*), nest in the ground, often in sandy soil in full sun – a closely clipped lawn or sunny ornamental border could be perfect for them.
- Red mason and leafcutter bees have not been recorded in all parts of Britain and Ireland – do check distribution maps before investing in a bee hotel.

Which bee hotels work best?

Bee hotels are a relatively new phenomenon and, as such, there's no definitive guide to making or using them. However, I've come up with the following advice, incorporating my years of experience, plus the knowledge I've gathered from others. As we gain more experience and as science proves or disproves current assumptions, this advice will surely change. But for now, here are some pointers to ensure your bees have the best possible chances in life.

I have come to learn that smaller is better with regard to bee hotels. When I first started making them, I would use huge boxes and fill them with a variety of different materials. These were heavy and difficult to manage. Now I make much smaller hotels, which are lighter and encourage bees to nest at lower densities. I like to experiment by using different materials and positioning them at different heights and locations – you never know what might pay a visit! In the table below I outline some of the main materials used to make bee hotels, along with their pros and cons and personal experience where relevant.

Materials you can use for home-made bee hotels

Material	Pros	Cons	Personal experience
Bamboo canes	They look good and attract leafcutters and mason bees. Holes come in a variety of diameters. They provide a safe, dry habitat. They make it hard for predators and parasites to attack.	You need to saw the canes to fit the box and sand off any splinters, avoiding nodes that can block the tubes. You may need to drill into each cane to remove pith and solid nodes. It's hard to identify parasite-infested nests or dead bees/larvae (there are always some that don't survive). Canes need replacing yearly to prevent diseases and parasites building up. Spiders and woodlice love them.	Labour-intensive. It seems wasteful replacing canes each year, and I couldn't see whether live bees were trapped behind dead ones when emerging in spring. Spider predation was also an issue.
Dry flower foam	Really easy – just arrange the foam in a box and use a pencil to make holes; the bees will resize them to fit. Inexpensive. Fairly easy to take apart in autumn (although dusty). Provides a dry habitat.	It's not very attractive and easily destroyed by birds. Foam needs replacing annually to prevent diseases and parasites building up. Due to the soft walls, parasitic wasps may be able to reach eggs in adjacent nests – therefore giving them an advantage over the bees. The effects of the synthetic materials used to make the flower foam on bees is not known – research is needed here. As foam is not biodegradable, it is a potential source of pollutants.	Really easy and quite successful but I've stopped using it due to the potential toxicity of the foam on bees. Higher level of parasite infestation than other types of hotel. Huge mess/dust generated when sorting in autumn. Produces microplastics as it breaks down.

Material	Pros	Cons	Personal experience
Cement / brick	Potential for a permanent home for solitary bees – you can buy bespoke bricks to include in new-build homes or walls of extensions. They provide a safe, dry habitat. Hard for predators and parasites to attack.	They're hard to clean. You have to wait until the new generation of bees has emerged in spring and use a pipe cleaner to clear out the nest.	I do have a bee block in my wall but it's never attracted nesting solitary bees. Gorgeous little *Ectemnius* wasps roost in it, however, which makes it worth having.
Gathered plant stems	Natural, easily gathered from the garden (and therefore easy and free to replace each year). Attractive to a wide range of bees and wasps. Provide a dry habitat.	If the stems aren't dried properly or get wet, they can rot, which can kill bees. Stems need replacing annually to prevent diseases and parasites building up. Thinner-walled stems may give parasites and predators an advantage.	I've only tried this once and the stems rotted. Would try again but need to make sure the stems are fully dried out first.
Glass tubes / test tubes	You can see what's going on inside! A joy to watch the bees in action.	Condensation can build up and lead to fungal infections, which kill the bees. Hard to get in to clean.	
Mud / loam	Looks good and could attract species that don't usually use bee hotels, such as the hairy-footed flower bee (*Anthophora plumipes*). Fairly easy and cheap to make – probably needs replacing every two years.	It's hard to identify parasite-infested nests or winter mortality. Impossible to clean or replace material. Might be easier than other materials for birds to pick at.	Bees have so far shunned my mud/loam hotel but it did attract roosting *Ectemnius* wasps (which are very welcome). Will keep trying.
Cardboard tubes	Easy and inexpensive. You can buy refills online or make your own to the right diameter. Bees use them. Really easy to clear out in autumn, plus you can remove a tube as soon as it fills up, thus reducing the likelihood of parasitism.	If not housed correctly, they can get wet. They need replacing annually to prevent diseases and parasites building up. Paper alone makes it easy for parasites to lay eggs in adjacent nests, giving them an advantage over the bees – make sure you use thick card, which you can line with paper.	Easy, clean and inexpensive. My preferred choice in home-made designs.
Untreated wood with holes drilled in	Looks good and is relatively easy to make. You can drill a variety of different-sized holes. Attractive to bees and solitary wasps. They provide a safe, dry habitat if given a roof. Hard for predators and parasites to attack.	Wood needs replacing every two years to prevent fungal diseases/rotting. Can get wet if not given a roof. It's hard to identify parasite-infested nests or winter mortality.	I love my little bee block. The bees have shunned it but it's home to *Ectemnius* wasps, which are absolutely gorgeous and worth reading up on (see page 80).

How to make a bee hotel

This easy bee hotel comprises a simple wooden box with tubes placed in it. It's simple to make and easy to maintain. You can use bamboo canes (you can cut them yourself or buy them pre-cut) or bespoke bee tubes from a specialist supplier. The great thing about this design is that when each tube fills up, you can easily remove it and pop it in your shed, to prevent a build-up of parasites. The bee tubes here comprise an external reusable tube and an inner lining. The advantage of using these over bamboo canes is that in autumn you remove the reusable external tube and then soak the inner lining in water to release the cocoons. You then leave these to dry before popping them in a matchbox or similar and storing them somewhere cool and dry (such as your shed) for winter.

You will need:
- Bee tubes or bamboo canes (I used tubes from masonbees.co.uk). They need to be a depth of around 16cm, with diameters ranging from 7mm to 12mm.
- Plank of untreated wood with a width of 12cm and a length of no less than 125cm
- Drill and drill bits
- Self-tapping wood screws

Steps...

1. Cut the plank into five lengths of 25cm and piece them together using the drill and screws to make an open-fronted box with a long back panel. Drill a hole in the long back panel so you can fix it to a wall.

2. Sand off any rough edges and place the tubes or bamboo canes in the box. (If using bee tubes, make sure the tube lining is flush with the external tube at the front, with the the liner protruding from the tube at the back.)

3. Fix the hotel to a south- or east-facing wall or fence, so it gets plenty of morning sun, around 1.5m off the ground. Make sure the tubes are pushed back against the back of the hotel so they are protected by the box from wind and rain.

If you don't fancy making your own bee hotel, you can buy one instead. But, as with home-made structures, some are better than others. Prices range from around £20–£30 up to more than £100. Here are a few things you should keep in mind when choosing a bee hotel:

What you should look for:
- Holes of different sizes with the biggest diameter being no more than 12mm
- Material – i.e. bamboo stems, wood, tray system or thick cardboard tubes – that you can replace or clean easily
- A good roof to protect the contents from rain

What you should avoid:
- Tubes made of paper (cardboard tubes that have paper inserts are OK), plastic or glass
- Holes with a diameter greater than 12mm
- Bee hotels that don't have a back wall
- Any bee hotels that contain pine cones, straw or wood chips
- Bee hotels with visible splinters

Always remember: the main thing to consider when buying a bee hotel is 'will it be a safe habitat for bees?'. The bottom line is that it needs to be dry, snug and easy to take apart for cleaning.

▲ Some bee hotels have viewing panels so you can watch the bees as they build their nests.

Don't be scared of solitary wasps!

This is just a reminder that there are lots of wasp species in the British Isles and only two – the common wasp and German wasp, which are both social wasps – turn up at barbecues and picnics to steal your food and sting you. You should find space in your heart to love them anyway, but they're not going to set up home in your bee hotel. Solitary wasps do sometimes use bee hotels, but they're harmless and won't sting you. They include the beautiful ruby-tailed wasps, which are well worth trying to lure in. See page 75 for more on lovely wasps.

▶ Ruby-tailed wasps lay eggs in solitary bees' nests, where the larvae kill the larvae of the host species.

How to manage your bee hotel

Bee hotel management isn't an exact science but it's universally accepted that some management is necessary to keep the bees healthy. Below I have suggested three management methods: beginner, intermediate and expert. Do what you feel comfortable with. Over time, you may find that you develop more confidence and interest in your hotel and want to try more advanced techniques for looking after your bees.

Beginner

At the very least, take the bee hotel down in October, brush off any cobwebs and pop it in your shed, which should remain cool and dry throughout winter (don't bring the hotel into your warm home – it needs to be kept cool). This will stop predators such as tits and woodpeckers from attacking and eating the bees (they can wipe out an entire colony of bees in a matter of minutes). Do remember to put the hotel out in spring. Aim to replace the container or its nest holes (bamboo, etc.) at least every two years to prevent parasite numbers building up.

Intermediate

Take the bee hotel down. Brush away cobwebs and debris and inspect it. Count the number of completed nest holes and make a note of this. Depending on the design, remove the nest tubes/wood with holes drilled in and store them somewhere cool and dry, such as your shed. Clean out the bee hotel housing with a stiff brush and boiling water, allow it to dry and then conduct any maintenance (sanding, etc.) before adding new nest material and storing the hotel in the shed. In spring, put your bee hotel in its usual place, placing the old nest tubes/wood next to it so the bees can fly out and use the new, clean material. Note: the only problem with doing this is that the bees may try to return to the old material and start nesting in it, so keep an eye out!

How to protect it from bird attacks

If you make your own hotel, consider adding a protective 'cage' of chicken wire to prevent bird attacks. Just as tits learned to take the cream from the top of milk bottles in the 1980s, so they are learning that a box of holes on a south-facing wall is likely to contain tasty larvae or adult bees. And as bee hotels increase in popularity, bird attacks will likely increase too. Chicken wire is usually enough to deter them. However, robust, commercially available tray-based bee-hotels usually come with good protection.

How to deal with parasites

Bee hotel parasites can include mites, flies and parasitic wasps, including the rather lovely ruby-tailed wasps. The jury is out on what to do about these. Some argue that parasites are a part of the ecosystem and a sign of a healthy population. Others remove and destroy all parasitised cocoons to boost the bees' numbers. I'm sitting on the fence here. Having been managing bee hotels for years, I've never experienced a great number of parasites; and the cocoons that were affected were at the front of the hotel, which are male (females are laid at the back) and therefore less of a threat to the population than if they had been female. If something changed, I might consider destroying the parasites. However, I simply move them to the front garden. This means that in spring, when the bees wake up in the back garden, the parasites don't have an immediate advantage by already being in the hosts' nest. I don't kill them, but I don't make life easy for them either. Also, if ruby-tailed wasps ever deigned to visit my bee hotels, I'd probably be quite pleased.

Expert

This management method involves 'harvesting' the bee cocoons from the hotel, sorting healthy ones from parasitised ones, storing them somewhere cool and dry, then cleaning the housing to be used again – see the step-by-step guide opposite. This method is only possible if your bee hotel is designed to be opened and cleaned, or if you are able to prise open the nest tubes and replace them. After years of trial and error I've found that this approach helps prevent the build-up of parasites and can also prevent fungal diseases such as chalkbrood from destroying the bees.

My approach to managing bee hotels

In October I take apart my bee hotels and separate the cocoons by species. Red mason bee cocoons are red and walled up in mud; leafcutter cocoons are encased in leaves, like long tubes of cigars. I'm extremely gentle with them – while red mason bees will have completed metamorphosis by October, some leafcutter bees won't have. So I pop these to one side and leave them until spring.

With the red mason bees, I identify dead larvae and any parasitised cocoons (recognisable by their curly orange-brown frass), which I overwinter in the front garden. I rinse the healthy cocoons in tepid water to dislodge frass (droppings), pollen mites and pollen residue, and then leave them to dry while brushing down and scrubbing the bee hotel in hot, boiled water.

Finally I gather the dry red mason cocoons and gently place them in a box, such as a matchbox, with the leafcutter cocoons. I place these in my north-facing shed with the clean and dry bee hotels, where they remain cool and dry in winter. In early spring I put the bee hotels back up, remove the overwintered cocoons from their matchbox and place them in the release chamber at the bottom. The bees hatch and fly when they're ready to, hopefully into the clean, disease-free bee hotel they started life in.

Things to note

- Female cocoons are bigger than those of males and they tend to be laid at the back of the nest.
- Male cocoons sometimes have dimples.
- Red mason and leafcutter bees emerge at different times of year but I put them all outside at the same time – they know what time of year it is. In Brighton, my red mason bees emerge around 10 April and have usually started to nest by the 25 April. So I set up my bee hotels and put the cocoons in the release chamber in mid to late March. Depending on where you live, you might want to put yours out a week or two later.

Steps...

1. Take the bee hotel apart and gently remove the cocoons (I use the end of a teaspoon to tease them out). Identify any leafcutter cocoons and gently lay these to one side.

2. Gently rinse the red mason bee cocoons in tepid water until all pollen and frass residue is removed (don't worry – they're waterproof).

3. Lay the wet cocoons out on kitchen roll to dry. While doing this, brush down and scrub your bee hotel with hot water. Make sure there's no visible frass or pollen mites, rinse well and leave to dry.

4. Gently transfer the leafcutter cocoons and dry red mason cocoons into a box such as a large matchbox (you may wish to overwinter them in separate boxes). Leave them somewhere cool and dry, such as a north-facing shed, for winter.

Butterflies and moths

Who wouldn't want butterflies tumbling through the border on a summer's day? There are around 50 species found in the British Isles, with 20 likely to come into gardens (and several unlikely to come into gardens but that sometimes turn up anyway).

As well as butterflies, there are roughly 2,500 species of British moth, many of which are also found in gardens. Some people don't like moths as much as butterflies, while others don't like them at all. If you're one of these people, I urge you to reconsider. With so many species out there living in a huge variety of different situations, there's a moth (or 10) for everyone.

Sadly, many species of butterfly and moth are suffering huge declines (see page 69), but there's a lot we wildlife gardeners can do to help them.

Together we can make our gardens important refuges for many species of butterfly and moth. By adding a few choice plants to your borders, you could attract around 20 butterflies and 100 moths; but there are several other ways to tempt them in – see the table opposite for suggestions.

Regardless of the size of your garden, think of it as a stepping stone between larger habitats. If you don't have room for a huge patch of nettles on which small tortoiseshell, red admiral and peacock butterflies can lay their eggs, you might have room for some nectar-rich flowers to provide them with the fuel they need to find those nettles. Large gardens planted with plenty of caterpillar food plants are essential for the long-term survival of some species, but every balcony, doorstep, small courtyard and patio planted with a pot of nectar-rich plants can create a nation of wildlife corridors linking all our habitats together. This makes it easier for butterflies and moths to find the caterpillar food plants they need to lay eggs on, but it also reduces the chances

▲ A small tortoiseshell butterfly feeds on *Allium* flowers.

of some populations becoming isolated and of eventual local extinction.

Nectar provides butterflies and moths with the energy to fly and find a mate. It's a vital source of food in autumn and spring, on either side of the overwinter period. Nectar helps migrating species as well. Some travel between Britain and southern Europe or Africa to breed – can they find the food they need to refuel in your garden?

When planting for butterflies and moths, remember to choose a variety of flower shapes to attract the widest number of species. It can also be useful to grow the same types or colours of plant together in blocks. Prolong flowering by deadheading flowers, mulching with organic compost around the base of the plants to conserve water, and keeping them well watered.

For plant ideas, see the information on the next page as well as the RHS and Butterfly Conservation plant lists in Resources.

Ideas for attracting butterflies and moths

	Suitable for...				
	Small garden	Medium garden	Large garden	Allotment	Balcony/patio
Grow a range of flowering plants from spring to autumn, and leave out ripe fruit in autumn as an extra source of energy for butterflies.	✓	✓	✓	✓	✓
Let an area of grass grow long, which some species will breed in.	✓	✓	✓	✓	✗
Grow nettles, and 'Chelsea chop' them to encourage fresh growth for egg-laying butterflies. Do check for caterpillars before cutting them though!	✗	✓	✓	✓	✗
Lay pieces of slate or stone on bare patches in the borders or patio so butterflies can bask and warm up in the sun.	✓	✓	✓	✓	✓
Grow nectar-rich flowers and plant them in blocks, so butterflies and moths find them easily.	✓	✓	✓	✓	✓
Grow known caterpillar food plants (see the Butterfly Conservation lists in Resources), including native shrubs and grasses.	✓	✓	✓	✓	✓
Plant a meadow (see page 67).	✗	✓	✓	✓	✗
Plant a hedge, cutting it every other year, in late winter only.	✗	✓	✓	✓	✗
Leave untidy areas for caterpillars to overwinter.	✓	✓	✓	✓	✓
Tolerate weeds, which many moths use as caterpillar food plants.	✓	✓	✓	✓	✓
Don't use insecticides – they kill many insects, including butterflies and moths.	✓	✓	✓	✓	✓
Don't use herbicides, which are designed to kill weeds that some species breed on.	✓	✓	✓	✓	✓
Don't buy peat compost, as peat bogs are a valuable and irreplaceable habitat for some rare species of butterfly and many other species.	✓	✓	✓	✓	✓
Plant a pot of caterpillar food plants, such as native primrose, field poppy, foxglove and dandelion.	✓	✓	✓	✓	✓
Don't clear away old brassica plants in autumn. Instead leave them in place, where they will flower in spring.	✓	✓	✓	✓	✗

Five nectar plants for butterflies and moths

Buddleias
(*Buddleja*)
Easy to grow and comes in a variety of colours – the 'Buzz' series can be grown in pots. Prune them back hard in May to promote flowering in July and August.

Oregano
(*Origanum vulgare*)
One of the very best nectar plants in my garden. Grow in full sun in free-draining soil.

Lavenders
(*Lavandula*)
Simple to grow in free-draining soils. Flowers throughout summer, attracting a variety of moths and butterflies. Useful as a low-growing hedge. Takes easily from cuttings.

Wallflower 'Bowles's Mauve'
(*Erysimum* 'Bowles's Mauve')
In my garden this flowers continually all year. Takes easily from cuttings. Flowers attract a wide range of butterflies and moths. Tolerates shade and dry soils.

Be careful...
- when cutting back long grass, as caterpillars may be living among it.
- when digging soil, as you might uncover a moth pupa.
- when clearing leaves/foliage from corners, as you may disturb overwintering caterpillars.
- when tidying or clearing out the garden shed in winter as butterflies that overwinter as adults, such as small tortoiseshell, could be hiding out under joists or benches.

Argentinian vervain
(*Verbena bonariensis*)
Simple to grow, if given plenty of sun. Takes easily from cuttings and seed. Flowers well into November and is hugely popular with butterflies and moths. Gorgeous. Not fully hardy.

Grow a bee and butterfly garden

Provide for bees and butterflies all year round by planting shrubs and plants that flower at different times.

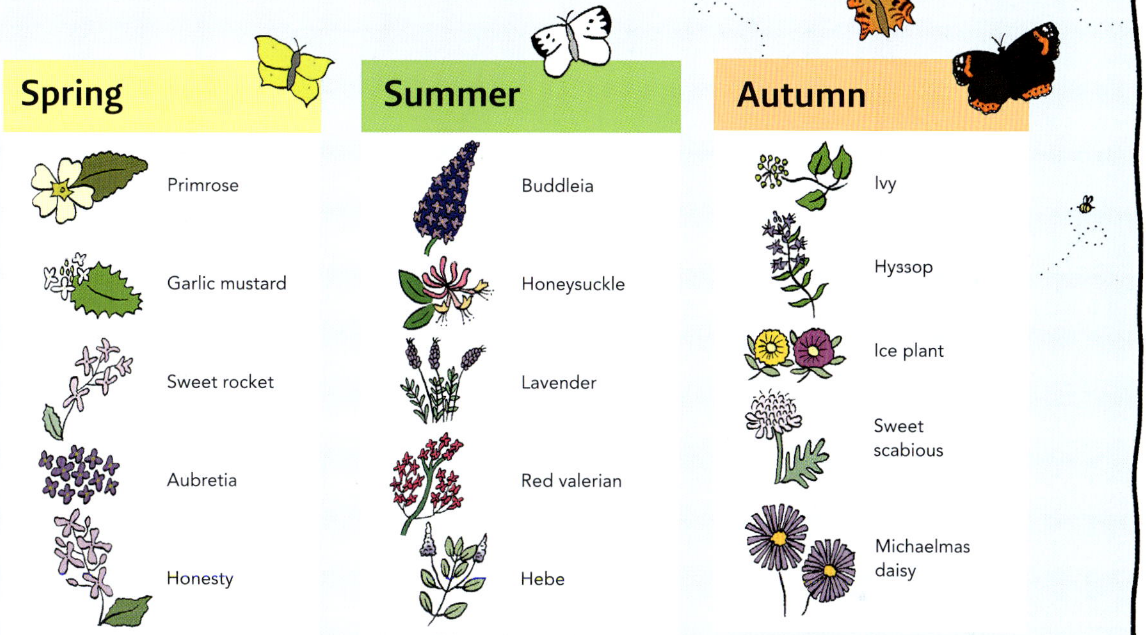

Spring	Summer	Autumn
Primrose	Buddleia	Ivy
Garlic mustard	Honeysuckle	Hyssop
Sweet rocket	Lavender	Ice plant
Aubretia	Red valerian	Sweet scabious
Honesty	Hebe	Michaelmas daisy

Create a wildflower meadow

Traditional hay meadows have declined by 97 per cent in Britain, so finding space, even for a small one, in your garden can make a dramatic difference. Many butterflies and moths breed in grasses, while grassland flowers provide a great source of pollen and nectar for a multitude of insects.

There are many types of meadow, but in gardening terms they fall into two categories: annual and perennial. Annual meadows aren't really meadows in the truest sense, but ornamental borders designed to look like a meadow. These are sown with colourful annuals that you would typically find in a cornfield, and require resowing every year. Perennial meadows imitate traditional hay meadows or 'grassland', which are extremely important habitats for a number of animal species. They contain grasses and wildflowers, and provide butterflies and moths with a huge range of egg-laying and nectar-gathering opportunities over many years.

Annual meadows

Annual meadows have become popular in recent years. They're full of colour and are turning up in municipal planting schemes across the country. While they look pretty and generate a lot of interest, the seed mixes don't contain grasses, so the butterflies and moths you would expect to find in traditional meadows can't breed here. However, they are easier to create than a traditional hay meadow and might be more appropriate for your garden. Some annual meadow seed mixes provide flowers right through to autumn, providing a long season of nectar and pollen.

To create an annual meadow, you need to prepare the ground as you would a seedbed, sow seed and wait. If sown and germinated evenly, you should have a long-lasting splash of colour throughout summer and into autumn.

Annual meadow seed or plug plant mixes often combine native and non-native plants including any of the following:

- Bishop's flower *Ammi majus*
- California poppy *Eschscholzia californica*
- Cornflower *Centaurea cyanus*
- Corn marigold *Chrysanthemum segetum*
- Dyer's tickseed *Coreopsis tinctoria*
- Field poppy *Papaver rhoeas*
- Larkspur *Consolida ajacis*
- Scabious *Scabiosa atropurpurea*
- Scorpion weed *Phacelia tanacetifolia*

No room for a full meadow?

Consider letting a patch of grass grow wild around the base of a tree, or make a wildflower feature of your lawn by mowing around a certain shape, such as creating a maze for children to explore. You could even grow a mini meadow in a pot.

▲ Transforming your lawn into a mini meadow will reward you with beautiful wildflowers and masses of wildlife.

Perennial meadows

There are several ways to create a perennial meadow. Ideally, it should contain a good mix of wildflowers that aren't outcompeted by grasses, so low-fertility soil is ideal. Garden lawns typically have rich soil. You can remove the top layer to reveal the less fertile subsoil, then sow a mix of wildflowers and grass seeds directly into this. You can also lay bespoke wildflower turf or plant wildflower plug plants. This option can be labour-intensive and expensive, but you should start seeing results instantly. In the first couple of years, you'll need to remove weeds such as dock and nettles. If you want a bit of colour in the first couple of years while the wildflowers become established, sow cornfield annuals such as cornflowers and field poppies.

The easier and cheaper way to create a perennial meadow is to reduce soil fertility gradually, by converting an existing grassed area, mowing twice a year (spring and autumn) and removing the nitrogen-rich grass clippings rather than letting them break down back into the lawn. This takes longer than the first option (up to 10 years). You can try this approach alone and see which wildflowers turn up or you can plant plugs to get things going. To help speed up the process, sow yellow rattle in early autumn – this is a hemiparasite (partial parasite) of grass and will slow down its growth, allowing wildflowers to flourish.

Grow your own mini meadow

You will need:

- Spare patch of the garden in an area that hasn't had fertiliser or compost added
- Packet of meadow flower seeds
- Watering can
- Rake

1. Remove grass, weeds and the top layer of soil, then lightly rake.
2. Sprinkle your seed mix (best in spring or autumn).
3. Walk over the soil and water lightly.

Cut in summer to 5–10cm high and compost the cuttings.

Don't take seeds from the wild – always buy specially grown seeds, and use pre-packaged seeds in your garden.

1–5g of seed per m² of soil (check pack)

Cornfield annuals will flower in the first year. Perennial meadows often need two years.

Perennial seed or plug plant mixes can include any of the following:

- Agrimony *Agrimonia eupatoria*
- Betony *Stachys officinalis*
- Bird's foot trefoil *Lotus corniculatus*
- Common knapweed *Centaurea nigra*
- Cowslip *Primula veris*
- Common mouse-ear *Cerastium fontanum*
- Common sorrel *Rumex acetosa*
- Field scabious *Knautia arvensis*
- Great burnet *Sanguisorba officinalis*
- Lady's bedstraw *Galium verum*
- Meadow buttercup *Ranunculus acris*
- Meadow grasses *Poa*
- Meadow vetchling *Lathyrus pratensis*
- Oregano *Origanum vulgare*
- Ox-eye daisy *Leucanthemum vulgare*
- Primrose *Primula vulgaris*
- Red clover *Trifolium pratense*
- Ribwort plantain *Plantago lanceolata*
- Selfheal *Prunella vulgaris*
- Yarrow *Achillea millefolium*
- Yellow rattle *Rhinanthus minor*

The life cycle of butterflies and moths

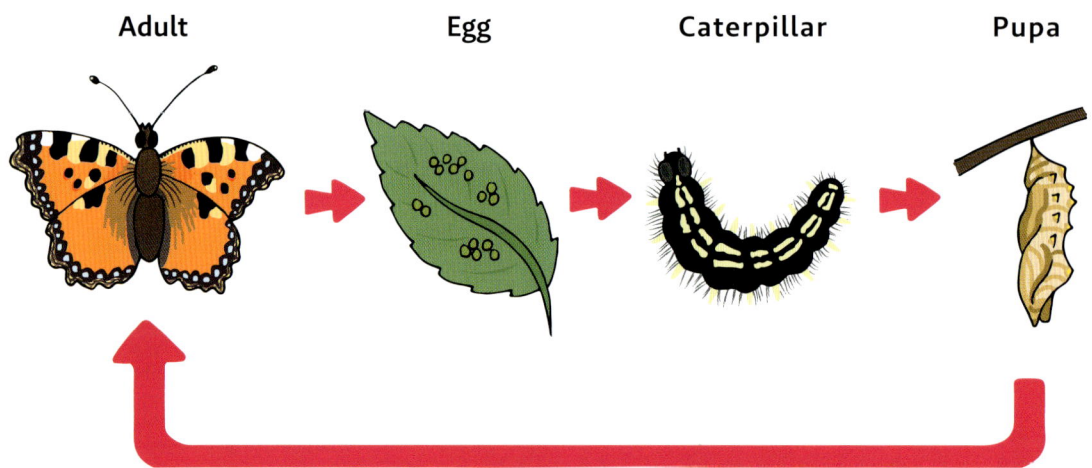

Like all insects, butterflies and moths go through changes in their development, known as metamorphosis. Butterflies and moths have four life-cycle stages: egg (ovum), caterpillar (larva), pupa (often called chrysalis in butterflies) and adult (imago). Eggs are laid throughout the year, although most species breed in spring and summer. Caterpillars develop over the course of a few weeks or months, with factors such as the weather, temperatures and environmental conditions affecting their development. Most species overwinter as a caterpillar but some overwinter as an egg, pupa or adult. The speckled wood butterfly overwinters as either a caterpillar or a pupa.

Caterpillars do very little other than eat, while the adults are focused on reproduction (and some species of moth don't eat as adults, preferring to just get on with the job of making the next generation). Pupation can last for anything from a week to several months, if over winter. In this time, the caterpillar gradually transforms into a butterfly or moth. When ready, it breaks out of its pupa, expands its wings (which can take several hours for some species) and then flies off in search of food or a mate.

Butterfly or moth?

There are few differences between butterflies and moths, and no real way to determine one from another – in essence a butterfly is just a type of moth. While many moths are nocturnal, some fly during the day; and many are just as beautiful as butterflies, if not more so.

Hungry for caterpillars

Some of Britain's favourite garden birds rely on caterpillars to rear their nestlings, with our blue tit chicks alone needing an estimated 35 billion a year.

Butterfly and moth declines

Roughly every three years, a partnership of conservation groups and charities jointly publishes the State of Nature report, outlining the population trends of a wide range of species across the British Isles. The charity Butterfly Conservation assesses information from national butterfly and moth recording and monitoring schemes, and makes recommendations for the conservation of UK butterflies and moths.

Key findings from The State of the UK's Butterflies 2022 report include:
- Butterflies continue to decline, with 80 per cent of species declining in abundance or distribution or both since 1976.
- 56 per cent of species increased in one or both measures in the same time frame.
- On average, UK butterflies have lost six per cent of their total abundance at monitored sites and 42 per cent of their distribution over the period 1976 2019.

Key findings from The State of Britain's Larger Moths 2021 report include:
- The total abundance of larger moths caught in the RIS light-trap network in Britain decreased by 33 per cent between 1968 and 2017.
- Moth species that occur in both southern and northern Britain fared significantly worse in the south (39 per cent decrease, compared to 22 per cent in the north).
- Despite the declines, some 53 species (16 per cent of the total) more than doubled their populations.

As indicator species (see box), butterflies and moths are telling us of catastrophic declines, with enormous implications for the rest of the natural world. Positioned at the very bottom of the food chain, their dramatic declines could affect numbers of birds, mammals, amphibians and other insect predators, and may already be contributing to the decline of some species that eat them, such as cuckoos (65 per cent decline since 1980) and hedgehogs (a decline of between 30 per cent and 75 per cent across different areas of the countryside since 2000).

With so many species reliant on insects such as butterflies, moths and their caterpillars for food, it's no wonder we're seeing such widespread declines across the board. Surely if we all grew more plants known to attract egg-laying butterflies and moths, we could make a difference.

Vital indicators

Because they're especially sensitive to environmental changes, butterflies and moths are known as 'indicator species'. This means they can tell us a lot about the general state of the environment, as well as the effects of certain habitat changes, employment of new pesticides or climate change. Ecologists monitor numbers closely – could the changes you make in your gardens alter statistics?

What's causing declines?

It's not known exactly what's causing these declines, but it could be a combination of the following:
- Loss of habitat due to land use changes from seminatural habitat to farmland and urbanisation.
- Changes in land use and management of farmland, including the grubbing out of hedgerows.
- Climate change, including milder winters, wetter summers and more extreme weather generally.
- Paving-over of gardens – loss of caterpillar food plants.
- Nitrogen run-off from farmland.
- Pollution, including air pollution and water contamination, which may potentially change the delicate chemical make-up of plants, and light pollution.
- Pesticides such as insecticides, herbicides and fungicides (see page 18).

In praise of moths

Moths are often divided into two groups: smaller micro-moths and larger macro-moths. Some micro-moths are absolutely tiny but, confusingly, some micro-moths are larger than the smallest macro-moths.

Moths are extremely varied in their appearance. There are brightly coloured ones, such as the olive and pink elephant hawk-moth; little brown ones, such as the light brown apple moth; and moths that have evolved to blend into lichen on trees, such as the marvellous merveille du jour. And did I mention the caterpillars? Once you have entered the magical world of moths, I challenge you not to be hooked. I absolutely love them and know they'll provide me with a lifetime of interest and fascination. For me, gardening for moths is all about seeing which species I can lure into my garden and catch (and release) in my moth trap – the more species I attract, the happier I feel.

With so many species in a wide range of habitats, moths play a huge part in the biodiversity of our gardens, not least because they're fundamental

Save the garden tiger moth

Ironically, despite its name, the beautiful garden tiger moth (*Arctia caja*) is now a rare sight in our gardens, especially in the south of the UK. Known for its 'woolly bear' caterpillars, it has declined by some 92 per cent in the last 40 years, probably largely due to climate change, habitat loss and use of insecticides (which kill them) and herbicides (which kill their food plants).

Adults fly from July to August and will turn up in moth traps. Their hairy larvae can be seen from August to June the following year. They sometimes feed in sunshine and you may spot one moving across bare ground when fully grown. They overwinter as caterpillars and then pupate among vegetation on or near the ground in spring.

How to help:
- Grow known caterpillar food plants. The garden tiger eats a variety of herbaceous plants, including broadleafed dock, burdocks, hound's tongue, nettles and others.
- Be less tidy. They need undisturbed areas of leaf litter/vegetation to pupate into an adult.
- Grow night-scented, nectar-rich plants, such as honeysuckle and night-scented stock, so they can refuel if they need to.

▲ The mint moth is a common visitor to gardens. Look out for it on catmint and lavender.

parts of the food web. This means that they and their eggs, caterpillars and pupae provide food for a wealth of other wildlife, including bats, frogs and toads, hedgehogs and many types of bird. So by gardening for moths, we not only make our gardens more interesting for ourselves, but we also make a difference to the wildlife that eats them.

Moth traps

A moth trap is a fantastic piece of kit that enables you to find out which moths visit your garden at night, and the best thing about them is that you can set them up and then go to bed! Many night-flying moth species are attracted to light. Moth traps work by using light to lure them in, then provide them with a safe place to rest until you check on them the following morning.

You can record moths by making your own trap using a white sheet and a table lamp or a torch, but you will have to stay up to see the moths coming in and fewer species are attracted to this method than to bespoke boxes. There are several designs to choose from. This trap is a Skinner design, comprising a simple box structure that can be taken apart after use, Perspex sheets and a strong light, mercury vapour (MV) if possible. Simply assemble the box and lay egg boxes in the bottom, so the moths can rest and hide safely. Turn the light on. The moths are attracted to the light and then fall into the trap. They rest among the egg boxes until morning.

Moth-trapping tips

Avoid trapping on rainy nights. If you have a greenhouse then you could pop it in there and leave the greenhouse door open, to provide cover for the trap. Hanging a white sheet near the trap can increase your chances of success.

Arm yourself with a good moth guidebook and make a note of all the moths you find, taking photos, too. You'll quickly build up an impressive species list and, if you start planting

▲ The elephant hawk-moth is one of the most striking moths you can attract to your garden.

caterpillar food plants, you may be able to gauge your success in luring more moths to your garden.

If you don't have time to go through your trap first thing the following morning, then move it into a shady spot and cover with a blanket or sheet so the moths remain comfortable. When you do empty the trap, transfer the moths to a dense shrub where they can take shelter from birds until dusk.

Don't trap every night, especially if you have a small garden. If you do, you will undoubtedly trap some of the same moths each night, thus potentially preventing them from being able to mate and feed.

What will you catch?

Macro-moths (large species) and micro-moths (tiny species). You're likely to also attract bumblebees, caddis flies, lacewings, some beetles species, many true flies and bugs, wasps and hornets.

Identifying moths can be daunting at first, but gradually you will know which part of the guidebook to look through. Better still, join one of the brilliant moth ID groups on Facebook, or download an ID app such as ID UK Insects, created by the Wildlife Trusts, or ObsIdentify.

ID parade
Butterflies

Brimstone
Gonepteryx rhamni

Description: A striking butterfly seen throughout the year but one of the earliest to emerge, the pale females appearing almost ghost-like against the first green shoots of spring. The wings of the female are very pale green, almost white, while males have yellow-green underwings and yellow upper wings. It's thought the word 'butterfly' originates from the butter-yellow colour of male.
When to see it: March to October.
Flowers visited: Betony (*Stachys officinalis*), bluebell (*Hyacinthoides non-scripta*), bugle (*Ajuga reptans*), carline thistle (*Carlina vulgaris*), cowslip (*Primula veris*), fleabane (*Pulicaria dysenterica*), dandelion (*Taraxacum officinale*), devil's-bit scabious (*Succisa pratensis*), knapweeds (*Centaurea*), oregano (*Origanum vulgare*), primrose (*Primula vulgaris*), ragged robin (*Lychnis flos-cuculi*), red campion (*Silene dioica*), selfheal (*Prunella vulgaris*), thistles (*Carduus* and *Cirsium*) and vetches, including common vetch (*Vicia sativa*) and kidney vetch (*Anthyllis vulneraria*).
Caterpillar food plants: Alder buckthorn (*Frangula alnus*) and purging buckthorn (*Rhamnus cathartica*).
Overwinters as: Adult.
Garden habitats: Flower borders and areas where caterpillar food plants are present.
Distribution: Widespread and common in England and Wales; less common in Scotland and Ireland.

Meadow brown
Maniola jurtina

Description: A brown butterfly with eyespots that usually have single white pupils, unlike the similar-looking gatekeeper (*Pyronia tithonus*), which has two and is smaller and more orange with a row of tiny white dots on its hind underwings. Hundreds may be seen together, flying low over the vegetation. Unlike many butterflies, adults fly in dull weather.
When to see it: Late May to September.
Flowers visited: A wide variety, including meadow plants such as clovers (*Trifolium*), dandelion (*Taraxacum officinale*), knapweeds (*Centaurea*), oregano (*Origanum vulgare*) and scabious (*Knautia* and *Scabiosa*).
Caterpillar food plants: Typically fine-leaved grasses such as bents (*Agrostis*), fescues (*Festuca*) and meadow grasses (*Poa*), but also coarser species such as cock's foot (*Dactylis glomerata*), downy oat grass (*Avenula pubescens*) and false brome (*Brachypodium sylvaticum*).
Overwinters as: Caterpillar.
Garden habitats: In and around long grass.
Distribution: Widespread and common throughout Britain and Ireland.

Orange-tip
Anthocharis cardamines

Description: One of the first butterflies to emerge in spring that hasn't overwintered as an adult. The male is white with bright orange wing tips and the female white with dark grey wing tips. Both have mottled green underwings, easily visible when resting.
When to see it: April to July.
Flowers visited: Bluebell (*Hyacinthoides non-scripta*), cuckoo flower (*Cardamine pratensis*), dandelion (*Taraxacum officinale*), wallflower 'Bowles's Mauve' (*Erysimum* 'Bowles's Mauve').
Caterpillar food plants: Cuckoo flower (*Cardamine pratensis*), garlic mustard (*Alliaria petiolata*), occasionally charlock (*Sinapis arvensis*) and hedge mustard (*Sisymbrium officinale*). In gardens it lays its eggs on honesty (*Lunaria annua*) and sweet rocket (*Hesperis matronalis*) but larval survival is thought to be poor on these plants.
Overwinters as: Pupa.
Garden habitats: Flower borders and areas where caterpillar food plants are growing.
Distribution: Widespread and common throughout England, Wales and Ireland, but scarcer further north and in Scotland.

Red admiral *Vanessa atalanta*

Description: A large, velvety black butterfly with dark orange-red bands. Primarily a migrant from the Continent, although more adults are choosing to spend winter here, especially in the south of England. This resident population is considered to be only a small fraction of the population seen in the British Isles, which is topped up every year with migrants arriving from central Europe in May and June.
When to see it: March to November.
Flowers visited: A wide range, including buddleias (*Buddleja*), daisies including tansies (*Tanacetum*) and Shasta daisies (*Leucanthemum* × *superbum*), and Argentinian vervain (*Verbena bonariensis*).
Caterpillar food plants: Primarily stinging nettle (*Urtica dioica*), occasionally small nettle (*U. urens*), hop (*Humulus lupulus*) and pellitory-of-the-wall (*Parietaria judaica*).
Overwinters as: Adult or migrates back to central Europe.
Garden habitats: Flower borders and nettle patches.
Distribution: Widespread and common in Britain and Ireland.

Small tortoiseshell
Aglais urticae

Description: Well known and good-looking, the small tortoiseshell is one of the first species to emerge in spring. Identified by its bright orange and black wings with a blue and black margin, and a white spot in each forewing.
When to see it: March to November.
Flowers visited: A wide range, including buddleias (*Buddleja*), daisies including tansies (*Tanacetum*) and Shasta daisies (*Leucanthemum* × *superbum*), and Argentinian vervain (*Verbena bonariensis*).
Caterpillar food plants: Small nettle (*Urtica urens*) and stinging nettle (*Urtica dioica*).
Overwinters as: Adult.
Garden habitats: Flower borders and nettle patches.
Distribution: Widespread and common throughout Britain and Ireland, although there are concerns about recent declines.

Moths

Angle shades
Phlogophora meticulosa
Description: A distinctive medium-sized buff-brown moth, with pinky-brown v-shaped markings on its wings. When folded, its scalloped wings give the appearance of a dead autumn leaf.
When to see it: May to October.
Flowers visited: A wide range.
Caterpillar food plants: Common nettle (*Urtica dioica*), red valerian (*Centranthus ruber*), hop (*Humulus lupulus*), broad-leaved dock (*Rumex obtusifolius*), bramble (*Rubus fruiticosus*), hazel (*Corylus avellana*), birches and oaks.
Overwinters as: Pupa.
Garden habitats: Walls, fences and any vegetation.
Distribution: Common and widespread throughout Britain and Ireland.

Elephant hawk-moth
Deilephila elpenor

Description: Gorgeous pink and olive-green moth, named after the caterpillar's resemblance to an elephant's trunk. Adults are nocturnal, flying from dusk and attracted to light, resting by day among its food plants. The larvae are usually seen when looking for somewhere to pupate, or when resting on stems in good weather, as they are very large, with noticeable eye markings. They overwinter as pupae in fragile cocoons at the base of plants in loose plant debris/litter, or just below the surface of the ground.
When to see it: May to early August.
Flowers visited: Honeysuckle (*Lonicera*) and other tubular flowers.
Caterpillar food plants: Bedstraws (*Galium*), enchanter's nightshade (*Circaea lutetiana*), fuchsias (*Fuchsia*), rosebay willowherb (*Chamaenerion angustifolium*) and other willowherbs.

Overwinters as: Pupa.
Garden habitats: Flower borders, especially where honeysuckle and other tubular flowers are present, and where there are fuchsias and willowherbs to lay eggs on.
Distribution: Common and widespread in Britain and Ireland.

Five-spot burnet
Zygaena trifolii
Description: A medium-sized moth with five red spots on each black forewing. Sometimes found commonly, it flies with a slow, buzzing flight during sunshine.
When to see it: May to August.
Flowers visited: A wide range.
Caterpillar food plants: Two subspecies occur in Britain Z. t. palustrella feeds on bird's foot trefoil (*Lotus corniculatus*). The caterpillar of subspecies Z. t. decreta feeds on greater bird's foot trefoil (*Lotus pedunculatus*).
Overwinters as: Caterpillar.
Garden habitats: Meadow areas with long grass and wildflowers, particularly trefoils.
Distribution: Found in England and Wales only.

Garden tiger *Arctia caja*
Description: Gorgeous moth with brown-and-white spotted forewings, orange-and-blue-spotted hindwings and a red face. If disturbed it displays its hindwings as a warning and can produce a clear yellow fluid from two ducts just behind the head. The larvae are hairy and known as 'woolly bear caterpillars'. They

sometimes feed and bask in sunshine and may be seen moving rapidly across bare ground when fully grown. They pupate in a thin cocoon among vegetation on or near the ground.
When to see it: July to August – it is attracted to light.

Flowers visited: Unlikely to visit flowers.
Caterpillar food plants: A wide variety, including broadleaved dock (*Rumex obtusifolius*), burdocks (*Arctium* spp.), hound's tongue (*Cynoglossum officinale*), stinging nettle (*Urtica dioica*) and many garden plants.
Overwinters as: Caterpillar.
Garden habitats: Areas of long grass, particularly those with weeds. Needs leaf litter to shelter beneath in winter.
Distribution: Found in Britain and Ireland but suffering huge declines.

Hummingbird hawk-moth *Macroglossum stellatarum*
Description: A large moth with grey-brown forewings, bright orange hindwings, and a greyish body with a broad, black-and-white 'tail'. It hovers and darts among flowers, with rapid wing movements, resembling a hummingbird.
When to see it: April to December.
Flowers visited: Tubular flowers like honeysuckle, red valerian (*Centranthus ruber*), phlox, jasmines, buddleias and petunias.
Caterpillar food plants: Lady's bedstraw (*Galium verum*), hedge bedstraw (*Galium album*) and cleavers (*Galium aparine*).
Overwinters as: Adult.
Garden habitats: Herbaceous border plants.
Distribution: Originally a summer migrant but now overwinters in southern regions of the British Isles. Found throughout Britain and Ireland.

Wasps

Wasps fall into three categories: social, solitary and parasitic. The social ones include the wasps we love to hate: the common and German wasps, which make huge nests and interfere with summer barbecues and picnics. They also include hornets, which many of us are scared of but which are actually quite placid. Most of us are barely aware of the solitary species, some of which (if you're lucky!) might use your bee hotel. The parasitic species lay eggs in other insects, the larvae eventually killing their hosts; they are more accurately called parasitoids as a true parasite doesn't usually kill its host.

Many people are scared of wasps and hornets, and understandably so. Social wasps can be aggressive if you get too close to their nest, particularly if you're in the flight line (i.e. standing in front of it, no matter how 'safe' your distance). While wasp stings are painful, and disturbing a social wasp nest can be dangerous, in reality wasps are no more aggressive than honeybees, and some would argue far less so. It's also worth remembering that there are 9,000 species of wasp in the UK, and only the social species – including the common and German wasp – are at all likely to sting you. Solitary and parasitoid wasps seem far more concerned with collecting or laying eggs in other invertebrates to bother stinging people.

Hornets too, while larger than other social wasps and more aggressive-looking, are actually quite passive and very unlikely to sting you. If you have a fear or have had a bad experience of flying insects or stinging bees and wasps, then be kind to yourself; it's OK to be wary of them. But try not to let this stop you from loving them and catering for them in your garden, because they really are wonderful. Honestly!

▲ This digger wasp collects caterpillars to feed its young.

Love 'em or hate 'em, wasps are expert 'pest' controllers and you'd do well to encourage them into your garden. While the adults of many species are pollinators, their larvae feed on caterpillars, aphids and flies. Some catch them for their young; others are parasitic, laying their eggs on or in prey; still others are cuckoos, or brood parasites. In my garden, tiny solitary wasps (see page 82) take aphids and caterpillars from my herbaceous plants, while *Ectemnius* wasps (see page 80) patrol my fennel, picking off hoverflies. On the allotment, common and German wasps work so hard taking small and large white butterfly caterpillars from my broccoli and cabbages that I don't bother netting them.

It's wasps, not us, that keep plant-eating species under control. So the more relaxed we are about aphids and caterpillars nibbling our plants, the more food we provide for wasp larvae, and the more adults there will be to maintain a happy equilibrium in return. What's not to like?

Learning to love social wasps

Social wasps like the common and German wasps give British wasps a bad name, but learning about the life cycle of these apparent troublemakers might make you like them a bit more.

The social wasp life cycle is similar to that of the social bees (particularly the bumblebees). In spring, mated queens wake from overwintering sites to find a nest. The nest comprises a series of hexagonal cells and is made using wood, which the queen scrapes off items such as fence panels and trees, chewing and mixing it with saliva until it resembles paper. She then lays eggs, and bears sterile worker females. In the first couple of weeks, she continues to forage for food (caterpillars and other insects) for her larvae while feeding on nectar, pollen and aphid honeydew herself.

Once she has built up a good number of adult workers, the queen stops leaving the nest and focuses on egg-laying; her workers take on the role of finding food to feed the larvae in the nest. In return for food the workers bring them, the larvae secrete a sugary solution, which the workers eat. This process continues all summer, with nests averaging 5,000 – 7,000 but occasionally reaching 40,000.

Towards late summer, the production of workers ends, and queens and males are produced. Once mature, these leave the nest to mate, the males then die while the new queens

The life cycle of social wasps

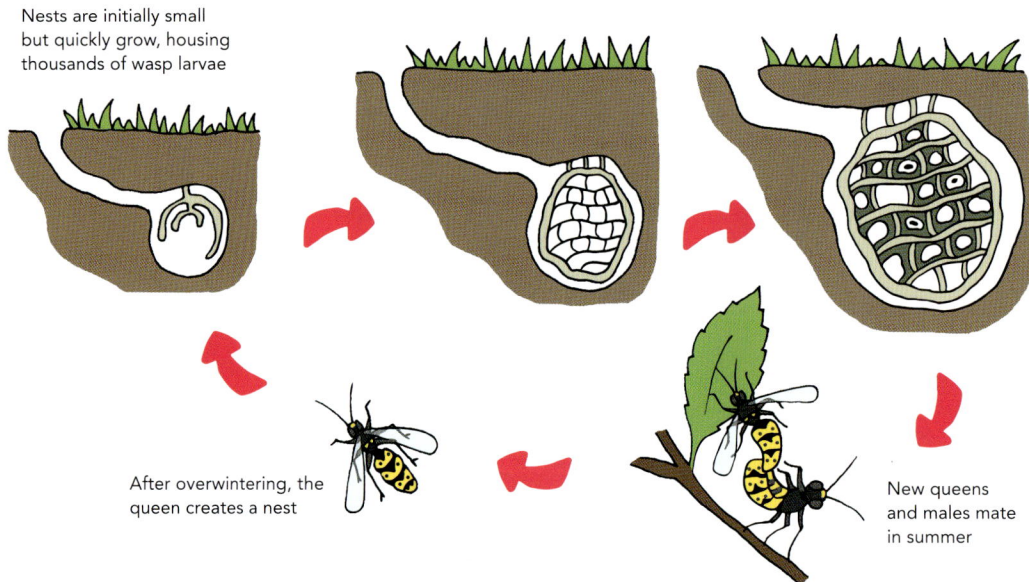

Nests are initially small but quickly grow, housing thousands of wasp larvae

After overwintering, the queen creates a nest

New queens and males mate in summer

store sperm in their bodies and find somewhere to overwinter. Eventually, the original queen stops laying eggs, and the workers have nothing to do. Without their sugary solution from the larvae, they crave a sweet hit, and that's when they start irritating us at barbecues and picnics.

Most of us notice social wasps only when they're annoying us, having spent all summer in blissful ignorance of how hard they've been working in removing our garden pests. Yes, they can be aggressive and sting us if we aggravate them, but I hope that understanding their life cycle and reasons for bothering us will make you more forgiving of them. As with human relationships, learning to love our neighbour requires only a little empathy and understanding. It's not just other people we should be reaching out to.

The life cycle of solitary wasps

Like their bee cousins, almost all wasps are solitary. Their life cycle is much the same as solitary bees (see page 43) and some of them will even use bee hotels, provisioning the nest cells with paralysed caterpillars, spiders or aphids rather than pollen and nectar. (This is the holy grail of bee hotel keeping in my book!)

▼ The common wasp has a bad reputation but it has an important role in the garden.

Gardening for wasps

Wasps are voracious predators of virtually anything that moves. Gardening for them involves tolerating aphids and caterpillars (as well as tolerating the wasps themselves!) as well as growing a wide range of flowering plants to attract more breeding insects for them to eat. It involves understanding that some species eat other pollinating insects, such as honeybees and hoverflies, but that they have been doing so for millennia and are not interfering with local ecosystems. There are a few other things you can do too, as listed in the table below.

▲ Solitary wasp on *Eryngium* flower.

Ideas for attracting wasps

	Suitable for...				
	Small garden	Medium garden	Large garden	Allotment	Balcony/patio
Grow as many plants for flying insects and their larvae as possible. For inspiration, see link to Butterfly Conservation's list of caterpillar food plants in Resources.	✓	✓	✓	✓	✓
Erect a bee hotel on a south-facing wall and keep your fingers crossed.	✓	✓	✓	✓	✗
Grow as many flowering plants as possible, including angelica and figwort, which wasps particularly seem to favour.	✓	✓	✓	✓	✗
Build log, stick and leaf piles, for overwintering wasp queens.	✓	✓	✓	✓	✓
Plant a wildflower meadow.	✗	✗	✓	✓	✗
Leave patches of bare earth in sunny borders for nesting solitary wasps.	✓	✓	✓	✓	✗
Provide water for thirsty wasps by including a pond with water lilies as landing pads, or a birdbath with stones in.	✗	✓	✓	✓	Birdbath with stones in
Don't net your cabbages. (Just try it – what's the worst that could happen?)	✗	✓	✓	✓	✗
Grow ivy on your walls and let it flower.	✓	✓	✓	✓	✗
Tolerate social wasps nesting in your roof / shed / compost bin. Remember, nests are annual.	✗	✓	✓	✓	✗
Leave a bit of your fence or shed untreated, so queen and worker social wasps can rasp off the wood to make their paper nests.	✓	✓	✓	✓	✗

ID parade
Social wasps

Common wasp
Vespula vulgaris
Description: Up to 2cm long, with an obvious 'waist' between the thorax and abdomen. It has bright yellow and black bands along its body, two

pairs of wings and long antennae. As with bees, the queens are larger than workers. Its facial markings look a bit like a ship's anchor, telling it apart from the German wasp (*Vespula germanica*).
When to see it: April to November.
Nests: Annual, usually made underground but are often found in wall cavities, roofs and tree hollows. They can contain several thousand wasps.
Flowers visited: A wide range, including cotoneasters (*Cotoneaster*) and other early-flowering shrubs for nectar. Males and the last workers are often found taking nectar from ivy flowers in autumn.
Larval food: Aphids, caterpillars, flies and other invertebrates, which it immobilises using its sting.
Overwinters as: Fertilised queen.
Garden habitats: Flower borders, particularly where larval foods are present.
Distribution: Widespread and common throughout Britain and Ireland.

European hornet *Vespa crabro*
Description: Britain's largest social wasp, at up to 3.5cm long. It has a red-brown thorax, and orange-yellow and brown stripes along the abdomen. Although it looks fearsome, it's actually quite placid and far less likely to sting you than a common wasp or honeybee; it is only aggressive if the colony is threatened.
When to see it: April to November.
Nests: The queen starts nest building in May, typically placing it off the ground (often in hollow trees) but occasionally in attics and outhouses or on or just below the ground. The queen and her workers build the nest using pulp collected from decayed wood.
Flowers visited: Several, including ivy (*Hedera helix*). Hornets also eat windfall fruit and tree sap – they can chew at the bark to pierce it and encourage sap to flow.
Larval food: Other species of social wasp, honeybees, flies, butterflies, moths and spiders. Hornets often hunt in wildflower meadows and take prey from flowers.

Overwinters as: Adult.
Garden habitats: Large, established gardens with plenty of tree cover, and flower borders where there is plenty of larval food.
Distribution: Found in many parts of England and Wales, spreading northwards. Absent from Ireland.

Solitary and parasitoid wasps

Chalcid wasps (superfamily Chalcidoidea)

Description: A large group of small parasitoid wasps that have a rounded abdomen, often metallic in beautiful shades of blue, green and red.
When to see them: April to September.
Flowers visited: Daisies such as tansies (*Tanacetum*) as well as umbellifers such as fennel (*Foeniculum vulgare*).
Larval food: They commonly lay their eggs in the eggs, larvae or pupae of other insects.
Overwinters as: Varied.
Garden habitats: Flower borders, particularly where hosts are present.
Distribution: Found throughout the British Isles.

Hunting *Ectemnius* wasps
Ectemnius spp.

Description: These wasps grow up to 1.5cm long and have large bulging eyes that look a bit like aviator sunglasses. There are 10 species in the British Isles, all fairly similar-looking, with some species likely to come into gardens. They have long legs for carrying prey and walk in a sidestepping or circular motion.

When to see them: May to October.
Nests: In rotting wood, such as tree stumps. In gardens *Ectemnius* wasps may use an artificial 'bee block' made out of a wooden post with holes drilled in. Nests are created individually, stocked with prey that the larvae may eat.
Flowers visited: Daisies such as tansies (*Tanacetum*) as well as umbellifers such as fennel (*Foeniculum vulgare*), often for pollen as well as prey.
Larval food: Hoverflies and other flies (some species of *Ectemnius* specialise only in hoverflies).
Overwinters as: Pupa.
Garden habitats: Flower borders, particularly where larval foods are present.
Distribution: Most species are found throughout Britain and Ireland, although are less common in the north.

European beewolf wasp *Philanthus triangulum*
Description: At nearly 2cm long, this is one of the largest solitary wasp species in the British Isles. Once considered a rarity, numbers have rocketed since the 1980s, thanks to climate change and a rise in the popularity of beekeeping. The beewolf can be identified by its pale face and red-brown markings behind its eyes. Females can be seen carrying honeybees back to the nest beneath their abdomen.
When to see it: July to September.
Nests: Solitary nests made in sandy soil, often in huge aggregations referred to as 'wasp cities'.
Flowers visited: A variety, including blackberry (*Rubus fruticosus*), ragworts (*Senecio*) and thistles (*Cirsium*).
Larval food: Honeybees, which it stocks in nest cells, around 4–5 per egg.
Overwinters as: Pupa.
Garden habitats: Not known in gardens yet but populations are increasing.
Distribution: It used to be very scarce but numbers are increasing in southern England and appear to be spreading northwards.

Field digger wasp *Mellinus arvensis*

Description: There are around 110 species of digger wasps in the UK, and the field digger is one of the most common and widespread. Long and thin with a clearly defined wasp 'waist', it has a yellow stripe across the front of the thorax and a yellow spot at the rear, with two large yellow bands across the abdomen and a red margin on the yellow tail.
When to see it: July to October.
Nests: Digs nest burrows in the ground, in sandy soil or vertical banks, even in gardens, sometimes in large aggregations and often alongside other species of digger wasp and some species of solitary bee. The burrow usually branches at the end and each branch will have a separate egg laid in it, stocked with insects. Instead of stocking the nest with prey and then leaving the young to fend for themselves, some digger wasp species leave a single prey item and then return with fresh supplies after the egg has hatched.
Flowers visited: A wide range. Males also take honeydew from leaves.

Larval food: A range of flies, which it uses to stock nest cells for its young.
Overwinters as: Pupa.
Garden habitats: Sandy soils, particularly coastal gardens, where they can find prey.
Distribution: Common and widespread in Britain and Ireland.

Ichneumon and braconid wasps Ichneumonidae
Description: A large group (some 2,500 species) of wasps that usually lay their eggs in, on or near the larvae of other insects. Some have a very long ovipositor (egg-laying tube) with which to penetrate logs and tree stumps where beetle or other wood-boring insect larvae are feeding; others lay eggs in the larvae of flies, bees, butterflies and moths. They are often very specific, for example the species of braconid wasp *Cotesia glomerata* lays its eggs exclusively in the caterpillars of large white butterflies (known to many gardeners as the cabbage white). Ichneumon wasps can be quite striking-looking, often with extremely pronounced waists, but are notoriously hard to identify.
When to see them: April to November.
Flowers visited: Unknown.
Larval food: Lays eggs in a variety of prey.
Overwinters as: Varies with the species.

Garden habitats: A variety of different locations, including rotten wood, and where they might find prey.
Distribution: Some are very rare and restricted, others are widespread and common throughout the British Isles.

Spider-hunting wasp *Dipogon variegatus*
Description: A tiny solitary wasp, this is one of three spider-hunting species, which patrol a variety of habitats looking for spiders to furnish their nest cells.
When to see it: May to September.
Nests: A variety of nest sites, including hollow plant stems, dead wood, in the mortar of old walls, and even old snail shells and bee hotels. Nest cavities are plugged with grains of sand and other soil and plant fragments bound together with spider's silk.
Flowers visited: A wide range.
Larval food: Almost exclusively the common crab spider (*Xysticus cristatus*). The female paralyses the spider by stinging it in the abdomen and then carries it back to her nest, where she seals it in a cell with a single egg. When the egg hatches into a larva, it has a fresh meal ready.
Overwinters as: Pupa.
Garden habitats: Flower borders, where the crab spider is found
Distribution: Widespread and common throughout the British Isles.

Solitary wasps that might turn up in your bee hotel

Aphid-hunting wasps *Passaloecus* spp.
Description: Black with a tiny wasp waist, yellow face and orange-red legs.
When to see them: May to September.
Nests: In cavities – mainly holes made by wood-boring insects but occasionally bee hotels. It seals each cell with clay.
Flowers visited: Unknown.
Larval food: Aphids.
Overwinters as: Adult.
Garden habitats: Bee hotels; anywhere aphids are found.
Distribution: Found throughout Britain and Ireland, apart from the far north of Scotland.

Ruby-tailed wasp *Chrysis ignita*

Description: The most common of several species of cuckoo solitary wasps, the ruby-tailed wasp is beautifully coloured with metallic shades of red, blue, green and bronze. A common sight at bee hotels, at just 1cm long you could easily miss her, but you might see her running around, using her antennae to detect her host insect, tentatively reversing into a nest hole or even curling into a ball and using her tough exoskeleton to defend herself against angry resident bees.
When to see it: April to September.
Nests: As with all brood parasites, instead of building her own nest, she lays her eggs in the nests of others, specifically mason bees and other solitary bees. Of all parasitoid wasp species, the ruby-tailed does the least damage to bee hotel populations.
Flowers visited: A wide range.
Larval food: Lays eggs in the nests of solitary bees. The wasp eggs hatch into larvae, which eat the newborn host species.
Overwinters as: Pupa.
Garden habitats: Found anywhere where their hosts are likely to occur, including gardens; bee hotels.
Distribution: Widespread and common throughout the British Isles, excluding Orkney and the Shetland Isles.

Willow mason wasp *Symmorphus bifasciatus*

Description: Black with a tiny wasp waist, yellow legs and yellow and black banding on its lower abdomen.
When to see it: June to August.
Nests: In cavities, such as plant stems, holes made by wood-boring insects, straws of thatched roofs, old walls and occasionally bee hotels. It seals each cell with clay.
Flowers visited: Unknown.
Larval food: Larvae of the blue willow beetle (*Phyllodecta vulgatissima*), which it stings to immobilise but not kill, so its larvae has fresh food to eat.
Overwinters as: Adult.
Garden habitats: Willow trees, bee hotels.
Distribution: Found throughout Britain and Ireland, apart from the far north of Scotland.

Have you seen the Asian hornet?

Native to the temperate regions of South East Asia, the Asian hornet (*Vespa velutina*) is thought to have inadvertently been shipped to France from China in a container of plant pots. Like our native European hornet (*Vespa crabro*), it eats honeybees. However, it eats them in far greater numbers than our native hornet and therefore poses a huge risk to honeybee colonies (although arguably still less than the threat posed by we humans!).

There have been several sightings of the Asian hornet in Britain. The first nest was recorded in Gloucestershire in 2016, and the following year one was found in Devon. In 2024, there were 71 credible sightings across the south of the UK, and 24 nests were located and destroyed ranging from Plymouth in the South West to Southend-on-Sea in the South East.

Although potentially a major predator of honeybees, it also feeds on other insects, including wasps, crickets, butterflies and flies, as well as spiders, flowers and ripe fruit.

With honeybees, the Asian hornet hovers around the entrance to the hive and catches returning workers. It forces its prey to drop to the ground before paralysing it and carrying it away. It's thought that one Asian hornet raid can destroy up to 30 per cent of a bee colony in just a couple of hours, and once they have weakened the hive, they may enter and raid it.

The Asian hornet is no more aggressive towards humans than a honeybee, although – as with all insect stings – some people are allergic. In France, where it has become established, it's predated by a variety of birds, including jays, tits and woodpeckers.

Identifying and reporting Asian hornet sightings

Smaller than our native hornet, at around 3cm long, the Asian hornet has a dark brown abdomen, each segment of which is edged with a thin band of yellow, except for the fourth segment, which has a wide yellow to yellow-orange band. The front section of its head, between its antennae, is orange and its legs have yellow tips.

If you think you have seen an Asian hornet, you should immediately notify the Great Britain Non Native Species Secretariat (NNSS) – see page 189.

▲ The smaller Asian hornet clearly showing its darker abdomen.

▲ Our native hornet is larger and has more of an orange body than the Asian hornet.

Wildlife gardening for beetles

Beetles don't tend to be high on wildlife gardeners' lists of priority species, but they should be. They are the largest group of insects in the world, with more than 300,000 species worldwide, and about 4,500 species of beetle in and around the British Isles. From colourful ladybirds and metallic ground beetles to huge, buzzing chafers and enormous stag beetles, there's a whole world out there waiting to be discovered. Some of them fall into the 'pollinators' category (see page 87).

British beetles vary in length from less than 1mm to 7cm. They have hardened forewings (elytra), which protect their fragile flying hindwings and soft abdomen. Some species, such as rove beetles, which you will find in your compost bin, have shortened elytra that cover only part of the abdomen.

Unlike true bugs (see page 100), beetles have biting mouthparts, which they use to bite and cut food. They go through complete metamorphosis, which means the larval stage differs greatly from the adult stage, and in some species only the larvae eat (the adults don't have functioning mouthparts and the only purpose is to breed). Some species with wood-boring larvae, such as stag beetles, have a larval stage that lasts several years, with the adults living for just a few weeks.

Sadly, many species of beetle are declining at a staggering rate (see page 88). There's still so much more research to be done on these falling numbers but, for the garden species at least, there's plenty we can do to help them.

▼ Rose chafer beetles are a gorgeous metallic-green and whir beautifully when flying.

Beetles are found everywhere in the garden. Look for tiny pollen beetles feeding on the pollen grains within flowers; great diving beetles rising from the bottom of your pond and whirligig beetles on the surface; leaf beetles and weevils among your foliage; rose chafers on your roses; rove beetles in your compost bin; and ground beetles in leaf litter and long grass.

Beetles should be welcomed for beetles' sake, but if you need any more incentives, remember that while some beetles damage plants, others help control pests. Many ladybirds eat greenflies and other aphids. Ground and rove beetles eat vine weevil larvae and many other problem invertebrates including slugs. Other beetles are detritivores – they help recycle decaying organic matter.

Gardening for beetles involves creating as wide a range of habitats as possible. That includes burying dead wood, composting your green waste, growing a huge range of flowering plants and letting patches of grass grow a bit long – see the table on page 86 for more suggestions. I like to encourage specific beetle species into my garden, so I grow wild carrot and cow parsley for soldier beetles; I make foul-smelling concoctions to attract dung beetles; I leave tussocks of grass and spent plant material, along with creating piles of twigs and sticks to help shelter ground beetles; and I look after my compost bins for rove beetles. In summer, on my allotment, I marvel at each tiny 22-spot ladybird that feasts on mildew in my courgette and winter squash leaves.

▸ Seven-spot ladybirds and their larvae eat a lot of aphids such as greenfly and blackfly.

Ideas for attracting beetles

	Suitable for...				
	Small garden	Medium garden	Large garden	Allotment	Balcony/patio
Plant a hedge, including field rose which may attract rose chafers.	✗	✓	✓	✓	✗
Tolerate aphids to attract ladybirds.	✓	✓	✓	✓	✓
Leave dead wood on trees for wasp beetles.	✓	✓	✓	✓	✗
Grow a variety of herbaceous plants.	✓	✓	✓	✓	✓
Let a patch of grass grow long.	✓	✓	✓	✓	✗
Mulch borders or pots.	✓	✓	✓	✓	✓
Compost your waste.	Compost bin	Large, open heap	Large, open heap	Large, open heap	Compost bin
Make a habitat pile of branches, twigs, leaves and other spent plants, allowing grass to grow among them.	✗	✓	✓	✓	Allow leaves to build up in a corner or behind pots.
Make a log pile, burying some logs if you can.	Small logs or twigs/prunings	Large, partially buried in the ground	Large, partially buried in the ground	Large, partially buried in the ground	✗
Leave tree stumps in place.	✗	✓	✓	✓	✗
Create areas of dense vegetation.	✓	✓	✓	✓	✗
Plant a native broadleaf deciduous tree, which many beetles use as a habitat.	✗	✗	✓	✓	✗
Grow nettles for aphid-eating ladybirds.	✗	✗	✓	✓	✓
Tolerate weeds, dandelions and ragwort.	✓	✓	✓	✓	✓
Grow as wide a range of flowering plants as you have room for.	✓	✓	✓	✓	✓
Tolerate mildew on your courgette and winter squash leaves to attract the 22-spot and orange ladybirds.	✓	✓	✓	✓	✓
Grow umbellifers for soldier beetles.	✓	✓	✓	✓	✓
Make a nettle feed, with twigs on top, for dung beetles.	Too smelly for a small space	✓	✓	✓	Too smelly for a small space
Grow climbers up walls and fences, including single roses, honeysuckle and ivy.	✓	✓	✓	✓	✓
Add a green roof to your shed.	✓	✓	✓	✓	✗
Plant a wildflower meadow.	✗	✓	✓	✓	✗
Make leaf mould and use it to mulch your borders.	✓	✓	✓	✓	✗

Beetles that pollinate

Despite being the first insects to have evolved a pollination relationship with flowers, beetles are not known for their role in pollination in Britain and Europe. However, there are a few species worthy of note, including the thick-legged flower beetle and red soldier beetle (pages 90–91). Some, such as pollen beetles, are regarded as a garden pest, although they don't actually damage the flowers – they're mainly just annoying if you cut the flowers for arranging and then find beetles all over your kitchen worktop (just give the flowers a good shake before bringing them indoors).

Beetles that do have a role as pollinators might exclusively feed on flowers, or they may supplement their (often carnivorous) diet with nectar and pollen. Some species of beetle visit flowers but aren't considered particularly useful as pollinators. These include ladybirds.

▲ Soldier beetles can be encouraged into rural gardens.

Gardening for pollinating beetles

Gardening for pollinating beetles involves making sure there are plenty of suitable flowers for them (see the RHS Plants for Pollinators lists in Resources). It also means providing safe spaces for them to breed and overwinter. As well as offering food and shelter, it's worth remembering that many beetles overwinter or pupate in the soil, and therefore leaving soil undisturbed can be hugely beneficial to them.

◂ The thick-legged flower beetle is one of the wonderful pollinating beetles that you might spot in your garden.

Beetle declines

Beetles such as the stag beetle are thought to be suffering similar declines to bees and other pollinators. However, there is less hard evidence than for other insect groups.

A report published in 2012 suggested that ground beetles are suffering staggering declines. The study of 68 of Britain's 360 ground beetle species at 11 locations in the British Isles was published in the *Journal of Applied Ecology*. It showed that more than three-quarters had declined in number over a 15-year period. Of these, half had declined so much that they are now considered 'threatened'. Numbers of eight species had dropped by more than 50 per cent – this level of decline means these species are now considered 'endangered'.

Many ground beetles have very specialised habitats (the beetle that suffered the greatest decline was *Carabus arvensis*, a species found on drier montane dwarf shrub heaths). However, some ground beetles will come into gardens, and indeed our gardens can help link more specialised habitats and could potentially even mitigate some of the losses experienced in the wild.

Possible causes of their decline include habitat loss or fragmentation, and climate change. However, different trends were found at each location studied.

The worst declines included 52 per cent in mountainous regions, 31 per cent in areas of moorland, and 28 per cent in pasture. Declines of beetles living in woodland and hedgerows were lower.

Monitoring dung beetles

▲ The minotaur beetle (*Typhaeus typhoeus*) is a specialist rabbit dung feeder. Only the male has the three horns.

Dung beetles are so-called because they feed and develop in and on dung. Some species roll the dung into a ball and bury it, while others tunnel into dung (such as a cowpat) or simply lay their eggs on the surface. Dung beetles play hugely important roles. The dung beetles help break down faeces and aerate the soil, improving drainage and nutrient recycling. They quickly dispose of animal droppings that harbour parasites harmful to livestock. What's more, the beetles and their larvae are a vital source of food for wild birds and mammals.

Dung beetles are suffering huge declines. The Dung Beetle UK Mapping Project (DUMP) helped confirm the 'alarming trend' of decline of some species. Reasons for the decline include coming into contact with drugs called anthelmintics, which are given to livestock to control intestinal worms. These drugs pass through the animals and are found in the faeces. Soil disturbance and a reduction in permanent pastures could also be factors. The scientists examined well-documented dung beetle locations, including sites in the Cairngorms, as well as previously unrecorded places.

ID parade
Beetles

Cockchafer
Melolontha melolontha

Description: A large flying chafer beetle also known as the May bug and Billy witch. About 2.5cm long, it has a stout, reddish-brown body and distinctive feathery antennae, which it uses to find a mate. Adults are attracted to light and will often come to moth traps or porch lights on May evenings. They have a distinctive low whirring sound when flying – you can certainly hear them coming!
When to see it: May.
Diet: Adults may feed on pollen and nectar. The larvae eat plant roots and tubers.
Flowers visited: Unknown.
Life cycle: Adults live for a few weeks at most. They emerge in late April or early May, mating takes place and the female lays eggs in the soil. The eggs hatch into larvae, which live in the soil for up to three years. They eventually pupate and emerge as an adult beetle in spring.
Garden habitats: Garden borders.
Distribution: Widespread in Britain and Ireland.

Devil's coach horse *Ocypus olens*
Description: One of 1,000 rove beetle species in the British Isles, the devil's coach horse is a black beetle about 2.5cm long. A nocturnal carnivorous predator, it is known for its aggressive posturing when handled or threatened – it lifts its abdomen in a scorpion-like posture to ward off predators. It can also emit a foul smell from its abdomen area (*olens* means 'smelling') and can excrete an unpleasant fluid. Although able to fly, it rarely does.
When to see it: April to October.
Diet: Adults feed on spiders, woodlice, worms and a range of other invertebrates, which they catch and cut using their enormous jaws. The larvae also feed on soil invertebrates.
Life cycle: Adults mate in autumn; two to three weeks later the female lays an egg in a damp, dark place such as leaf litter or moss. After around 30 days, the larva hatches, living mainly underground. It goes through three stages of growth (instars) before pupating and finally emerging as an adult.
Garden habitats: A wide range of habitats with damp conditions, including compost heaps.
Distribution: Widespread and common throughout Britain and Ireland.

Great diving beetle *Dytiscus marginalis*
Description: One of our largest beetles at 3.2cm long, the great diving beetle lives in ponds and is a voracious predator. It's black-green with a yellow margin around the thorax and elytra. You might spot these beetles coming to the surface of the pond periodically; and if you watch carefully, you can see them point the tip of their abdomen out of the water to restock the air supply they store beneath their wing cases and use to breathe. Despite spending most of their lives underwater, they can also fly and will do so to colonise new habitats.
When to see it: April to October.
Diet: Both adults and larvae eat small aquatic invertebrates, including tadpoles and even small fish.

Life cycle: Mating takes place in spring and the female lays eggs in plants just above the water's surface. The larvae are yellow-brown and grow to about 5cm long. They have large heads and large jaws, which they're not afraid to use on pond dippers! When ready to pupate, they leave the pond and find damp soil. As new adults, they return to the pond and feed for a few weeks before overwintering at the bottom until spring.
Garden habitats: Garden ponds, areas of damp soil.
Distribution: Common and widespread.

Pollen beetles
Meligethes spp.
Description: Just 2–3mm long, these tiny black or green beetles have clubbed antennae.
When to see them: May to September.
Diet: Both adults and larvae feed on pollen.
Flowers visited: They seem to prefer yellow flowers such as daffodils (*Narcissus*), dandelion (*Taraxacum officinale*), sunflower (*Helianthus annuus*) and brassicas including oilseed rape (*Brassica napus*). They may aid pollination.
Life cycle: Emerging in spring, the female lays eggs in the buds of flowers – usually brassica crops or wildflowers. The larvae feed inside the flower buds and then drop to the soil to pupate, emerging as adults in late summer. The adults overwinter in sheltered spots such as leaf piles and log piles.
Garden habitats: Anywhere with flowers.
Distribution: Widespread across the British Isles.

Red soldier beetle
Rhagonycha fulva
Description: About 1cm long, the red soldier beetle has a narrow body and red wings with a black tip. Also known as the 'bonking beetle', it's rarely seen without a mate.
When to see it: June to August.
Diet: Adults feed on aphids and other insects, as well as pollen and nectar. Larvae eat invertebrates.
Flowers visited: Cow parsley (*Anthriscus sylvestris*) and other umbellifers.

Life cycle: Adults emerge in summer and mate before the female lays eggs in the soil. The eggs hatch and the larvae spend their time on the ground, typically in long grass. They overwinter as larvae and pupate in spring, then emerge as adults in summer.
Garden habitats: Wilder gardens and allotments closer to rural areas, with a good range of long grass and umbellifers.
Distribution: Widespread and common throughout Britain, although scarcer in the north and in Ireland.

Seven-spot ladybird
Coccinella septempunctata
Description: One of our most common and easily recognisable ladybirds, the seven-spot is about 1cm long and has red wings with seven black spots.
When to see it: April to September.
Diet: Both adults and larvae eat aphids (and lots of them).
Life cycle: Adults emerge from overwintering sites in spring, mate and the female lays eggs on plants supporting aphid colonies. The eggs hatch and the young feed on aphids before pupating and emerging as an adult a week or so later. The new adults feed for a few weeks before finding somewhere to overwinter.
Garden habitats: Gardens with plenty of foliage and spaces to overwinter.
Distribution: Widespread.

Stag beetle
Lucanus cervus
Description: Males are red-brown with enlarged antler-like jaws. The stag beetle is the UK's largest beetle at up to 7.5cm long. Adults fly on early evenings in search of a mate. Males often get into fights with rival males, using their large, antler-like mandibles.
When to see it: May to August.
Diet: Adults eat very little, although they may nibble on soft fruit. The larvae feed on dead wood especially rotting tree roots.

Life cycle: The adults emerge in May and are dead by August, having spent most of their time mating. Eggs are laid in rotting tree roots, where the larvae live for up to seven years before pupating and becoming adults.
Garden habitats: Decaying wood buried in the soil, in old roots of deciduous trees and shrubs (including buddleia) and occasionally in rotting fence posts.
Distribution: Found only in south-east England (particularly the New Forest and Southampton, parts of Essex, and south and west London) and declining.

Thick-legged flower beetle *Oedemera nobilis*
Description: A metallic-green beetle around 8–10mm long, it is often seen on flowers – particularly ox-eye daisies – on warm, sunny days. The males have thickened hind legs and both sexes have elytra that don't fully meet at the base, leaving the wings below partially exposed.

When to see it: All year round.
Diet: Smaller soil invertebrates. Violet ground beetles are particularly helpful to gardeners, as they prey on many 'pest' species, including the occasional small slug.
Life cycle: After mating in spring, females lay their eggs in soil and the larvae hatch, becoming active predators.
Garden habitats: Leaf litter, log piles, compost heaps.
Distribution: Widespread.

Wasp beetle
Clytus arietis
Description: This beetle belongs to the family of longhorn beetles, which typically have long antennae that they use to find mates and suitable breeding sites. For a longhorn  beetle, the wasp beetle typically has relatively short antennae and a narrow body up to 1.8cm long. It mimics the colour and movements of the common wasp to deter predators, and can even buzz if you get too close. However, it doesn't have a sting and is completely harmless.
When to see it: June to August.
Diet: Adults feed on pollen. The larvae eat rotting deciduous wood above ground, such as untreated old fence posts and dead branches left on trees.
Flowers visited: A variety of flowers including umbellifers such as cow parsley (*Anthriscus sylvestris*).
Life cycle: The adults emerge in spring, then mate, and the female lays eggs in rotting wood. These grow and pupate, emerging as adults the following year.
Garden habitats: In gardens, it prefers well-vegetated areas with plenty of dead wood.
Distribution: Widespread in England and Wales, scarcer in Scotland. Not present in Ireland.

When to see it: Adults from April to September. The larvae are rarely seen – they live within the plant stems.
Diet: Adults feed on pollen, larvae feed on plant stems.
Flowers visited: Umbellifers such as cow parsley (*Anthriscus sylvestris*), ox-eye daisy (*Leucanthemum vulgare*) and wild carrot (*Daucus carota*); thistles (*Carduus* and *Cirsium*).
Life cycle: Mating takes place in summer on or in flowers. The female lays eggs in the dried stems of plants such as thistles, where the larvae feed and grow.
Garden habitats: Garden areas planted with umbellifers, thistles and long grass.
Distribution: Widespread across England and Wales, but scarce in Scotland. Not present in Ireland.

Violet ground beetle *Carabus violaceus*
Description: About 3cm long and metallic black with violet edges, this common beetle is a nocturnal hunter so often goes unnoticed.

Wildlife gardening for true flies

▲ The Batman hoverfly (*Myathropa florea*) lays its eggs in decaying waste, rot holes or stagnant water, and its 'rat-tailed maggot' larvae breathe through a long, tail-like tube, which they send to the surface, like a snorkel.

Much under-appreciated, flies come in many guises – from those that look like bees and wasps to those with gorgeous metallic colourations. Some lay eggs in other insects, in faeces and rotting matter, but plenty have slightly less gruesome life cycles. And what's wrong with gruesome, anyway? Many flies are nature's recyclers or important pollinators, while some are both. It's time we paid them more attention.

Unlike bees and wasps, flies have only one pair of wings; the second pair is converted into halteres, or balancers, which look like little stems with a rounded knob on the end, and help them to balance while flying. Adult flies usually feed on fluids. Like other insects, flies can taste with their feet as well as in or near their mouth – the feet of blowflies are up to 200 times more sensitive to the taste of sugar than the human tongue. Most flower-visiting flies have large eyes and have developed colour vision, which helps them find flowers to feed from. Some of them have absolutely wonderful names.

You have probably never considered gardening for flies before. You may consider the life cycle of some unhygienic and therefore you may be unsure about welcoming them into your garden – let alone taking deliberate actions to encourage more flies. If that's the case then I urge you to reconsider. As well as being nature's recyclers and often important pollinators, many flies are hugely important as food for other wildlife and for the garden ecosystem in itself.

Gardening for flies involves respecting the fact that they exist and allowing them to share your garden with you. Some pollinating flies (including some hoverflies – see box, page 95) lay eggs in stagnant water such as in tree stumps, branch forks or in the roots of trees, known as rot holes. They also lay eggs in rotting waste, such as wet compost heaps, piles of sludge and leaves, so creating these habitats and then tolerating fly larvae (maggots) would be a good start. You could go further and actively encourage flies into your garden, as I do. Make a 'hoverfly lagoon' (see page 96). See the table below for more suggestions.

Ideas for attracting flies

	Suitable for...				
	Small garden	Medium garden	Large garden	Allotment	Balcony/patio
Grow a variety of flowering plants, particularly umbellifers.	✓	✓	✓	✓	✓
Dig a pond or bog garden, which many species will use to breed.	✓	✓	✓	✓	Container pond
Let an area of grass grow long to provide shelter for crane flies.	✓	✓	✓	✓	✗
Build an open compost heap.	✓	✓	✓	✓	✓
Leave an old tree stump in place, which some hoverflies may breed in.	✓	✓	✓	✓	✗
Make a hoverfly lagoon.	✓	✓	✓	✓	✓
Grow known caterpillar food plants (see Resources) to increase numbers of caterpillars for parasitic flies.	✓	✓	✓	✓	✓
Grow climbers, including honeysuckle, ivy and single roses, up walls and fences.	✓	✓	✓	✓	✓
Plant a wildflower meadow.	✓	✓	✓	✓	✗
Leave fox and hedgehog poo for flies to 'clear up' for you – you'll be surprised how quickly it disappears. Brush it onto your borders if necessary. Do clear up after dogs and cats, however, as many are treated with pesticides for fleas and worms.	✗	✓	✓	✓	✗
Rather than disposing of dead birds and mammals, move them to a sheltered part of the garden for flies to deal with.	✗	✓	✓	✓	✗

Hoverflies

Despite their superficial resemblance to bees or wasps, hoverflies are not related to these groups, but make up the family Syrphidae within the insect order Diptera (true flies). Unlike bees and wasps, hoverflies have two wings rather than four, mostly fly in a darting or hovering manner with fast-moving wings, and they don't have a sting. Hoverflies vary greatly in size and appearance, with the smallest around 4mm long and the largest around 16mm.

Many have bright and ornate body patterns to mimic bees and wasps, making themselves look more fearsome than they are and thereby protecting themselves from predators. Certain species bear very specific resemblances, such as the hornet hoverfly (*Volucella zonaria*), which looks like a hornet, and the bumblebee hoverfly (*Volucella bombylans*), which looks like a bumblebee.

Adult hoverflies feed from plate-like flowers such as daisies and umbellifers, which enable them to land on the source of food and feed from it. They use their proboscis like a sponge to dab pollen and nectar. Popular with gardeners as a source of natural pest control, many species lay eggs near to greenfly and other aphid populations, and their larvae eat these before pupating and becoming adults (for more on aphids, see page 103). A few species can damage garden plants – for example, the large bulb fly lays its eggs at the base of daffodil and snowdrop plants, and their larvae eat the bulbs beneath, usually killing the plant. But remember that a garden pest is only a pest when numbers have reached damaging proportions.

There are about 270 species of hoverfly in Britain, some of which are rare and associated with very specific habitats but a large number of them come into gardens.

Gardening for hoverflies involves making sure there are plenty of suitable flowers for them (see below) as well as creating habitats that enable them to breed (such as tolerating aphid colonies and making hoverfly lagoons). In my garden,

◀ The hoverfly *Eristalis pertinax* on *Euphorbia palustris*.

hoverflies can't get enough of the fennel. I grow it next to my cardoons, which are usually covered in blackfly by mid-June. Hoverflies buzz about, feeding from the fennel flowers, and mating and laying eggs on the cardoons. The cardoons don't appear to be harmed by the aphids at all – by the time they flower, the hoverflies have eaten all the aphids, leaving nothing but a glorious display. By late summer, *Ectemnius* wasps have joined the party to feed on the hoverflies, so I have a four-tier food chain existing on the two plants. It's wonderful to watch.

▸ Aphids collect on the leaves and buds of roses, providing food for some hoverfly larvae.

Flowering plants for hoverflies

- Composite or daisy-like flowers: astrantia (*Astrantia major*), cosmos (*Cosmos bipannatus*), French marigold (*Tagetes patula*) or pot marigold (*Calendula officinalis*), dandelion (*Taraxacum officinale*), ragworts (*Senecio*), sea holly (*Eryngium*), Shasta daisy (*Leucanthemum × superbum*), single-flowered dahlias (*Dahlia*), sunflower (*Helianthus annuus*), Argentinian vervain (*Verbena bonariensis*).
- Ivy (*Hedera helix*).
- Umbellifers: bishop's flower (*Ammi majus*), cow parsley (*Anthriscus sylvestris*), fennel (*Foeniculum vulgare*), orlaya (*Orlaya grandiflora*), parsnip (*Pastinaca sativa* subsp. *sativa*), wild carrot (*Daucus carota*).

You may see them take pollen from flowers with long filaments, such as honeysuckle and phacelia, dabbing it off the anthers. Hoverflies also drink honeydew, which is secreted by aphids.

▸ Argentinian vervain is a fantastic flowering plant for hoverflies and other pollinators.

How to make a hoverfly lagoon (silage lagoon)

While many species of hoverfly lay eggs near established aphid colonies, some breed in stagnant water, with their larvae feeding on the decaying organic matter and associated bacteria and fungi. Most of us don't have stagnant water in the garden, so this project helps you create the perfect conditions for them. The larvae use an elongated tube to breathe air like a snorkel. This has earned them the unfortunate name of 'rat-tailed maggot'. Try not to let this put you off – they turn into the most beautiful hoverflies such as *Myathropa florea* (pictured on page 92). I'm very fond of them.

You will need:
- Large plastic bottle such as a milk bottle, or similar watertight container
- Cut grass
- Water
- Leaves or leaf litter
- Sticks

1. Cut the bottle into two pieces, recycling the half with the handle. Fill two thirds with grass clippings.

2. Add water to the grass clippings so that it completely covers them.

3. Add your leaves or leaf litter, so the adult female hoverflies have somewhere to land when they come to lay eggs.

4. Place sticks around the edge of the container so that the new hoverflies can climb out of the lagoon when they're ready.

5. Over time, the grass and leaves will break down, creating the perfect stagnant conditions for these hoverfly to breed. Top up the water periodically and add more grass or leaves if you need to.

ID parade
Flies

Bluebottle
Calliphora vomitoria
Description: A species of blowfly 10–14mm long with pretty metallic-blue colouring and large red eyes.
When to see it: All year.
Diet: Adults feed on nectar, sugar as well as carrion. Their larvae eat rotting material such as food waste, faeces and carrion.
Flowers visited: Strong-scented flowers such as goldenrods (*Solidago*).
Life cycle: Mating takes place all year round and the female lays eggs on or near rotting food waste, faeces or carrion. The larvae pupate in the soil and emerge as adults within three weeks. They are sexually mature almost immediately.
Garden habitats: Anywhere with flowers and larval food.
Distribution: Widespread and common throughout the British Isles.

Broad centurion
Chloromyia formosa

Description: One of a number of species of soldier fly, named after their smart appearance and apparent resemblance to military uniforms. Around 9mm long, the broad centurion has large eyes, a flattened body with a squared-off abdomen, and rounded, translucent wings. The female is blue-green, while the male is more yellow-green. Superficially similar to hoverflies, they are often found basking on leaves in sunshine. It is said that broad centurions are a good indicator of a healthy habitat.
When to see it: May to September.
Diet: Adults feed on pollen. The larvae feed on decaying vegetable matter.
Flowers visited: Umbellifers, particularly cow parsley (*Anthriscus sylvestris*).
Life cycle: Lays eggs in damp, rotting vegetation, including compost heaps and waterlogged soil.
Garden habitats: Mature, well-vegetated gardens.
Distribution: Widespread and common in the British Isles.

Crane fly *Tipula paludosa*

Description: Sometimes known as daddy-long-legs, this is one of the most common of the 300 crane fly species found in Britain. Adult flies are about 60mm long, with thin bodies and gangly legs that easily break off. The male has a squared-off abdomen, while the female's abdomen ends in a pointed ovipositor, which she uses to lay eggs in the soil. The 'leatherjacket' larvae, named for their tough skins, can be an important source of food for starlings and other birds.
When to see it: July to September.
Diet: The adults probably do not feed, concentrating instead on mating and laying eggs. The leatherjacket larvae feed on plant roots. If present in large numbers they can cause damage to lawns but they rarely cause significant damage.
Life cycle: Eggs are laid in soil in autumn. They pupate and emerge as adults the following autumn.
Garden habitats: Areas with short grass where the females can lay their eggs.
Distribution: Widespread and common in the British Isles.

Golden dung fly
Scathophaga stercoraria
Description: A dung fly, it is often seen on cowpats in rural areas but is fond of dog faeces in urban areas. It will also come to organic nettle and comfrey feeds. This pretty golden-yellow fly is 7–9mm long with a hairy abdomen.
When to see it: March to November.
Diet: Adults are largely predatory on other insects but also visit flowers. The larvae will eat faeces but may also prey on other invertebrates within it.
Flowers visited: A wide variety, particularly daisies such as tansies (*Tanacetum*) and umbellifers such as cow parsley (*Anthriscus sylvestris*).
Life cycle: Dung flies have several broods per year. Mating takes place on or near dung, particularly cowpats, and the female lays eggs in mammal faeces.
Garden habitats: Flower borders, dung.
Distribution: Widespread and common in the British Isles.

Hornet hoverfly
Volucella zonaria

Description: One of our largest hoverflies at 2cm long, this hornet mimic has a red-orange thorax and yellow-and-black striped abdomen; but its large eyes, broad body and single pair of wings identify it as a fly. Only a rare visitor to the British Isles up until the early 1940s, it has become more common in southern England and continues to spread north.
When to see it: May to November.
Diet: Adults feed on nectar and pollen. The larvae eat wasp detritus and larvae.
Flowers visited: Flat-headed flowers such as yarrow (*Achillea millefolium*) and umbellifers.
Life cycle: The female lays her eggs in social wasp nests and the larvae scavenge in the bottom of the nest for dead workers and larvae.
Garden habitats: A variety of habitats, particularly where common wasps are present.
Distribution: Widespread in the southern half of England and steadily expanding its range northwards. Not present in Ireland.

Batman hoverfly
Myathropa florea
Description: A large and distinctive hoverfly that has a wide, flat abdomen with black and yellow stripes.
When to see it: May to October.
Diet: Adults feed on nectar and pollen. The larvae eat bacteria found in stagnant water.
Flowers visited: Umbellifers such as fennel (*Foeniculum vulgare*) and ivy (*Hedera helix*).

Life cycle: Lays eggs in rot holes, compost bins, bog gardens or ponds with a large amount of decaying matter. Will come to hoverfly lagoons and home-made comfrey and nettle feeds (please leave twigs in the top to prevent them from drowning).
Garden habitats: Compost bins, manure heaps and buckets of stagnant water.
Distribution: Widespread and common in the British Isles.

Large bee-fly
Bombylius major

Description: Around 1–2.5cm long, this parasitic bee-fly superficially resembles a bumblebee. It has a long, thin proboscis, which it uses for sucking nectar from various flowers, and flies with the proboscis extended. In flight it tends to dart from one place to the next, hovering and feeding from flowers before landing on them.
When to see it: Spring.
Diet: Adults feed on nectar and pollen. The larvae eat the larvae of their host species.
Flowers visited: Aubretias (*Aubretia*), forget-me-nots (*Myosotis*), hyacinth (*Hyacinthus orientalis*), grape hyacinth (*Muscari armeniacum*), primrose (*Primula vulgaris*) and lungworts (*Pulmonaria*).
Life cycle: In spring the female drops eggs near the nests of ground-nesting solitary bees, particularly *Andrena* species. Sometimes wasp and beetle nests are also used.
Garden habitats: A frequent visitor to gardens, where you might see it hovering around flowers or hanging around the nests of ground-nesting solitary bees.
Distribution: Widespread and common throughout the British Isles, although less common in Ireland.

Marmalade hoverfly
Episyrphus balteatus
Description: About 9–12mm long, this is a very common wasp mimic whose orange-yellow abdomen is distinctively marked with double black bands – the thinner, often broken bands resembling a moustache. Adults feed on nectar and pollen from flowers.

When to see it: January to December. In summer, numbers can be boosted by migrants from the Continent.
Diet: Adults feed on nectar and pollen. The larvae eat aphids.
Flowers visited: A wide variety, particularly umbellifers, poppies and daisies, such as cow parsley (*Anthriscus sylvestris*), field poppy (*Papaver rhoeas*), ragworts (*Senecio*) and tansy (*Tanacetum vulgare*).
Life cycle: The female lays eggs on plants infected by aphids. The larvae develop into teardrop-shaped pupae and emerge as adults either later the same year or the following year.
Garden habitats: Flower borders, particularly near aphid infestations.
Distribution: Common and widespread in the British Isles.

Large bulb fly
Merodon equestris

Description: This hoverfly species is about 10–15mm long with a hairy body that varies in colour. It is a bumblebee mimic, although its single pair of wings and large fly eyes help reveal its true identity. Can be a bit of a nuisance in the garden, as it breeds in the bulbs of daffodils and other plants.
When to see it: March to August.
Diet: Adults feed on nectar and pollen. The larvae feed on flower bulbs, often destroying them.
Flowers visited: A wide variety of flat-headed blooms, including dandelion (*Taraxacum officinale*).
Life cycle: The female lays eggs on the bulb necks of daffodil (*Narcissus*), snowdrop (*Galanthus nivalis*) and bluebell (*Hyacinthoides non-scripta*). The larvae hatch and burrow into the bulb.
Garden habitats: Anywhere bulbous plants are found.
Distribution: Widespread and common in the British Isles.

Owl midges
Psychodidae family
Description: Also known as moth flies, drain flies and sewage flies, there are 99 species in the British Isles. Tiny (2–4mm) and covered in grey or light brown hairs, it looks just like a small, furry moth. Owl midges are an excellent source of food for bats. Like moths, they can be attracted to light.
When to see it: All year round.
Diet: Adults don't feed but spend their time mating and laying eggs in stagnant water. The larvae feed on decaying matter or bacteria in stagnant water.
Life cycle: The female lays eggs in stagnant water, such as in drains, guttering and waste pipes; also in rot holes, the water that can accumulate among fallen leaves between tree roots and wet compost heaps. The larvae pupate and emerge as an adult fly within a couple of weeks.

Garden habitats: Compost heaps, ditches, drains and sinks.
Distribution: Widespread and common in the British Isles.

Thick-headed fly
Sicus ferrugineus
Description: One of many species in the family Conopidae, which are all parasitoids that prey on bees. Around 8–13mm long, it is mostly orange-brown with a yellow head, large red eyes and pronounced antennae.
When to see it: May to September.
Diet: Adults drink nectar and are good pollinators. The larvae feed inside the host bee, initially keeping it alive by feeding on body fluid before moving on to the essential organs, which eventually results in the bee's death.
Life cycle: The female lays eggs in bees' abdomens. She often waits near flowers and attacks as soon as a bee arrives, injecting a single egg between the abdominal segments into the bee's body. The larva pupates in the host's body and overwinters as a pupa. The adult fly emerges in the following year.
Flowers visited: A variety, including meadow buttercup (*Ranunculus acris*).
Garden habitats: Anywhere bees are present.
Distribution: Widespread and common in the British Isles.

Wildlife gardening for true bugs

The term 'bug' is often used to describe any and all invertebrates, but in scientific terms a true bug is one that belongs to the insect order Hemiptera. Insects in this order are many and varied, and include aphids, pond skaters, shield bugs and water boatmen. All of them have tubular, piercing mouthparts called stylets, which they use to suck juices from plants or animals.

Hemiptera is further divided into several suborders, including Heteroptera and Homoptera. Bugs in Heteroptera often bear a similarity to beetles, with toughened, protective forewings held flat over the body when at rest. But the wings usually have a soft membranous tip which overlap instead of meeting in the middle. Example groups include capsid bugs and shield bugs. Bugs in Homoptera include aphids, leafhoppers, mealybugs and whiteflies. They are very variable: some don't have wings as adults, or if they do they can have hard or soft forewings, which are often held tent-like over the body when resting.

Bugs go through incomplete metamorphosis, which means the young, often known as nymphs rather than larvae, look like and have similar habits to the adults, but are always wingless.

There are around 2,000 true bug species throughout the British Isles and you'll find bugs everywhere in the garden, ranging from sap-sucking aphids on your plants to pond skaters and water boatmen in your pond.

▶ The green shield bug is one of the more obvious bugs we see in our gardens.

As with many other types of wildlife, gardening for some bugs is more to do with tolerating them than actively encouraging them in – aphids, for example, are prey for many other insects and are therefore extremely valuable to those species further up the food chain. Simply leaving bugs on your plants rather than washing or spraying them off can make a huge difference to the health and vitality of your whole garden.

There's no 'one size fits all' habitat for bugs, but a good mix of leafy and shrubby plants, long grass, a nice wildlife pond plus spaces to overwinter will do admirably.

▼ The striking red-and-black froghopper is easy to spot and common throughout Britain.

Ideas for attracting bugs

	Suitable for...				
	Small garden	Medium garden	Large garden	Allotment	Balcony/patio
Plant a hedge.	✗	✓	✓	✓	✗
Let border perennials and shrubs fill out to maximise the amount of vegetation in your garden.	✓	✓	✓	✓	✓
Plant a garden tree suitable for your size of plot to support plenty of aphids.	✗	✓	✓	✓	✗
Grow a variety of herbaceous plants.	✓	✓	✓	✓	✓
Let a patch of grass grow long.	✓	✓	✓	✓	✗
Compost your waste.	Compost bin	Large, open heap	Large, open heap	Large, open heap	Compost bin
Make a leaf pile.	✓	✓	✓	✓	Allow leaves to build up in a corner or behind pots.
Cover your fences and walls with climbing plants to provide shelter and food.	✓	✓	✓	✓	✓
Dig a pond with plenty of shallows and submerged plants.	Small	Medium	Large (make sure it has shallows)	Large	✗
Tolerate weeds, including sorrel and dock.	✓	✓	✓	✓	✓
Grow as wide a range of flowering plants as you have room for.	✓	✓	✓	✓	✓

All about aphids

Aphids are tiny bugs that suck sap from plants and most are able to reproduce parthenogenetically (without mating). Commonly referred to as greenfly or blackfly, they come in a wide range of colours, including yellow, pink and white. Some, such as the woolly aphid, cover themselves in a fluffy white waxy secretion and can be confused with scale insects or mealybugs. Most feed on foliage, stems and flowers but some species suck the sap from roots. Some aphids transmit plant viruses on plants such as cucumbers, dahlias, raspberries, strawberries, sweet peas, tomatoes and tulips.

Aphids have traditionally been the scourge of gardeners, but it's time we reconsidered them. There are around 500 species in the British Isles, including the black bean aphid, which is known for the damage it causes to bean crops, and the nettle aphid, which you would hardly notice at all.

Aphids can cause damage to plants by distorting plant growth, and also excrete a sticky substance called honeydew onto leaves. Sooty mould often grows on the honeydew, reducing plants' ability to photosynthesise. However, the myriad of predators known to eat aphids can redress the balance particularly as the growing season progresses. What's more, the fear of plant damage can be greater than the damage itself. In my 35 years of gardening, I've lost only one crop of broad beans to black bean aphid. They were growing on a small patch of land close to a road with hardly any other nearby plant cover. I believe the lack of surrounding habitat meant there were fewer birds around to eat the aphids for me, and so this 'pest', which never caused me problems before and hasn't since, was able to multiply its numbers to pest proportions. If you are constantly battling aphid infestations and wonder why, take a look at your habitat – could it be that you just aren't providing a complete habitat, one that caters for those predators that eat aphids?

▲ Aphids can quickly multiply and can damage your plants, but they are eaten by a wide range of species further up the food chain.

▲ Aphids come in a range of colours, like these mottled arum aphids (*Aulacorthum circumflexum*).

The aphid life cycle

Typically aphid colonies consist of wingless females that give birth to live young. (Winged forms develop only when overcrowding occurs, the host plant dies, when there is a shift in seasons or another reason that causes them to up sticks and move to another plant.) Most species overwinter as eggs but some can remain active, particularly in mild winters or on indoor plants.

Many species have an annual cycle that involves two or more host plants – these often overwinter as eggs on trees and migrate to herbaceous plants in summer. Others live year-round on one type of plant, though may be active for only part of the year.

Ants love to drink aphid honeydew and can be seen 'farming' the aphids for this secretion. If you spot ants and aphids on a plant together, watch their behaviour – you may see the ants gently stroking the aphids with their antennae to encourage them to secrete more honeydew.

What eats aphids?

Abundant, highly productive and prone to form big aggregations, aphids are an important food source for a huge range of other species. And you don't need to worry that these predators won't find the aphids on your plants. When attacked by aphids, plants release stress hormones that encourage hoverfly larvae, ladybirds and other insect predators to zone in on infestations. We should cherish aphids as food that brings so much else to the table.

Aphid midge larvae *Aphidoletes aphidimyza*
When wholly grown, aphid midge larvae are yellow-orange maggots up to 3mm long. They insert their mouthparts into the aphid's body and suck out the contents. When fully fed, they drop to the soil to pupate and emerge as tiny flies, which feed on honeydew.

Green lacewing larvae
These insatiable predators are so good at eating aphids, they are sometimes known as 'aphid lions'.

Hoverfly larvae
Many hoverfly species lay eggs on aphid infestations and their larvae feed on the aphids.

Ladybirds and their larvae
Several ladybird species eat aphids. Look out for crocodile-like orange and black ladybird larvae, which can consume hundreds of aphids a day.

Parasitoid wasps (*various species*)
Several species of small parasitoid wasps (see page 75) attack aphids. The adults lay single eggs inside the bodies of young aphids. The egg hatches into a larva that feeds on body fluids within the host insect. Eventually the parasite larva kills the aphid, usually by consuming the entire body contents, and pupates inside the dead aphid's body. By then the aphid's body has become whitish brown with an inflated appearance and is often called an aphid mummy. The adult parasite emerges through a hole cut in the aphid's body.

Earwigs
Earwigs are omnivorous, feeding on small invertebrates and plant material. On fruit trees they can offer useful control of fruit aphids and do not cause damage to the trees or fruit.

Birds
Sparrows rely on aphids to feed their young, while blue tits take aphids when there is a shortage of caterpillars.

▲ The 'aphid lion' (lacewing larvae) lives up to its name.

◀ Ladybirds are important predators of aphids.

▼ Earwigs occasionally damage garden flowers, but on fruit trees they are useful aphid predators.

ID parade
True bugs

Common green shield bug *Palomena prasina*
Description: One of several shield-shaped bugs found among plants, it is sometimes called a stink bug as it may release a marzipan-like odour when handled. Adults are about 10mm long and are broad, flat and green with brown wing tips. In autumn they become a darker purple-brown. Easily confused with the southern green shield bug (*Nezara viridula*), a species that is native to Africa but arrived in southern England in 2003. This is green with white or transparent wing tips, and can cause some damage to plants such as bean crops.
When to see it: May to September.
Diet: Plant sap from a range of herbaceous plants, but they generally don't do any damage.
Life cycle: Adults emerge from overwintering sites in spring and spend a month feeding before mating. Females lay greenish eggs on the underside of leaves in hexagonal batches. The nymphs are pale green with black markings and have more of a rounded shape than the adults. They remain in groups, close to where they were laid as eggs. Towards the end of summer, they metamorphose into adults and spend a few weeks feeding before changing colour and finding somewhere to overwinter.
Garden habitats: Areas with leafy and shrubby plants. Overwinters in leaf litter or log piles.
Distribution: Widespread and common across the British Isles.

Froghopper *Philaenus spumarius*
Description: A tiny (6mm long) sap sucker, most notable for its nymphs covering themselves in a whitish froth known as cuckoo spit. Gently wipe away the spit and you will see a tiny green froghopper nymph, which will quickly re-cover itself in protective bubbles. The adult looks similar to the nymph but is rarely seen, as it can jump up to 70cm into the air to avoid predators! It comes in a range of colours and patterns – including almost black, black and white, and brown – and its wings are held tent-like over the body.
When to see it: May to August.
Diet: Both adults and nymphs feed on plant sap, but do no harm the plant.
Life cycle: Adults mate back to back in spring. Eggs are laid among plants and the nymphs go through five instars (stages) before becoming adults.
Garden habitats: Areas with plenty of leaf cover.
Distribution: Widespread and common throughout the British Isles.

Hawthorn shield bug *Acanthosoma haemorrhoidale*
Description: Similar looking to the common green shield bug but larger (15mm long) and with red markings across its abdomen, wings and 'shoulders'. It can be found anywhere near shrubby food plants. Attracted to light, it may turn up in moth traps.
When to see it: May to September.
Diet: Adults suck leaf sap and fruit juices. The nymphs feed on ripening red berries, including cotoneasters (*Cotoneaster*), hawthorn (*Crataegus monogyna*), rowan (*Sorbus aucuparia*) and whitebeam (*Sorbus aria*).
Life cycle: Mating takes place in spring and eggs are laid on suitable plants. Over the summer, the nymphs go through five nymphal instars before the adult stage, in time to feed for

a few weeks prior to overwintering. Like the common green shield bug, adults may become darker when they overwinter.
Garden habitats: Mature gardens with hedges and shrubs.
Distribution: Common and widespread across the British Isles, apart from in Scotland where it is less common.

Pond skater *Gerris lacustris*
Description: Commonly found skating over pond surfaces, this predatory bug is around 1–2cm long and has a thin, brownish body with long, widely spaced middle and hind legs that help it balance as it moves. Like the water boatman, it's covered in tiny sensitive hairs, which it uses to detect prey on the surface.

When to see it: May to September.
Diet: Aquatic larvae and insects caught on the pond surface.
Life cycle: Adults emerge from overwintering sites in mid-spring and begin mating immediately. Eggs are laid among pond plants and take up to two weeks to hatch. The young undergo five instars before becoming adults. In autumn, the adults leave the pond to overwinter.
Garden habitats: Ponds with plenty of shallow areas and submerged plants.
Distribution: Widespread and common throughout the British Isles.

Water boatman *Notonecta glauca*
Description: A large (16mm) boat-shaped bug that swims on its back just below the water surface, using its long, oar-like hind legs as paddles. It traps air beneath the surface using its wings and tiny hairs.
When to see it: May to September.
Diet: Water boatmen are voracious predators, hunting tadpoles, water beetle larvae and insects drowning on the surface. They use their mouthparts to pierce their prey and suck out their juices.
Life cycle: Mating takes place in spring and eggs are laid singly among the stems of aquatic plants.
Garden habitats: Ponds with plenty of shallow areas and submerged plants.
Distribution: Widespread and common throughout the British Isles.

Wildlife gardening for other minibeasts

Over the next eight pages I look at the underdogs – the invertebrates that we might take for granted but which have important roles in the garden. They include insects such as ants, earwigs, crickets and grasshoppers, damselflies and dragonflies. They also include many species that are not insects but belong to other animal groups. Among them are valuable decomposers such as earthworms, millipedes and woodlice, voracious predators such as centipedes and spiders, and slugs and snails (see page 110), which provide food for a host of other wildlife.

You'll spot minibeasts everywhere in the garden, especially in cracks and crevices, under rocks and logs, in your soil and compost bin. Damselflies and dragonflies will visit your pond, crickets and grasshoppers will find a haven in long grass, and countless other beasties will live virtually everywhere else.

▲ Brown seed heads provide the perfect camouflage for similarly coloured harvestmen.

▲ Azure damselflies mating on a leaf beside a pond.

Gardening for most of these species is simply letting them get on with living – tolerating slugs and snails where you can, letting spiders erect webs and giving centipedes and woodlice free rein of your compost bin. Dig a pond for damselflies and dragonflies, allow areas of grass to grow long for crickets and grasshoppers, but otherwise just carry on gardening. Provide habitats, don't use pesticides, mulch the soil, compost waste and grow plenty of plants. See the table opposite for more suggestions.

Ideas for attracting other minibeasts

	Suitable for...				
	Small garden	Medium garden	Large garden	Allotment	Balcony/patio
Plant a hedge.	✗	✓	✓	✓	✗
Tolerate aphids.	✓	✓	✓	✓	✓
Leave dead wood on trees.	✓	✓	✓	✓	✗
Grow a variety of herbaceous plants.	✓	✓	✓	✓	✓
Let a patch of grass grow long.	✓	✓	✓	✓	✗
Mulch borders or pots.	✓	✓	✓	✓	✓
Compost your waste.	Compost bin	Large, open heap	Large, open heap	Large, open heap	Compost bin
Make a leaf pile.	✓	✓	✓	✓	Allow leaves to build up in a corner or behind pots.
Make a log pile, burying some logs if you can.	Small logs or twigs/prunings	Large, partially buried in the ground	Large, partially buried in the ground	Large, partially buried in the ground	✗
Leave tree stumps in place.	✓	✓	✓	✓	✗
Create areas of dense vegetation.	✓	✓	✓	✓	✗
Plant a native broadleaf deciduous tree.	✗	✗	✓	✓	✗
Dig a pond.	✓	✓	✓	✓	✗
Tolerate weeds.	✓	✓	✓	✓	✓
Grow as wide a range of flowering plants as you have room for.	✓	✓	✓	✓	✓
Grow climbers to provide cover.	✓	✓	✓	✓	✓

Slugs and snails

◀ Garden snails can cause a great deal of damage to plants but are also a significant part of the food chain.

▶ Not all snails cause as much damage as the garden snail, including this white-lipped banded snail.

Slugs and snails are gastropods, meaning 'stomach foot', which describes the way they appear to crawl on their bellies. All species have a flat, muscular 'foot', which releases mucus and enables it to move across hard surfaces. They belong to a larger group of soft-bodied invertebrates known as molluscs, most of which have shells, but slugs' shells are tiny and hidden inside their body.

As herbivores and detritivores, most slugs and snails munch on live and decaying plant or animal material, and some species have a fondness for garden plants. The plants we tend so well grow faster and lusher than those growing without such attention in the wild, and our slimy friends like them so much they tend to eat all of them in one go. I know few gardeners who have good things to say about them.

I've lost many plants to slugs and snails, but I've lost just as many to mice, frost, disease and simple bad gardening. And I lose far fewer on my allotment, where I have an army of slow-worms, frogs, toads and newts, song thrushes and blackbirds to eat the slugs and snails, than I do in my tiny walled garden that provides less of a habitat for their predators. Not all slugs and snails cause damage to your plants, and some can even be good for the garden. There are several different species, some of which you can find out more about in the ID parade on pages 113–115.

How to deal with them

In my experience, the best way to deal with slugs and snails is to create better habitats for their predators. Reptiles, amphibians and some mammals and birds eat them – so the more habitats you create for those in your garden, the fewer slugs and snails you'll have. Dig a pond, plant a hedge and open up your compost heap. It might take a few years for the ecosystem to balance itself out, but in time you'll find you can live with slugs and snails quite peacefully because other garden wildlife are doing the job of getting rid of them for you.

Slug pellets containing metaldehyde are thankfully now banned in the UK, so all pellets for sale contain ferric phosphate. This is said to be harmless to wildlife but hasn't fully been tested, and there are suggestions that the chelate (EDTA) used to make the iron soluble could harm other species, including earthworms. I've seen birds feeding these slug pellets to their chicks. Can we really use them with confidence?

▲ Regularly collecting snails in buckets can reduce the numbers of snails in your garden.

Nematodes

Nematodes are microscopic worm-like animals. There are thousands of nematode species that naturally occur in most environments. You can buy packets of one species, *Phasmarhabditis hermaphrodita*, that is pathogenic and specific to molluscs which can be watered into the soil. The nematodes enter slugs' bodies and infect them with bacteria that cause a fatal disease. They attack and kill slugs, which often reside just below the soil's surface, but they don't eliminate snails.

Hand-picking

You can conduct nightly patrols and hand-pick slugs and snails off your plants. This works best if you do it regularly, preferably every night, but especially after rain. What you do with them once you've caught them is your business – I take mine 'on holiday' to the local park where there's plenty of wildlife to eat them. Don't simply throw them next door – this isn't neighbourly and they'll only come back. Both slugs and snails have homing instincts, and studies have shown if discarded within a 20m radius or more, they can get themselves back to your garden.

Beer traps

Strange but true, slugs and snails love real ale. By setting beer traps – simply filling a container with ale and placing it in your border overnight – you can lure them to their death. If you choose to do this, then please make sure you minimise risk to other wildlife – check the container sits proud of the soil surface so centipedes, beetles and other beasties don't fall in. And do clear the intoxicated slugs and snails away first thing in the morning so they're not snaffled by hedgehogs and birds.

Copper tape and other deterrents

Slugs and snails are supposed to not like travelling over copper. You can buy copper tape to fit around your plant pots. Prickly leaves such as holly are also said to deter them, as slugs and snails don't like moving over them, but you will have to mulch your beds and borders with lots of fresh holly leaves on a regular basis which isn't always practical. Indeed, a recent RHS study found no reduction in slug damage from barriers made of copper tape, bark mulch, egg shells, sharp grit, holly leaves or wool pellets.

ID parade
Insects

Black or garden ant
Lasius niger

Description: One of the most common species found in the UK. Workers (sterile females) are 4–5mm long, brownish-black and covered in small hairs. Queens (reproductive females) are 8–9mm long, mid-brown and have a large pair of clear wings (these are lost soon after mating). Males are 4–5 mm long and also have wings. Ruled by just one queen, black ants live in social colonies that contain several thousand workers (up to 15,000) and can last for many years.
When to see it: All year round.
Diet: Aphids (which they 'farm' for their sweet honeydew), caterpillars and other insects; sugary foods including nectar and rotting fruit, which they forage for along scent-marked trails.
Life cycle: The queen establishes a nest and lays her eggs. The larvae develop into the first generation of workers, which tend the queen, forage for food and expand the nest. The queen continues to produce successive generations of workers, and once the colony is well established, she lays eggs that will develop into males and fertile females. In summer, on 'flying ant day' (which usually includes a number of warm, humid days, typically in July and August), these winged adults leave the nest and take to the skies to find a mate and establish new nests. They are predated by a huge number of birds, and those males that do succeed in mating die shortly afterwards anyway. Only the females survive. After returning to earth, they shed their wings and start a new colony.
Garden habitats: Any and all gardens, particularly in dry soil such as sunny borders and dry compost heaps.
Distribution: Widespread and common.

Common blue damselfly
Enallagma cyathigerum

Description: One of several similar-looking blue damselflies, the male is blue with black markings, while the female is either blue or green with similar black markings. Males and females often perch together on emergent plant stems, facing the same way. In common with most damselflies, when at rest they hold their wings along the length of their abdomen.
When to see it: June to September.
Diet: Mosquitoes, midges and small flies.
Life cycle: Mating takes place near water. The male and female form a 'mating wheel', where the male clasps the female by the neck and she bends her body around to his reproductive organs. She lays eggs in plant material just below the water's surface.
Garden habitats: Ponds.
Distribution: Common and widespread throughout the British Isles.

Common darter *Sympetrum striolatum*

Description: One of our most common dragonflies. Mature males are orange-red with a brown thorax; the female has a very varied colouration and can be green, yellow or brown, sometimes with red patches. Males can be spotted holding territory around garden ponds – a male will pick a perch, such as a large stone at the edge of the pond or a branch growing out over the water. From here he will defend territory against other males, as well as hunt prey, which he will scoop up in his front legs and return to his perch to eat.
When to see it: June to October.
Diet: Mosquitoes, midges, small moths and flies.
Life cycle: Mating takes place near water and egg-laying involves both partners: the male holds on to the female and pushes her abdomen down to break the water's surface.
Garden habitats: Ponds.
Distribution: Common and widespread in England, Wales and Ireland; less common in Scotland.

Common earwig
Forficula auricularia

Description: A brown, shiny insect around 11–16mm long with large 'tail pincers'. It is so named due to the ancient belief that while a person slept, an earwig would crawl into their ear, bore into their brain and lay its eggs. Many gardeners wrongly regard earwigs as pests, as they have a tendency to nibble dahlias and other ornamental flowers, but they also eat aphids and are a valuable part of the garden ecosystem.
When to see it: April to October.
Diet: Adults nibble flowers and other plant material, decaying matter, carrion and eat insects including aphids. The young nymphs feed on regurgitated scraps of plant and insect material from their mother, while older nymphs feed on the same material as the adults.
Life cycle: After mating in autumn, the female lays eggs beneath stones and in crevices. She is an excellent mother, gently cleaning the eggs and staying with the young nymphs until they're old enough to fend for themselves in late spring. The nymphs go through four instars and gradually transform into adults, leaving the nest when they're ready to fend for themselves.
Garden habitats: Under stones and logs, in log and twig piles as well as areas of dense vegetation.
Distribution: Widespread and common.

Field grasshopper
Chorthippus brunneus

Description: Grasshoppers have short antennae (shorter than the body) while crickets usually have antennae that are at least as long as the body. Mottled brown, with barring on the sides, the field grasshopper is one of the most common grasshoppers. It's readily found in any open, sunny, grassy area, including our gardens and allotments. The male rubs his legs against his wings to create a repetitive chirping, which he uses to lure a female (if she's interested, she'll sing back).
When to see it: June to November.
Diet: Mostly grass.
Life cycle: Mating usually takes place in summer and eggs are laid in the soil. These hatch the following year. The nymphs go through four instars before becoming adults.
Garden habitats: Long grass.
Distribution: Common and widespread across the British Isles.

Speckled bush cricket
Leptophyes punctatissima

Description: Unlike grasshoppers, crickets have long antennae (longer than the body). Predominantly grass green, as its name suggests, its body is covered in tiny black spots. Adult females have a large ovipositor, used to deposit eggs. Bush crickets tend to be less obvious than grasshoppers – both the male and female calls are very high pitched and are best heard using a bat detector. They hide among foliage and are rarely seen.
When to see it: June to September.
Diet: Shrubs and herbaceous plants.
Life cycle: Mating usually takes place in summer and eggs are laid in the bark of trees.
Garden habitats: Shrubs and trees.
Distribution: Widespread in England and parts of Wales and Ireland, but absent from Scotland.

Other minibeasts

Brown-lipped snail
Cepaea nemoralis

Description: Smaller than the garden snail (see page 115), the brown-lipped snail is named after the brown 'lip' around the shell opening. Shell colour varies enormously and can be cream-yellow through to pink. The body of the snail is usually green-grey, becoming yellow towards the rear.
When to see it: March to November.
Diet: Different types of plant material, including fresh new growth, although it may prefer dead and decaying plant material, so is less of a nuisance than the garden snail.
Life cycle: Like all slugs and snails, it's hermaphrodite (having both male and female reproductive organs). Breeding takes place in early summer and mating involves fertilising each other. Within a week of mating, they each dig a hole in the ground with their foot and lay between 30 and 80 eggs. The eggs hatch around a fortnight later.
Garden habitats: Almost everywhere in the garden.
Distribution: Common and widespread across the British Isles, except the far north of Scotland.

Centipedes and millipedes

Description: Centipedes and millipedes belong to a group called myriapods, which typically have long bodies composed of many segments – centipedes having one pair of legs per segment and millipedes two. Most centipedes are predatory and venomous, with jaw-like mandibles and a pair of venomous claws that are used in defence and to capture prey. Millipedes tend to be detritivores and some often protect themselves by curling into a tight ball; but many can produce irritating or poisonous chemicals. Both centipedes and millipedes are prey to numerous animals, including insects, spiders, birds, mammals, reptiles and amphibians.

When to see them: All year round.
Diet: Centipedes eat a variety of invertebrates, including caterpillars, small slugs, spiders, woodlice and worms. Millipedes mainly eat decaying plant matter.
Life cycle: Mating usually takes place in summer and eggs are laid in the soil.
Garden habitats: Beneath rocks, stones and logs; in compost bins and log piles.
Distribution: Common and widespread.

Common earthworm *Lumbricus terrestris*

Description: Earthworms are annelids – soft-bodied organisms with bodies made up of numerous segments or rings. This species is our largest earthworm, reaching up to 35cm long. Its pinky-brown body is made up of many ring-like segments that are covered in tiny bristles, which help the worm move through the soil. Older worms have a saddle-like band called a clitellum, which secretes mucus to form a cocoon for the worm embryos. As recyclers of organic waste, earthworms are invaluable to the wildlife garden, maintaining soil health by aerating and fertilising it. They're also eaten by a wide range of predators, including birds and hedgehogs.
When to see it: All year round.
Diet: Leaf litter and other organic matter.
Life cycle: Earthworms are hermaphrodites, but they still need other earthworms to reproduce. Mating takes place in summer, when two worms 'exchange sperm'. Each worm then makes a cocoon, fills it with eggs and sperm, and deposits in the soil. Young worms hatch after 1–5 months and are ready to reproduce 6–18 months later.
Garden habitats: Moist, humus-rich, undisturbed soil.
Distribution: Common and widespread.

Common shiny woodlouse
Oniscus asellus

Description: Woodlice are terrestrial crustaceans, with a hard outer skeleton, segmented body and jointed legs. There are about 45 species in the British Isles, which range from pink to brown to grey. One of our most common woodlice, it's grey with lighter patches and is about 16mm long. It spends the day hiding in damp places, especially in hot, dry weather.
When to see it: All year round.
Diet: Mildew, rotting wood, decomposing organic matter, fruit and vegetable crops.
Life cycle: Mating takes place at night. The male climbs onto the female's back and drums her with his front legs while 'licking' her head with his mouthparts. After mating, females carry their fertilised eggs in a small brood pouch under their bodies. The young hatch inside the pouch and stay there until they are big enough to survive on their own. A common shiny woodlouse can live for three to four years. Its main predators are centipedes, toads, shrews and spiders.
Garden habitats: Dark and damp habitats which they can hide in, including compost heaps, log piles, leaf litter and under stones.
Distribution: Common and widespread.

Garden slug
Arion hortensis

Description: Medium-sized (up to 3cm), black with paler side stripes and, like all *Arion* species, characterised by its rounded cross section. It has a yellow/orange foot and mucus.
When to see it: All year round.
Diet: Plant stems, young leaves, flower heads, root crops and bulbs.
Life cycle: Like all slugs and snails, it's hermaphrodite. Living for only around 18 months, it usually mates in autumn and eggs are laid throughout winter, hatching in January and

February. The young slugs grow through the summer months, maturing in September and October. They mate, lay eggs and die before July of the following year.
Garden habitats: Everywhere.
Distribution: Common and widespread across the British Isles.

Garden snail *Helix aspersa*
Description: Brownish all over with a soft, mucus-covered body and a yellow or cream shell with brown spiral stripes. The shell develops a lip with maturity. It has a flat, muscular foot that releases mucus to help it move with a gliding motion.

When to see it: All year round.
Diet: Living plants, especially young, lush ones, and occasionally decaying food, such as the contents of your compost heap.
Life cycle: Like all slugs and snails, it is hermaphrodite. Breeding takes place in early summer and, while self-fertilisation is possible, they usually mate with another, which can take as long as 12 hours. Within a week of mating they each dig a hole in the ground with their foot and lay around 80 eggs. The eggs hatch around a fortnight later. Garden snails can lay up to six batches of eggs per year.
Garden habitats: Almost everywhere in the garden.
Distribution: Common and widespread across the British Isles.

Garden spider
Araneus diadematus
Description: Spiders are arachnids, which usually have two body segments, eight legs, no wings or antennae and are not able to chew. The garden spider is abundant in gardens and is easily recognised by the large white cross on its abdomen, which ranges from pale yellow to blackish-brown. Adult females grow up to 15mm and males up

to 9mm. Garden spiders are most often seen in late summer to autumn, when females spin large and elaborate orb webs across paths, and between shrubs and herbaceous plants. She spins her web and then waits, head down, to dispatch any prey unlucky enough to get stuck.

When to see it: May to November (most obviously in autumn).
Diet: Flying insects such as bees, beetles, butterflies and moths, and flies.
Life cycle: Mating takes place in autumn, usually on the web. Afterwards, the female makes a silken sac to lay her eggs in, and then spends the rest of her life looking after them. She dies in late autumn and her eggs hatch out the following spring. These lie low, feeding on small invertebrates, until they're big enough to mate the following autumn.
Garden habitats: Mature gardens and allotments with plenty of plant material and insects to eat.
Distribution: Widespread and common.

Harvestmen *Opiliones*
Description: Harvestmen belong to a group of arachnids called Opiliones, which superficially look like spiders, with their round bodies and long, thin legs. However, harvestmen are quite different beasts. They don't have a waist,

they're not able to spin webs, they don't have fangs or produce venom, and they can chew food with their pincer-like jaws. For defence, most harvestmen have a pair of specialised glands, which secrete a noxious fluid.
When to see them: June to August.
Diet: Harvestmen are omnivores, so eat a wide variety of food: bird droppings, small invertebrates, carrion, fungi, fruit and other plant material. In turn, they are eaten by amphibians, ants, beetles, centipedes, spiders, birds and small mammals.
Life cycle: Mating takes place in summer. Unlike spiders, male harvestmen have a penis. The female has an ovipositor and lays around 100 white, spherical eggs in the soil, moss and rotting wood. The eggs hatch in spring.
Garden habitats: Well-vegetated gardens with plenty to eat.
Distribution: Common and widespread.

Green cellar slug
Limacus maculatus
Description: As the name suggests, this is a greenish-yellow slug with a pale, mottled body. They are found in gardens (often in compost heaps) and in damp, dark areas of houses.
When to see it: May to November.
Diet: Fungi and decaying matter.
Life cycle: Like all slugs and snails, they are hermaphrodite. Mating takes place in summer and autumn and eggs are laid in autumn or the following spring.
Garden habitats: Compost heaps.
Distribution: Common and widespread.

Wildlife gardening for birds

Sometimes colourful, often noisy, birds are the most obvious wildlife we most commonly encounter in our gardens. From the humble blue tit to the chatterbox goldfinch, birds offer a window into a wider world of garden wildlife, which includes the aphids, caterpillars, slugs and snails they rely on for food.

Traditionally associated with the woodland edge, birds such as the blackbird and robin have adapted to the similar landscape of lawn, trees and shrubs in our gardens, and many of them thrive living in such close proximity to humans. And as more pressure is put on agricultural land and more green belt is lost to build new towns and cities, so some birds continue to adapt: gardens are now increasingly important to some species of farmland bird, particularly the goldfinch. Since 2007, the goldfinch has consistently appeared in the top 10 species recorded in the RSPB's annual survey of UK garden birdlife, the Big Garden Birdwatch. It's thought that milder winters are encouraging more goldfinches to stay in the UK rather than migrate to Spain, but also that they are adapting to suburban and urban habitats, possibly due to supplementary feeding.

Birds all have slightly different habitat requirements, but as a general rule they need a good mix of shrubs and trees in which they can shelter and nest, water to drink and bathe in, and food to eat and feed their young – this means planting more caterpillar foodplants and other native shrubs and trees that cater for lots

▸ Goldfinches are common in gardens, where they will feast on the seeds on flowering plants such as dandelion, greater knapweed and teasel. They nest in dense hedges and in the forks of trees.

of the invertebrates that birds eat. Not all of us can meet all these requirements, but even those of us with a balcony can grow native plants and fill a birdbath with fresh water – you never know what might come along. You'll find further suggestions for encouraging birds in the table on the next page and a list of plants to provide for them on pages 120–21.

▶ Berries provide an important source of food for a variety of birds, such as blackbirds (*Turdus merula*).

Make your own winter birdbath

You will need:

- Three bricks 
- Trowel (if it's been snowing) 
- Shallow dish or pet bowl 
- Tealight candles and matches 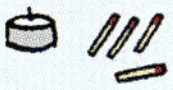
- Warm water (not too hot) 
- A large stone

① Find a flat area sheltered from the wind. Clear any snow and make a level patch.

② Arrange the bricks in a triangle.

③ Light a tealight and place it in the middle.

④ Rest a ceramic dish on the bricks and fill with warm water.

⑤ Place a stone in the middle for birds to sit on.

Ideas for attracting birds

	Suitable for...				
	Small garden	Medium garden	Large garden	Allotment	Balcony/patio
Plant a hedge.	✗	✓	✓	✓	✗
Grow fruit, including crab apples, and leave windfalls in situ.	✓	✓	✓	✓	✗
Grow native plants.	✓	✓	✓	✓	✓
Grow as wide a range of flowering plants as you have room for.	✓	✓	✓	✓	✓
Keep areas of grass short for blackbirds, robins and green woodpeckers.	✓	✓	✓	✓	✗
Let a patch of grass grow long. It will bear seed and caterpillars.	✓	✓	✓	✓	✗
Mulch borders or pots with compost or leaf mould.	✓	✓	✓	✓	✓
Compost your waste.	Compost bin	Large, open heap	Large, open heap	Large, open heap	Compost bin
Make a leaf pile.	✓	✓	✓	✓	Allow leaves to build up in a corner or behind pots.
Make a log pile.	Small logs or twigs/prunings	Large, partially buried in the ground	Large, partially buried in the ground	Large, partially buried in the ground	✗
Install a birdbath.	✓	✓	✓	✓	✓
Dig a pond with plenty of shallows and submerged plants.	Small	Medium	Large (make sure it has shallows)	Large	✗
Tolerate weeds, including dandelions.	✓	✓	✓	✓	✓
Let flowering plants such as lavender, sunflower and teasel seed in autumn.	✓	✓	✓	✓	✓
Plant a broadleaf tree, especially one that provides seeds in autumn, such as birch and alder.	✗	✓	✓	✓	✗
Grow climbing plants up walls and fences.	✓	✓	✓	✓	✓
Erect bird boxes.	✓	✓	✓	✓	✗
Grow as many berry-bearing trees and shrubs as you have space for, including rowan, hawthorn, guelder rose, holly and ivy.	✓	✓	✓	✓	✗
Offer mud in spring for nesting house martins and swallows.	✓	✓	✓	✓	✗
Leave hips on your roses in autumn.	✓	✓	✓	✓	✗

How to make a nest box

You will need:
- Rough cut timber
- Some old rubber or a hinge
- 20mm nails
- Tools: saw, hammer, hand brace or drill, pencil, ruler and scissors

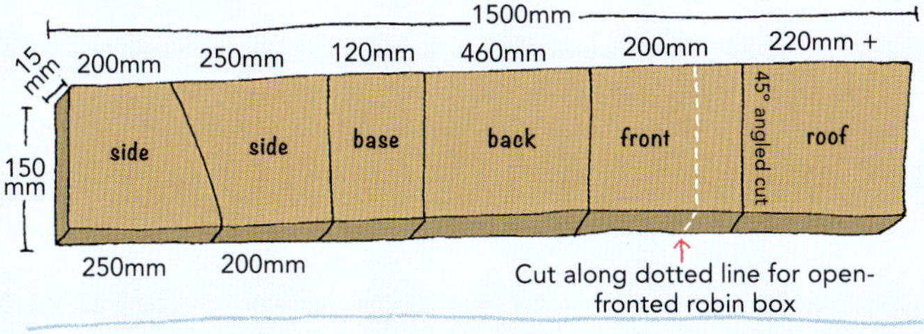

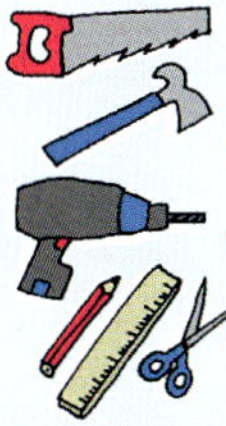

Panels (from 1500mm length, 150mm wide, 15mm thick): side 200mm, side 250mm, base 120mm, back 460mm, front 200mm, roof 220mm+ (with 45° angled cut). Sides also marked 250mm and 200mm.

Cut along dotted line for open-fronted robin box

1. Mark out and saw panels
Use diagram above, and write the name of each panel onto the marked-out wood.

2. Choose your box type
- hole-fronted box:*
  - blue tits (25mm)
  - great tits (28mm)
  - sparrows (38mm)
  - starlings (45mm) 
- open-fronted box for robins

3. Assemble the box
Nail the panels together.

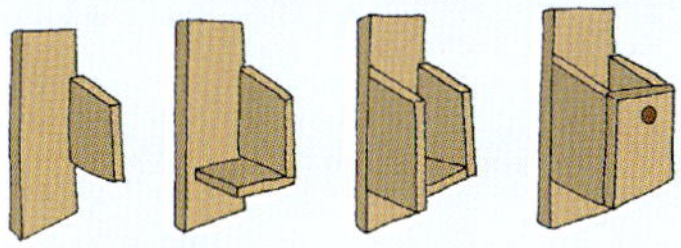

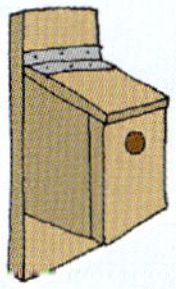

Fix on the roof panel with a hinge or strip of old rubber.

Where to put it:
2–5m above the ground, somewhere sheltered.

2–5m above ground

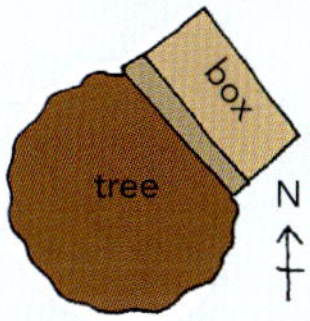

* Remember to sand the edges smooth.

◀ Nuthatch (*Sitta europaea*) using a home-made garden nest box.

Plants for birds

Plant	Native/non-native	Provides
Alder *Alnus glutinosa*	N	insects, seeds, shelter
Alder buckthorn *Frangula alnus*	N	berries, insects, shelter
Apple *Malus domestica*	N	fruit, insects, shelter
Beech *Fagus sylvatica*	N	insects, seeds, shelter
Bird cherry *Prunus padus*	N	fruit, insects, shelter
Blackberry *Rubus fruticosus*	N	berries, insects, shelter
Blackthorn *Prunus spinosa*	N	berries, insects, shelter
Cotoneaster	NN	fruit, shelter
Crab apple *Malus sylvestris*	N	fruit, insects, shelter
Dandelion *Taraxacum officinale*	N	insects, seeds, shelter
Devil's bit scabious *Succisa pratensis*	N	insects, seeds, shelter
Dog rose *Rosa canina*	N	fruit, insects, shelter
Elder *Sambucus nigra*	N	berries, insects, shelter
Evening primrose *Oenothera biennis*	NN	seeds
Field scabious *Nautia arvensis*	N	seeds
Greater knapweed *Centaurea scabiosa*	N	seeds
Guelder rose *Viburnum opulus*	N	berries, insects, shelter
Hawthorn *Crataegus monogyna*	N	berries, insects, shelter
Hazel *Corylus avellana*	N	insects, seeds, shelter
Holly *Ilex aquifolium*	N	berries, insects, shelter
Honeysuckle *Lonicera periclymenum*	N	berries, insects, shelter
Hornbeam *Carpinus betulus*	N	insects, seeds, shelter
Ivy *Hedera helix*	N	berries, insects, shelter
Lavenders *Lavandula*	NN	seeds

▲ Blackbird (*Turdus merula*)

▲ Robin (*Erithacus rubecula*)

Plant	Native/non-native	Provides
Lemon balm *Melissa officinalis*	NN	seeds
Mistletoe *Viscum album*	N	berries, insects, shelter
Oak *Quercus robur*	N	insects, seeds, shelter
Oregon grape *Mahonia aquifolium*	NN	berries, shelter
Pear *Pyrus communis*	N	fruit, insects, shelter
Pyracantha	NN	fruit, shelter
Rowan *Sorbus aucuparia*	N	berries, insects, shelter
Sea buckthorn *Hippophae rhamnoides*	N	berries, insects, shelter
Silver birch *Betula pendula*	N	insects, seeds, shelter
Snowberry *Symphoricarpos albus*	NN	fruit, shelter
Snowy mespilus *Amelanchier lamarckii*	NN	fruit, shelter
Spindle *Euonymus europaeus*	N	fruit, insects, shelter
Stinging nettle *Urtica diocia*	N	insects, seeds
Stranvaesia *Photinia davidiana*	NN	berries, shelter
Sunflower *Helianthus annuus*	NN	seeds
Teasel *Dipsacus fullonum*	N	insects, seeds
Thistles *Carduus* and *Cirsium*	N	insects, seeds
Argentinian vervain *Verbena bonariensis*	NN	seeds
Wayfaring tree *Viburnum lantana*	N	berries, insects
Whitebeam *Sorbus aria*	N	fruit, shelter, insects
Wild cherry *Prunus avium*	N	fruit, shelter, insects
Wild privet *Ligustrum vulgare*	N	fruit, shelter, insects
Wild service tree *Sorbus torminalis*	N	berries
Yew *Taxus baccata*	N	fruit, insects, shelter

▲ Blue tit (*Cyanistes caeruleus*)

▲ Chaffinch (*Fringilla coelebs*)

Feeding garden birds

We used to put our kitchen scraps out for garden birds in winter. Now, every year, we spend millions of pounds on bird food and bird feeders. Feeding garden birds feels like an obvious, easy and enjoyable way to help our garden wildlife while learning more about it.

Around half of UK householders feed the birds in their garden, providing them with 50,000–60,000 tonnes of food annually. We know the most appealing high-calorie foods to help them maintain their bodyweight in winter and the best protein-rich options to help them prepare for breeding in spring. New foods and feeders are continually developed and many of us see a wider variety of species at bird tables than we did a couple of decades ago. But is what we're doing for garden birds actually good for them?

Supplementary feeding has certainly benefitted declining species like house sparrows, tree sparrows and starlings. However, when some species increase, it can create problems for others. In suburban and rural areas, dominant species such as great tits and great spotted woodpeckers outcompete less competitive species like willow and marsh tits, for nest sites and food resources. So gardeners may, unwittingly, be giving dominant birds an advantage at the expense of less dominant ones.

Diseases can also spread easily at garden feeding stations. In 2005, the protozoan parasite *Trichomonas gallinae* jumped from woodpigeons to finches – two species unlikely to have otherwise come into such close contact. This resulted in a 66 per cent loss of greenfinches per year, for 10 years. Avian pox and salmonella can also spread at feeding stations, particularly at bird tables. Sick birds who don't have the energy to cling to a feeder may still feed from bird tables or ground

▲ Squirrel-proof bird feeders can deter squirrels and larger birds, leaving more food for smaller birds like this blue tit.

feeders in gardens. At the time of writing, the RSPB has suspended sales of bird tables and table feed mixes while they review the evidence of diseases being more easily spread on flat structures.

Imported bird food also has its own environmental footprint, including habitat loss, pesticide exposure and carbon emissions. And by replacing natural food sources with commercial seeds, we contribute to environmental harm while losing control over how the food is produced. A better approach might be to make our gardens wilder, allowing birds to feed themselves naturally.

How to feed birds naturally

▲ Blackcaps feed on a variety of fruits and berries, like these crab apples, in winter.

It's time to reconsider how we feed garden birds. Essentially, we need to improve our garden habitats to ensure there's more food as nature intended, so birds can feed themselves.

I used to love watching birds at my feeder, but I love seeing them find natural food even more – sparrows on grass stems, goldfinches on knapweed, and blackbirds on crab apples. Since removing my feeders, I see fewer crowds but more variety. Whether or not you feed birds, creating natural habitats helps them thrive – that's what wildlife gardening is all about.

What if I stop feeding the birds?

If we all stopped feeding birds in our gardens, most species would remain very common. Dr Richard Broughton, author of *The Marsh Tit and the Willow Tit*, says he took down his bird feeders years ago, and doesn't miss them. 'I still get lots of birds using my garden, but no diseases and no rats, and the money I save helps support a few wildlife charities', he says.

If we do continue buying food to put out for the birds in our gardens, it's essential we buy products that are developed and produced with nature in mind. The RSPB sells only bird food that meets its Fair to Nature standards and that's packaged sustainably in compostable paper bags. The BTO works with a UK supplier that grows much of its bird food on its own farm, some of it cultivated organically. Profits from sales of bird food from both the RSPB and BTO are directed back to the conservation of birds.

Plant native tree and shrubs

Native trees and shrubs attract more egg-laying insects than non-natives. Plant a mixed native hedge (to include hawthorn, hazel and dog rose), or grow standard trees such as birch, crab apple or field maple. Many birds seek out insects, their eggs and larvae all year round.

Stop controlling 'pests'

House sparrows and chiffchaffs eat aphids, while thrushes and starlings eat slugs and snails. As well as earthworms, blackbirds eat vine weevil larvae and robins eat moths. Take a more relaxed outlook to the usually less welcome garden inhabitants, and let the birds control them for you.

Leave areas of long grass

Long grass provides habitat for a huge number of species, from moth and butterfly larvae to grasshoppers and ground beetles. In summer the grass seed will be eaten by sparrows but all year round there will be insects.

▲ Thrushes eat snails, smashing them against an 'anvil' – which can be any stone or rock – to release the juicy food inside the shell.

▲ Caterpillars, sawfly larvae and other grubs make a protein-rich meal for birds and their chicks.

Make habitat piles
Piling up logs, sticks and other plant material will create an invertebrate-rich feast for all sorts of birds, such as robins and wrens, which will seek out insects and spiders.

Leave seedheads standing
The easiest way to feed birds over winter is to not cut down seedheads in autumn. Anything from sunflowers to lavender, teasel, greater knapweed, cardoon, asters and lamb's ear will attract seed-eating birds, and they look good too.

Grow more fruiting plants
Birds eat the fruits of holly, rowan, hawthorn, honeysuckle, dogwood, roses and crab apples.

Grow caterpillar foodplants
Many small birds feed caterpillars to their chicks. Allow caterpillar-friendly 'weeds' such as dandelion, bedstraws and dock to flourish in areas you will tolerate them, and grow foxgloves, nasturtiums and primroses.

Feed the soil
Mulching with home-made compost and leafmould will support worms and other soil invertebrates, while letting autumn leaves remain where they fall – except on lawns and paths – will mimic the natural cycle of woodland. Look out for blackbirds sifting through the leaves for larvae and other grubs.

Avoid burning waste
Burning garden waste destroys habitats and kills invertebrates such as spiders, beetles and woodlice sheltering within. Make a large, open compost heap instead, which will break down slowly and provide lots of feeding opportunities for birds such as wrens and blackbirds.

Dig a pond
A pond provides bathing and drinking water, as well as food for birds, including tadpoles and froglets, and invertebrate larvae such as dragonfly and damselfly nymphs.

Leave windfalls be
Apples and pears will be eaten by blackbirds and migrant thrushes such as redwings and fieldfares, which might arrive in large groups. You don't have to give up your prized crop, simply leave windfall fruit in place, so the birds can make the most of it.

A guide to commercial bird food

If you are still keen to provide supplementary food for birds, use the following as a guide.

Seed mixes
These vary in quality. Some companies bulk out their mixes with cheap grains like barley and wheat, or split peas, beans, lentils or even rice, which attract pigeons. A lot of them will end up on the ground, which will either germinate and cause a weed problem, or attract rats, which you may then be obliged to control (see page 125). Choose mixes that contain kibbled peanuts, maize and sunflower seeds or hearts. Avoid mixes containing whole nuts at all times except winter.
Popular with: House sparrows, robins and tits.

Sunflower seeds
Packed with energy-rich oils and antioxidants. Choose black seeds over striped seeds as the oil content is higher so birds spend less energy eating per seed. Shelled sunflower hearts where the outer seed husk has been removed are even more energy efficient. Mostly imported from Ukraine, Turkey, Romania and Argentina.
Popular with: Goldfinches, house sparrows, robins and tits.

Niger (or nyjer) seeds
Small and black with a high oil content, these are the seed of choice for goldfinches. They can be fiddly to handle, and you will need a special feeder to hold them in. Imported from Africa, India and South East Asia.
Popular with: Goldfinches and siskins.

▲ Always keep an eye out for unusual visitors to your feeders, such as tree sparrows (*Passer montanus*).

Peanuts
Calorie-rich, these come whole, crushed or kibbled. Only buy nuts intended for bird consumption and ensure they have been tested and guaranteed not to contain aflatoxin, a poisonous mould that can kill birds. When providing whole nuts, use a wire mesh feeder so the nuts cannot be taken away in one piece. Mainly imported from Africa.
Popular with: Great spotted woodpeckers, greenfinches, house sparrows, nuthatches, siskins and tits. Chopped nuts attract dunnocks, robins and wrens.

Check for eco-friendly seeds and nuts

Many seeds and nuts are grown far from the British Isles, on land that could be used to provide habitats for native species or to grow food for people. They are often freighted in single-use plastic bags. They may also have pesticide residues on them if they were grown in countries with poor pesticide regulations.

Suet products

Suitable for winter feeding only, products made from beef fat are highly calorific. Remove fat balls from their nylon mesh, which can trap birds' legs (and harm other wildlife if they fall to the ground). Never use fat left over from cooking, even if unseasoned, as it is too soft and can damage feathers.
Popular with: Great spotted woodpeckers, house sparrows, nuthatches and tits.

Mealworms

Providing protein-rich mealworms for birds in the breeding season to make up for any lack of caterpillars or other live food is often recommended. Robins eat them year-round. They are available live or dried; the latter can be rehydrated in water. Most are imported from China.
Popular with: Blue tits, house sparrows, robins, blackbirds, wrens and starlings.

Cat and dog food

In dry summers when birds can't find earthworms to eat, small amounts of meaty tinned cat and dog food can be used to feed birds. Dry biscuits are not suitable, but small amounts of water-soaked dog biscuit are OK.
Popular with: Blackbirds

Dairy products

Birds can't digest cow's milk so never leave it out. They can digest cheese, however, and small amounts of grated mild cheese can attract robins and wrens.
Popular with: Dunnocks, robins and wrens

Coconut

While a coconut shell packed with suet is a popular method for feeding birds, desiccated coconut can kill birds. Choose fresh pieces of coconut only.

Rice and cereals

Cooked rice, without salt, can be good for birds. Uncooked porridge oats are OK, as are small amounts of dry breakfast cereal if they don't contain too much salt or sugar.

▲ Blue tits are regular visitors to the garden, feasting on a number of supplementary foods, such as suet in a coconut shell.

What not to feed birds

- Dried fruit such as raisins and sultanas (which can kill dogs)
- Mouldy or stale food
- Salty and sugary food

Feeding birds may be driving evolutionary changes. Part of Eastern Europe's blackcap population now migrates to the British Isles rather than Spain and North Africa for the winter. These birds have evolved longer, narrower beaks, possibly an adaptation to using bird feeders.

How to make your own winter bird feeder

What you need:

- **Dry ingredients**
  - bird seed
  - cooked rice
  - grated cheese
  - dried fruit (not raisins or sultanas)
  - breadcrumbs
  - chopped nuts

- **Hard cooking fat (lard or suet)**

- **A pine cone, coconut shell or yoghurt pot**

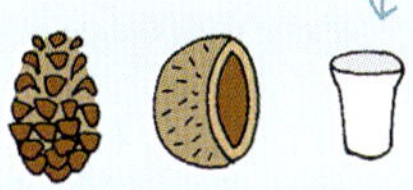

  Use an old yoghurt pot for this and always recycle after it's been used

- **String**

1. Mix all the dry ingredients together in a bowl.

2. Add the fat and give it a good mix around.

   You may need to melt the fat to mix it in

3. Choose your feeder.

   Plaster all over a fir cone

   Put it round the inside of a coconut shell

   Press into a yoghurt pot

   You can hang this upside down like a bell or turn it out like a cake

4. Hang your feeders with string (you may need to make holes and tie the string in before adding the mix).

Hang your feeder where you can watch birds without disturbing them.

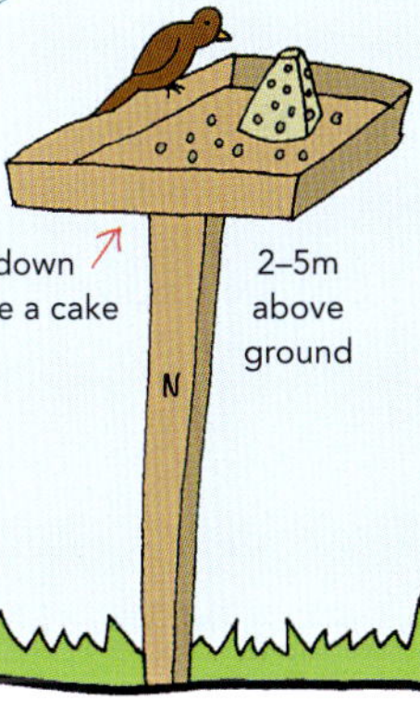

2–5m above ground

Health risks for garden birds

Just like us, birds exposed to certain infectious organisms, such as bacteria, viruses and parasites, can become ill. And, just like us, the more birds that gather in the same area (think busy Tube train on a Monday morning), the more likely they are to pick something up. Bacteria and viruses can build up on the surfaces of birdbaths and feeding stations or be transmitted from bird to bird, but good hygiene and common sense can reduce the risks for spread.

Diseases

Garden birds are susceptible to a number of infectious diseases, but the two major conditions affecting birds at the time of writing are avian pox and trichomonosis.

Avian pox

Avian pox is caused by the avian pox virus. It has been recorded sporadically in garden birds for many years, affecting species such as the dunnock, house sparrow, starling and wood pigeon.

However, since 2006 the virus has been found in tits. Infected tits have been reported with tumour-like growths next to the eye or beak, on the legs, wings or other body parts, with great tits apparently most frequently and worst affected. Sightings of great tits with these growths started in south-east Britain and have gradually moved west and north.

The tumour-like growths in other species are typically less aggressive than in great tits, and may recede as the birds recover. Affected birds can often feed and move around normally. But in great tits the growths can become so big that they affect the bird's ability to see, feed or move. This makes them much more susceptible to starvation and predation by cats and other predators.

It's thought that avian pox is spread between birds in three ways: by biting insects (e.g. mosquitoes), by direct contact with other birds, and by indirect contact via contaminated surfaces such as perches or bird tables. The virus can survive in the environment for long periods of time.

Trichomonosis

Caused by a single-celled parasite called *Trichomonas gallinae*, trichomonosis typically affects pigeons and doves and occasionally birds of prey that feed on them. However, it was first confirmed in British finches in 2005 and has since spread to epidemic proportions among greenfinches and chaffinches. The disease is now widespread throughout the British Isles. A number of other songbird species are also susceptible to the disease.

Affected birds show non-specific signs of ill health, such as fluffed-up plumage, and are often too lethargic and slow to fly away. They may also display any of the following signs of disease: drooling saliva, regurgitating food, showing difficulty in swallowing or laboured breathing. They may have matted, wet plumage and food stuck around the face and beak.

The parasite is spread in fresh saliva from affected birds and is killed when it dries out in the environment. Transmission between birds is most likely via birds feeding each other with regurgitated food during breeding season, or through food or water contaminated by an infected bird. Trichomonosis causes ulcers to develop in the gullet of affected birds so that they have difficulties in swallowing. They then regurgitate food, which still contains the parasite: if this contaminated food waste is eaten by another bird at a feeding station they can become infected.

Between 2006 and 2009, the UK breeding greenfinch population declined by around 35 per cent, and the average number of greenfinches visiting gardens declined by 50 per cent over the same period. The population decline of greenfinches continues and the most recent Breeding Bird Survey data indicates a 60 per cent reduction in the UK breeding population since the disease emerged.

Mites and leg lesions

Knemidocoptes mites burrow into birds' legs and around their beak, resulting in scaly dry encrustations.

The *Fringilla* papilloma virus causes warty growths on finches. These vary in size but can cover a whole leg, and eventually leaving to a loss of digits or lameness.

Minimising disease risk

To reduce the spread of disease at feeding sites:

- Consider taking down supplementary feeders and instead focus on natural ways to feed birds, such as leaving seedheads standing, and growing berries and caterpillar foodplants.

- Clean and disinfect feeders and feeding stations regularly. Suitable disinfectants include a weak solution of domestic bleach or other products designed specifically for disinfecting bird feeders – a number of bird food retailers now stock disinfectant. Thoroughly rinse feeders and allow them to fully air-dry before refilling.

- Wear rubber gloves when cleaning feeders. Thoroughly wash hands and forearms afterwards with soap and water, and do this outside in a bucket with a dedicated brush.

Controlling disease outbreaks

If you spot birds with signs of disease:

- Empty, clean and air-dry birdbaths.

- Stop feeding for a minimum of two to four weeks.

To report signs of disease or dead garden birds, contact Garden Wildlife Health (see page 189). This will help the team of vets monitor the conditions affecting garden birds.

Should we light our gardens?

Artificial light at night (known as ALAN) affects wildlife in several ways. It can attract migrating birds to urban areas where they could collide with buildings. Street and garden lights affect how birds forage, potentially preventing them from feeding due to fear of predation. Some birds, like robins, thrushes and blackbirds, sing all night in intensively lit areas. Many bats that have evolved to fly at night to avoid predation, avoid foraging in areas with lots of light pollution, which can reduce how much they eat. Some delay when they emerge from their roost as artificial light makes them think it's still daytime.

The charity Buglife claims that, in some areas, light pollution reduces nocturnal pollinator visits to flowers by 62 per cent and moth populations by around half. Buglife estimates that a third of insects attracted to lights die due to exhaustion, increased predation and a disrupted ability to navigate.

Light pollution can also interfere with the life cycles of insects, such as the time of year they hatch or emerge from hibernation. Mating and breeding can be affected too; for example, female glow-worms are less able to attract mates by 'glowing'.

Our towns and cities are responsible for most light pollution. Urban residents can push for darker skies by asking councils and local businesses to turn lights off that aren't in use.

If we have lighting in our garden, here's how we can reduce its impact on wildlife:

- Use warm yellow or amber light, not harsh white light, as they are believed to be less disruptive to insects
- Use solar lights that emit a dull glow
- Turn lights off when you're not using them, or use motion sensors so lights turn on only when you're in the garden
- Position lights low to the ground or aim them downwards so they don't light up the sky
- Fit hoods over lights to reduce glare where bright lighting isn't needed
- Avoid hanging lights from or directing light into trees and shrubs where insects and birds might be sheltering.

These measures will help but we should also consider whether we should light our gardens at all. Away from steps and outdoor dining areas, let's welcome the dark for connecting us with the moon and stars. Let's work together to ensure the UK's 30 million gardens are a safe refuge for birds, insects, bats and other wildlife by keeping them in their natural state at night: darkness.

ID parade
Birds

Blackbird *Turdus merula*
Description: Males are black with a bright yellow bill and yellow eye rings; the female has a dull brown body with a mottled chest, and a brownish beak. Fiercely territorial, the male sings well into the evening in spring, often in quite urban areas, singing loudly from rooftop TV aerials. I think the blackbird is quite a jumpy character – one minute singing his lungs out and the next sending out alarm calls, seemingly over nothing. His song is melodious and rich, fluty almost, and his alarm call is a quick '*pink-pink-pink*'. In early spring you might see one flying quickly from one place to the next in a territorial dispute.
When to see it: All year round.
Nests: The nest is made with grass, twigs and mud, and is usually low down in a hedge, tree or mature climber, but may sometimes be found in buildings or even on the ground.
Diet: Invertebrates such as worms and insects, often taken from lawns and borders or compost / leaf mould / mulch. In winter they eat windfall fruit and berries. The young are fed worms and caterpillars.
Life cycle: Breeding takes place from March to late July, producing up to five broods of three to four eggs, the last of which may still be in the nest in late August. The female incubates the eggs for around two weeks and the young fledge after 14–16 days.
Garden habitats: Untreated lawn; mixed, mature native shrubs or hedging, in which they can forage for caterpillars for their young, nest and eat fruit in autumn.
Distribution: Widespread and common. However, numbers have been declining in southern England since 2020.

Blue tit
Cyanistes caeruleus
Description: A well-known garden bird with blue wings, tail and crown, yellow underparts, greenish back, white face with a black eye stripe. The sexes are hard to tell apart, but the female is slightly paler. Fledgling blue tits look like adults that have been dipped in a lemon wash. Blue tits are often seen at the edge of trees hanging upside down, scouring branches for insects. In winter they join forces with other tits as well as goldcrests, and search for food in large roving flocks.

When to see it: All year round.
Nests: Like robins, blue tits are known to nest in unusual places, such as letterboxes and pipes and even cigarette bins; but they will also use holes in trees and bird boxes. The female makes the cup-shaped nest using leaves, moss, wool and spiders' webs, lining it with feathers.
Diet: Mostly insects, especially caterpillars, as well as spiders and seeds. They eat pollen, nectar and tree sap in early spring, and berries in autumn. They feed caterpillars to their young, and scour plants for aphids when caterpillars are in short supply.
Life cycle: The female lays just one brood of 8–10 smooth, brown-spotted white eggs and incubates them for 13–15 days. The young fledge after 18–21 days.
Garden habitats: Mature gardens, especially where there are plenty of caterpillars for raising young.
Distribution: Widespread and common. The blue tit has a green UK breeding status, so is not considered threatened or declining. However, cold winters can dramatically reduce numbers.

Coal tit *Periparus ater*
Description: Smaller than the great tit at 12cm long, the coal tit has a grey back, buff underparts, a black cap and a white patch at the back of its neck. It has a sort of sepia hue to it, like watching a blue tit on an old black and white film. It has adapted a smaller bill than other tits – perfect for foraging among the spike-like conifer leaves. In winter it joins other tit species, along with goldcrests, in roving groups in search of food.

When to see it: All year round.
Nests: The nest is made from leaves, moss, wool and spider webs, and lined with moss, and can be found in a variety of locations including tree hollows, tree stumps and even old mouse and rabbit burrows. Coal tits will sometimes use nest boxes, and seem to prefer those placed closer to the ground.
Diet: Insects, beech mast and conifer seeds, plus black sunflower

seed. Coal tits often cache food to eat later, but these hidden morsels are well known – and raided! – by great tits.
Life cycle: The female lays one brood of 9–10 small, smooth, speckled white eggs and incubates them for 14–16 days. Both parents feed the young. The young fledge after 16–19 days.
Garden habitats: Mature gardens.
Distribution: Widespread and common. Numbers have remained consistent over the years and are no cause for concern. Coal tits have a green conservation status.

Goldfinch
Carduelis carduelis

Description: Gorgeous, twittering finch with a bright red face and yellow wing patches. The rest of the body is biscuit-brown, with black and white bars on the head. Its call is not dissimilar to that of a swallow, reminiscent of squeaky trolley castors or constant chatter. Some goldfinches migrate south as far as Spain in winter, although others stay at home and roam in large flocks in search of food.
When to see it: All year round.
Nests: Goldfinches nest in loose colonies in trees or hedges. The female makes a deep, cup-shaped nest using grass, moss, roots, lichens, wool and even hair.
Diet: Seed-eaters, goldfinches appear to prefer the seeds of plants in the daisy family, including dandelions (*Taraxacum officinale*), ragworts (*Senecio*) and thistles. They feed regurgitated seeds and insects to their young.
Life cycle: Nesting starts later than many other species, with the first eggs laid in June. The female bears up to 3 clutches of 5 pale blue, speckled eggs, which she incubates for 13–15 days. Both parents feed the young, which fledge after 14–17 days.
Garden habitats: Mature bushes and trees; wild areas where dandelions and thistles can grow.
Distribution: Widespread and common across the British Isles, except the far north of Scotland. Increasing in numbers, goldfinches are spreading northwards and have a green conservation status.

Great tit *Parus major*
Description: Our largest tit at 14cm long, the great tit is grey-green and yellow with a black cap, white cheeks and a black breast stripe, or tie (more noticeable in males). With a crisp, high-pitched '*tee-cher, tee-cher*' song, it's easy to know when great tits are around. Despite flocking with blue tits and coal tits in winter to scour for food, it can bully smaller birds away from the bird table.

When to see it: All year round.
Nests: Great tits build a nest using moss, grass and down in a variety of locations including holes in trees and nest boxes.
Diet: Like blue tits, great tits eat insects, particularly caterpillars, beetles and flies; they eat more tree seeds, especially beech mast, during autumn and winter. In spring they feed insects and spiders to their young.
Life cycle: The female typically lays a single clutch of 7–9 white, glossy eggs with purple-red spots. She incubates them for 13–15 days and the young fledge after 18–21 days.
Garden habitats: Shrubs, trees and hedges, where they can nest and forage for food.
Distribution: Widespread and common, with a green UK conservation listing.

Greenfinch *Chloris chloris*

Description: A sturdy finch, slightly larger than the house sparrow. The male is olive-green with green-yellow on the breast and lower back, and bright yellow wing flashes. Females are grey-green with less yellow. Juveniles are paler still, with streaked plumage. Known for its familiar wheezing call in spring, it also makes nasal, twittering calls similar to other finch species.
When to see it: All year round.
Nests: Greenfinches tend to nest in loose colonies in dense shrubs. The female builds the nest, using grass, plant roots, twigs and soft material such as hair.

Diet: Seeds, buds and berries. They feed their young a regurgitated mix of seeds and insects.
Life cycle: The female lays up to two clutches of 4–5 white, glossy eggs with black markings are produced, which the female incubates for 14–15 days. The young are fed by both parents and fledge after 14–16 days.
Garden habitats: Mixed, mature gardens full of insects and seed-bearing plants.
Distribution: Widespread and common, but numbers have fallen due to trichomonosis (see page 128), a disease caused by a parasite that stops the birds from feeding properly. This is thought to have contributed to a decline of around a third.

House sparrow *Passer domesticus*

Description: Noisy, gregarious little brown bird. The male has a chestnut back with black streaks and pale grey underparts. It has a dark grey crown, pale grey/white cheeks and black around its eyes, beak and on its throat (bib). The female is paler with no grey crown or black markings, but has a straw-coloured stripe above the eye. The house sparrow congregates in extended family groups, in a hedge, scrubby bush or similar, where you might hear its 'cheep-cheep-cheep' before spotting any birds. Populations are sedentary, meaning the birds stay in the same area, even if the habitat becomes unsuitable. This means local populations are more vulnerable than other species to habitat changes such as the paving-over of gardens – rather than moving on, they simply stay in the location and suffer the consequences (such as a sudden reduction in insects to feed their young).
When to see it: All year round.
Nests: Untidy cup- or dome-shaped nests in holes or crevices in buildings, or among ivy growing on buildings. They also use nest boxes, especially when there are several placed together, allowing the birds to nest communally.

Diet: The adults eat a variety of seeds, suet and grains, but feed their young exclusively on insects (particularly aphids) and caterpillars.
Life cycle: Mating takes place from spring to late summer. Each pair produces up to four broods of 4–5 speckled white eggs per year. Eggs are incubated for 13–15 days and the fledglings emerge after 15–17 days.
Garden habitats: Long grass provides a habitat for insects, which house sparrows feed their young, as well as seeds to forage for themselves. Areas of bare ground enable them to dust bathe. A range of shrubs and herbaceous plants provide insects, particularly aphids. Large shrubs provide shelter to hide and socialise. Nooks, crevices and nest boxes enable them to nest. A birdbath or small pond provides water for drinking and bathing.
Distribution: House sparrow numbers dropped by 71 per cent between 1977 and 2008. Numbers now appear to be levelling off, at least in some parts of the UK, but the species is still a cause for concern and has been given red conservation status. Population declines have been evident in urban areas, with some now absent from areas where they were previously abundant. Reasons for declines include: loss of nesting habitat – in urban areas, it's thought that new-style buildings and house renovations are reducing the availability of nooks and crannies for house sparrows to nest in; loss of food – reduced numbers of insects and caterpillars in intensively farmed and urban areas.

Long-tailed tit *Aegithalos caudatus*

Description: Not really a tit, although distantly related to tits, the long-tailed tit is like a tiny flying badger – small (14cm long), fluffy and pinkish with black and white markings, and with a very long black and white tail (the longest tail of any British bird in relation to its body). It tends to gather in family groups throughout the year, with unpaired relatives sometimes helping out with feeding their sibling's young.
When to see it: All year round.

Nests: The nest is a complex ball of hair, moss and spiders' webs, camouflaged with lichen and lined with feathers, and can take up to three weeks to build.
Diet: Insect eaters, they typically eat butterfly and moth eggs, bugs and small insects. They will eat berries in winter.
Life cycle: The female lays one clutch of 6–8 glossy white eggs with purple-red spots. She incubates them for 15–18 days and the young fledge from 16–17 days.
Garden habitats: Trees and dense, thorny bushes.
Distribution: Widespread and common. Populations are increasing, possibly due to milder winters or their recent adaption to use garden feeders. They have a green conservation status.

Robin *Erithacus rubecula*

Description: Small and brown with a red breast and huge black eyes, there's no mistaking the robin (although the young have a brown and white speckled breast before developing their red breast after around three months). Its song is easy to recognise too, reminiscent of a trickling water fountain. Some say its song becomes mournful in winter.
When to see it: All year round.
Nests: Nests are made using grass, moss and leaves in a variety of locations, including dense vegetation, tree hollows and the ground. They will also use open-fronted nest boxes.
Diet: Invertebrates such as worms and beetles, which they tend to eat on the ground; berries in autumn and winter.
Life cycle: Usually two (sometimes three) broods of 4–5 eggs are produced per year, which are incubated for 14–16 days. The young fledge 13–16 days after hatching.
Garden habitats: A wide variety of garden habitats can support the robin, especially those with mature plants and good soil fauna, which provide them with a variety of invertebrates to eat.
Distribution: Widespread and common, it has a green conservation status.

Starling *Sturnus vulgaris*

Description: Slightly smaller than a blackbird, the starling is black with iridescent green and pink flashes in summer, and duller but with white speckles in winter. This sharp-suited bird gathers in large flocks, often in trees or on rooftops. Known for its ability to mimic a variety of different sounds, it can imitate car alarms, telephone rings and emergency vehicle sirens, and often makes a series of noises not dissimilar to R2-D2 from *Star Wars*.
When to see it: All year round.
Nests: Starlings nest in holes and cavities, especially in trees, but also cavities in buildings and under the eaves of houses; they use nest boxes too. The male starts the nest, using dry grass and leaves. He then sings to attract a female and finishes the nest by shaping it and lining it with grasses, moss and feathers.
Diet: A wide variety of food including insects, worms, snails and berries. They feed insects and larvae to their young. Their beak is strong and has evolved to probe the ground for invertebrates, such as leatherjackets, beneath the surface.
Life cycle: From spring to summer, one or two broods of 4–5 eggs are laid. Both parents incubate the eggs (for 12–15) days and feed the chicks. The young fledge after 19–22 days.
Garden habitats: Untreated lawn; mixed, mature shrubs and some suitable nest sites.
Distribution: Widespread and common. However, breeding populations have declined by around 80 per cent since the early 1980s, especially in woodland and in south and west Britain, and starlings now have a red conservation listing. Reasons for the decline are unclear, but a reduction in food and loss of habitat are the most likely causes, particularly the loss of permanent pasture (the starling's preferred feeding habitat) in rural areas. As numbers have decreased, the numbers of fledglings per breeding attempt has increased; clutches are now larger than they used to be.

Wildlife gardening for amphibians and reptiles

Amphibians and reptiles are an absolute joy to have in the garden. They bring me enormous cheer, from the gentle splash of a frog as it disappears into the pond when it hears me coming, to the 'pip-pips' of mating toads or the glimpse of a slow-worm patrolling my greenhouse in search of slugs. I only wish I had space to accommodate more of them.

Provided they have access, common frogs, common toads and smooth newts are regularly found in gardens and allotments, with some of us lucky enough to attract slow-worms, lizards and even grass snakes. I've visited gardens teeming with great crested newts – if the right habitat is nearby, you never know what might turn up.

While often lumped together in the same category, amphibians and reptiles have quite different sets of needs. Although both groups are cold-blooded, amphibians are typically associated with damp, cool habitats, while lizards (including slow-worms) and snakes need warm spots to bask in the sun. In this section you'll find all the information you need to attract both amphibians and reptiles, including feeding and breeding requirements, and where to find them.

▲ Garden ponds make a perfect habitat for common frogs (*Rana temporaria*).

Amphibians

The most obvious habitat to create for amphibians in the garden is a pond (see page 139 for a guide on how to make one). But you needn't feel that's the only amphibian habitat. Frogs, toads and newts use ponds to breed in, but for the rest of the year they might take shelter under a log or in a leaf pile, sit out summer in your greenhouse or patrol a particularly fly-infested corner of your patio.

Gardening for them is also about ensuring there is plenty of food for them (see box, page 143). So while you're unlikely to see any on your balcony or doorstep, you can still help amphibians by growing plants that cater for the invertebrates they eat. A well-mulched soil or plant pot encourages beetle and worm activity; single, open flowers create feeding opportunities for flying insects; and certain caterpillar food plants will bring egg-laying moths to your door (see the Butterfly Conservation lists in Resources). By clothing every available space in plants, whether we have a large garden or a tiny balcony, we can increase the number of species that are foundational to the food web, thereby benefitting many others.

▲ Common toads (*Bufo bufo*) are found in varied habitats after breeding.
▼ Garden ponds are a valuable contribution to the local ecosystem.

Reptiles

There are six species of native reptile in Britain: three lizards – common lizard, sand lizard and slow-worm; and three snakes – adder, grass snake and smooth snake. Of these, just three are likely to turn up in gardens – the common lizard, grass snake and slow-worm.

Like much of our native wildlife, populations of grass snakes, lizards and slow-worms are declining. Gardening for reptiles involves bringing a bit of wildness to your garden: growing your grass a bit longer, providing opportunities for them to bask and warm up in the sun. A compost heap is a must – the warmer the better.

In my garden and allotment, I have created habitats for common lizards and grass snakes, but the only reptiles I have seen are slow-worms. They love to bask beneath the refugium (see box, page 142)

Be careful...
- when mowing or strimming the lawn, as frogs like to sit in long, damp grass in summer.
- if you have a cat, or cats come into your garden. Make sure you provide extra hiding places for amphibians and reptiles to escape quickly if they need to.
- when netting plants, such as peas, as this can trap amphibians and reptiles. Lift netting 22–30cm off the ground, but ideally don't use it.
- if you feed the birds fat balls. Make sure you remove and dispose of any plastic netting, as it can not only trap birds but can harm amphibians and reptiles.
- to provide shade at the edge of your pond if it is edged with paving stones. On hot, sunny days, froglets leaving the pond can become stuck on these and die.
- if you have a drain (gully pot) in or around your garden. Amphibians (and hedgehogs) can become trapped in these and are often washed into sewers. Consider fitting an escape ladder.

▲ Slow-worms (*Anguis fragilis*) are common and beneficial in the garden.

I made for them, and sometimes I see them above ground, chasing after prey. They seem to love the hot, moist, slug-rich conditions of my greenhouse. Of my four allotment compost heaps, they prefer the black plastic ones that reach 40°C on sunny days. I'm convinced they breed here but I don't want to disturb them to check. My compost bins are emptied strictly in April only – between overwintering and breeding – to ensure minimal disturbance of anything living within them.

You'll find further suggestions for attracting amphibians and reptiles in the table overleaf.

Ideas for attracting amphibians and reptiles

	Suitable for…				
	Small garden	Medium garden	Large garden	Allotment	Balcony/patio
Dig a pond – the larger the better, ensuring you have plenty of shallow margins, where aquatic larvae can congregate, and hedgehogs and amphibians can enter and exit easily.	✓	✓	✓	✓	✗
Make a container pond, using bricks as a 'frog ladder' so amphibians can enter and exit easily.	✓	✓	✓	✓	✓
Compost your waste and leave the heap undisturbed as much as possible.	✓	✓	✓	✓	✓
Make a habitat pile using logs, branches, twigs and leaves.	✓	✓	✓	✓	✓
Let an area of grass grow long, especially around your pond.	✓	✓	✓	✓	✗
Pile stones up together or build a drystone wall.	✓	✓	✓	✓	✓
Grow groundcover plants to create areas of dense vegetation.	✓	✓	✓	✓	✗
Make leaf mould.	✓	✓	✓	✓	✗
Avoid killing slugs and snails.	✓	✓	✓	✓	✓
Make a reptile refugium.	✓	✓	✓	✓	✗
Make an amphibian hibernaculum (see page 142).	✓	✓	✓	✓	✗
Join your local Toads on Roads group (see the Froglife website in Resources).	✓	✓	✓	✓	✓
Create basking sites for lizards and snakes.	✓	✓	✓	✓	✗

Top tips for tailoring your pond

Frogs, toads and newts all have slightly different needs, so you might want to tailor your pond to suit one over another. That said, amphibians don't read books! You may find all three species happily using the same pond, so use this as a guide only.

- Frog ponds should be shallow or have plenty of shallows – the spawn is laid here, as shallow water warms up more quickly in spring.
- Toad ponds should be larger and deeper, and have plenty of submerged and emergent plants, such as marsh marigold and water lilies. Females wrap their spawn around the stems of these plants in spring.
- Newts typically prefer deeper ponds and lay eggs individually in the leaves of marginal plants, such as water forget-me-not.
- Newts can eat frogspawn and frog tadpoles.

 ## Make a wildlife pond

You will need:
- A big patch of garden
- Spade 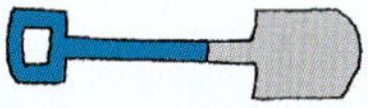
- Plank of wood 
- Spirit level 
- Butyl pond liner 
- Sand 
- Water (use rainwater for best results) 
- A variety of pond plants 
- Large rocks

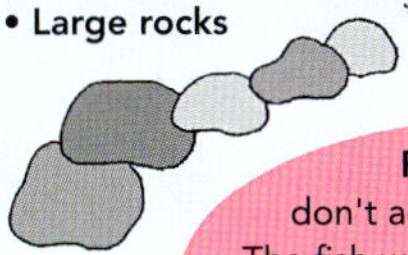

Remember: don't add fish or a pump. The fish will eat smaller animals (including frog and newt tadpoles) while the pump may suck them up!

1. Choose your spot.* Draw your pond outline and dig out, including some shallow areas.

   Use a plank and spirit level to ensure that the edges are level

2. Put a layer of sand at the bottom (don't use it all, you'll need some later).

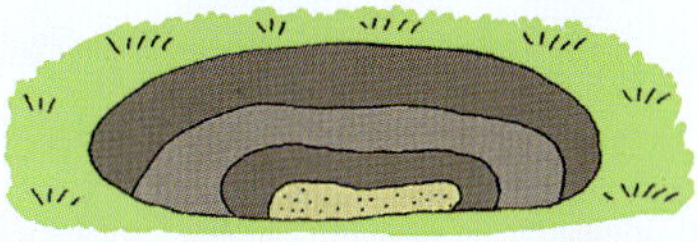

3. Make a trench all around the edge of your pond, and lay the edge of the liner into this. Weigh it down with large rocks.

4. Fill the bottom with the remaining sand.

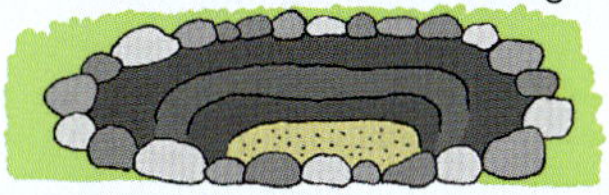

5. Fill the pond up with water.

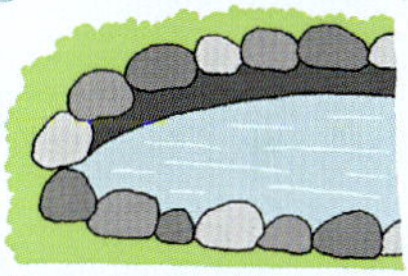

   If you fill it from a tap or hose your water might turn green – don't worry this is just the minerals.

6. Leave your pond to settle for about a week before adding your plants.

7. Watch and see what wildlife visits.

   Make sure you add a plank of wood or something similar as a ramp to help any wildlife that may have fallen in.

* Look for a spot with plenty of sun, ideally with some shade in the afternoon. Try to avoid positioning it near trees, as fallen leaves can pollute the pond.

- Toad tadpoles are poisonous to fish and other predators, including newts. This means that in a pond with frogs, toads and newts, the toads will be at an advantage because the predators will eat the frog and newt tadpoles.
- When emerging from the pond, immature frogs, toads and newts are susceptible to the attentions of predators such as blackbirds. You can help them hide by providing plenty of low-growing plant cover around the edge of the pond (such as edging it with grass rather than paving slabs).
- Frogs can breath through their skin and may shelter at the bottom of the pond over winter (particularly males, so they're ready and waiting for the first females in spring).
- Ponds dug beneath trees can become clogged up with leaves in autumn. Small amounts of leaves aren't a problem, but it is best to scoop larger amounts out before they sink to the bottom.

Provide easy pond access

When digging a pond, make sure there are plenty of shallows with gently sloping edges, not only for amphibians but also for birds and mammals, such as hedgehogs, so they can enter and exit easily. Hedgehogs are known to drown in steep-sided ponds. They might fall in, or take a dip in summer, and be unable to climb out. Hedgehogs can swim but they quickly get exhausted, so make life easy for them with a shallow exit. If you already have a steep-sided pond, add a log or ladder so they can exit easily.

Don't be tempted to introduce spawn

Don't be tempted to introduce spawn or animals to your pond. You may inadvertently also introduce diseases or invasive plants, and there may be good reasons why those animals aren't in your garden or allotment in the first place. By creating the right habitats (see the pond above) and ensuring animals can access your garden, you have every chance of attracting them naturally.

Keeping children safe around ponds

Very few children drown in ponds, but there are risks and we should take all precautions to reduce them. The most obvious of these is to supervise children at all times when at the edge of, or near, a pond. According to the Freshwater Habitats Trust, children aged between one and two are most at risk as they are mobile but lack adequate coordination. The risk of drowning reduces at the age of four or five, when children start to understand the dangers associated with water.

That said, a pond is one of the most valuable wildlife habitats to have in your garden, and is extremely educational, potentially giving your child a lifelong love of ponds and the wider natural world. By choosing to not have a pond, or by filling in an existing pond, you are potentially harming wildlife and cutting off a vital entry point for your child to the wonders of the natural world. Here's how to safely have a pond in your garden and hopefully instil a lasting fondness and respect for ponds in your children.

- Don't let children near your pond, or go pond dipping, unsupervised.
- Check with friends and neighbours as to the whereabouts of their ponds.
- Talk to children about the possible dangers of ponds from a very early age, as you would regarding baths.
- Consider fencing off or placing a childproof frame over your pond while the children are very young, but make sure wildlife are still able to enter and exit easily.
- Set an example – never stand at the edge of the pond but kneel instead, and teach children to do the same.

Make habitats for reptiles

One of the best habitats you can make for grass snakes and slow worms is a reptile refugium – a place where reptiles can hide. It's a great way to ascertain whether the species are using your garden or allotment in the first place. Simply lay a bespoke reptile mat or piece of corrugated iron flat on the ground in a sunny spot (ideally over long grass or straw). As it heats up during the day, slow worms and grass snakes will shelter beneath it.

How to build a hibernaculum

Great for overwintering amphibians and reptiles!

You will need:

- Spade 
- Logs and branches 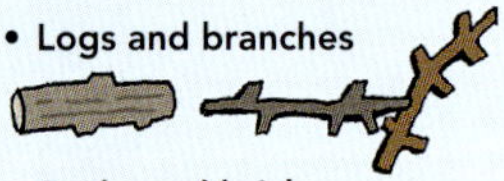
- Rocks and bricks 
- 2–3 drainpipe offcuts or cement pipes

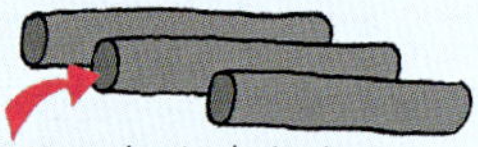

If using plastic drainpipes roughen the insides with sandpaper so that they are not too slippy for animals to climb

- Turf or meadow flower seeds (optional)

1. In a sunny spot dig a hole about 50cm deep and 1.5m across.

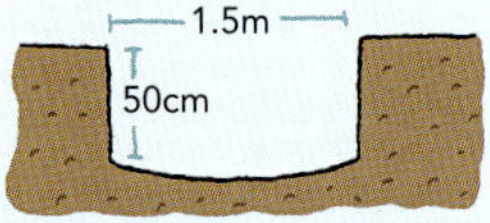

2. Fill with logs, branches, bricks and rocks, leaving plenty of gaps in between.

3. Insert entrance tubes (drainpipes) at ground level into the pile.

4. Cover the pile with soil (to about 50cm high).

5. You can plant meadow seeds or turf over the mound.

Amphibian and reptile declines

▲ A garden pond with a good shallow area for breeding amphibians and aquatic invertebrates, surrounded by stones and foliage that provide plenty of hiding places for froglets when they leave the pond in summer.

While many species remain common, amphibians and reptiles are suffering general declines across the British Isles, owing to a loss of breeding habitat, such as traditional dew ponds or drinking pools in farmland, and the loss of garden ponds in suburban and urban areas. Locally, species such as toads may be affected (or even die out) due to having to cross a busy road or due to their breeding ponds being compromised in some way because of pollution residue or local infection. Diseases play a part in declines too, particularly for amphibians (see next page).

Amphibians and reptiles are wonderful garden residents. Taking the time to dig a pond – or even fill a container with water and load it with aquatic plants – creates one of the best garden habitats you can provide for amphibians, and one of the most rewarding too. Reptiles tend to be trickier to attract, unless they are present in neighbouring plots, but it's easy and fun to see how simple measures can make huge differences.

What do amphibians and reptiles eat?

Frogs eat a wide range of crawling and flying invertebrates, including slugs and worms.

Toads eat a wide range of ground living and flying invertebrates, including spiders and worms. Larger toads may occasionally also eat small slow-worms, grass snakes and even harvest mice, which are swallowed alive.

Newts eat flies, mites, slugs, small snails, spiders, worms and other invertebrates. In ponds they eat small fish, frog tadpoles and invertebrates such as leeches, nymphs, shrimps and water fleas.

Lizards eat earthworms, insects, slugs, snails and spiders.

Grass snakes eat amphibians, fish, small mammals and young birds.

▲ Watching a frog eat a worm is one of life's great pleasures.

Amphibian diseases

As well as habitat loss, amphibians are also susceptible to diseases and other problems, some of the most notable of which are listed below.

Ranavirus

Whilst there are several types of ranaviruses worldwide, the majority of reports in British amphibians are caused by frog virus 3-like strains, thought to have been introduced from North America in the 1980s. Ranavirus most commonly affects adult common frogs and common toads but can affect tadpoles as well as other amphibians.

Signs of disease: Affected adults may be lethargic, have skin reddening or ulceration, loss of toes or entire feet, or show signs of internal bleeding. Sometimes, large numbers of amphibians may be found dead with, or without, obvious signs of disease.

Chytridiomycosis

There are two types of chytrid fungi known to cause skin disease in amphibians. The first, known as 'Bd', was discovered in the 1990s and has caused mass die-offs and species extinctions of amphibians across multiple continents. The second, known as salamander chytrid or 'Bsal', was more recently identified and has caused collapse of some fire salamander populations in the Netherlands. Bd is present in wild amphibians with a patchy distribution in Great Britain. All species of amphibian are susceptible, but in Great Britain, toads appear to be more susceptible. Whilst Bsal is present in captive newts and salamanders in Great Britain, it is not yet believed to be present in the wild.

Signs of disease: These vary. Affected adults may have skin ulceration or reddening, excessive shedding of skin, abnormal posture, or display unusual behaviours such as 'seizures' or nocturnal species being active during the day. In most cases, there are no visible signs of disease and apparently healthy animals can be found dead.

Amphibian spawn failure

Spawn failure (when spawn doesn't develop properly or fails to hatch) isn't known to be caused by an infectious disease. It may happen because the spawn hasn't been fertilised by a male, which could be for a number of reasons – sometimes due to a poor male–female ratio at the spawning site. Temperature, frost, light and water quality can also affect spawn development. What's more, spawn is highly likely to be predated by anything from fish and newts to ducks. Fungal infections don't cause spawn failure, but fungus may colonise dead spawn, giving it a cloudy or white appearance.

If you observe sick or dead amphibians in your garden, please report them to the Garden Wildlife Health project (see page 189). Tips to help prevent and control disease in wild amphibians are available on the Garden Wildlife Health website.

Snakes in the garden

Of the three snakes native to mainland Britain, just one – the adder – is venomous. Only the grass snake is likely to come into gardens. It's absolutely gorgeous and completely harmless. However, if you live near adder habitat and you're lucky enough to get them coming into your garden, then don't panic. Adders tend to shy away from humans so you're unlikely to get them visiting in great numbers. The Amphibian and Reptile Groups of UK includes helpful advice and information on its website.

▸ It's a lucky wildlife gardener who can attract grass snakes (*Natrix helvetica*) to their garden.

ID parade
Amphibians

Common frog
Rana temporaria

Description: Olive-green or brown (sometimes with pink or orange colouration), with black markings on the back and nearly always with a black patch behind the eyes. It has smooth, moist skin and long, striped legs. It jumps rather than crawls. Males grow up to 9cm long, females up to 13cm. In spring, its repetitive croaking, sounding a bit like the distant sound of a woodpecker pecking, can be heard from garden ponds.
When to see it: February to November.
Diet: A variety of invertebrates, including insects (particularly flies), small snails, slugs and worms.
Life cycle: Adults return to ponds in spring to breed (some spend the winter beneath the water, breathing through the skin). The female lays clumps of spawn at the pond edge and the male fertilises them as they are being laid (in a position known as amplexus). The spawn hatches into brown tadpoles, which feed on algae before developing a taste for meat. They develop legs after a few weeks and eventually absorb their tails, before they emerge from the pond as tiny froglets in midsummer. After spawning, adults leave the pond and spend time in patches of long grass, log piles or near a particularly good source of food. The females develop spawn in summer and carry it around with them through winter.
Garden habitats: Ponds with shallow edges, damp areas, log piles, greenhouses, areas of long grass, compost bins or heaps, or growing bags.
Distribution: Widespread but suffering general decline.

Common toad *Bufo bufo*

Description: Slightly broader than frogs, growing up to 13cm long (males 9cm), common toads can be brown, green, grey or even orange, and they have golden eyes with a horizontal pupil. The main feature that sets them apart from frogs is their dry, warty skin, which can secrete toxins, making them distasteful to predators. They also have shorter legs, which they use to crawl rather than jump. In spring, their mating call is a high-pitched '*pip-pip*'.
When to see it: March to November.
Diet: A variety of invertebrates, including flies, worms, slugs and snails; larger toads have been known to feed on small vertebrates such as slow-worms and mice.
Life cycle: Toads are more likely to use ancestral breeding grounds than frogs, so may be less likely to use a new pond. However, there are always a few that try out a new habitat. Similar to frogs, breeding takes place in ponds in spring, but spawn is laid in ribbons rather than clumps. Tadpoles are black and slightly poisonous. Like frog tadpoles, they feed on algae and inscets (sometimes each other). Their tails are absorbed after their legs have grown and the toadlets emerge from the pond by midsummer. After breeding the adults leave the pond and can be found in a range of locations – their dry skin means they can spend time in drier habitats than frogs.
Garden habitats: Deep ponds, compost heaps, log piles, areas of long grass and within drystone walls.
Distribution: Widespread but suffering general decline. Absent from Ireland.

Smooth newt *Lissotriton vulgaris*

Description: Our most widespread newt and the one you're most likely to spot in your garden or allotment. Thin and up to 10cm long, it is greenish-brown with a yellow or orange belly, marked with dark blotches, and its smooth skin becomes rough when on land. During the breeding season the male develops an impressive wavy crest along its back and tail.
When to see it: March to November.
Diet: Aquatic invertebrates such as water shrimps and water lice, tadpoles, water boatmen, as well as land invertebrates such as slugs and worms.
Life cycle: After spending the winter beneath logs and leaves,

smooth newts return to ponds for breeding. The males leave a spermatophore (package of sperm) at the bottom of the pond and 'waft' pheromones at the female to encourage her to pick it up. The female uses it to fertilise her eggs, which she lays individually in the leaves of marginal plants, such as water forget-me-not, folding each leaf over the egg. The eggs hatch into baby newts, or efts, which develop over spring and leave the pond by midsummer.
Garden habitats: Deep ponds, low-level vegetation, logs and log piles, leaf piles and stones.
Distribution: Widespread but suffering general decline.

Reptiles

Common lizard *Zootoca vivipara*

Description: The only terrestrial reptile native to Ireland, the common lizard is around 15cm long and varies in colour but is usually brownish with darker markings down the back and sides. It can lose its tail when threatened.
When to see it: May to October.
Diet: Invertebrates such as small insects, spiders and snails.
Life cycle: Mating takes place in spring. The females incubate their eggs internally and give birth to live young in summer.
Garden habitats: Warm walls, rockeries, brick or stones piles, wood or log piles, where they can bask to warm up. Long grass where they can hunt for spiders and insects.
Distribution: Widespread but suffering general decline. Absent from most Scottish islands and the Isles of Scilly.

Grass snake *Natrix helvetica*
Description: The only snake likely to come into gardens, the grass snake is completely harmless and non-venomous. Despite its name, it is often found in or near ponds, where it feeds on amphibians such as frogs. It's typically grey-green with a distinctive yellow and black collar, black bars down the side of the body and a forked tongue. The UK's longest snake, it can reach over a metre long.
When to see it: May to October.
Diet: Mainly amphibians and fish, and occasionally small birds.

Life cycle: Mating takes place in spring and, unlike other British native snakes, the females lay eggs – usually in warm spots such as large grass heaps or compost heaps. The eggs hatch in late summer.
Garden habitats: Ponds, compost heaps, grass heaps.
Distribution: Widespread and common in England and Wales, especially in the south, but largely absent from Scotland. Absent from Ireland.

Slow-worm *Anguis fragilis*
Description: Neither slow nor a worm, this legless lizard grows to 40cm long and has smooth, shiny skin. It is typically greyish brown or golden brown, with females and juveniles having dark sides and the female often having a black stripe down her back. Like all lizards, slow-worms can shed their tail when threatened. Unlike snakes, they have eyelids.
When to see it: May to October.
Diet: A variety of invertebrates including woodlice, slugs and snails.
Life cycle: Mating takes place in spring and the females incubate their eggs internally, giving birth to live young in late summer, in warm spots such as a compost heap. They may use compost heaps for overwintering or bury themselves in the ground.
Garden habitats: Long grass, greenhouses, compost bins, paving slabs and refugia.
Distribution: Widespread and common but suffering general decline; often predated by cats. Absent from Ireland.

Wildlife gardening for mammals

Almost all gardens will attract some mammals. However, this doesn't necessarily mean you will see them – most British mammals are nocturnal or crepuscular (active at dawn and dusk) and some are so small it's easy to miss them. The easiest way to discover if mammals are using your garden is to set up a camera trap or learn to identify their tracks – be they footprints, droppings, food caches or fur caught on the splinter of a fence.

As a wildlife group, mammals often get bad press. Many are considered a nuisance and most are unwelcome in gardens, while some are routinely persecuted by gardeners and hunters alike. I've always lived in urban areas, and the mammals that have come into my gardens have reflected the location – I've never had rabbits, badgers, deer or moles visiting, and I wonder how I'd react if I had a garden where they did (I hope I'd be tolerant and understanding). I do have foxes, hedgehogs, mice, voles and squirrels. I adore the mice and voles and tolerate them eating my pea and broad bean seeds (I always manage to grow plenty, regardless). And it didn't take too much effort to repair the pond liner after the foxes had chewed holes in it. If you're reading this and you think certain mammals are to be discouraged rather than encouraged, then I'm not going to attempt to change your mind. But perhaps I could persuade you to take a step back and relax a little to embrace a life working with rather than against these mammals. There's little you can actually do to stop them entering your garden, so being cross about the damage they cause is a waste of energy – why not spend it creating habitats for other wildlife instead?

Aside from cats, which don't count as wildlife but are usually present in our gardens, the mammals

▲ If you open your garden to them, you could see hedgehogs visiting.

we're most likely to see are mice, grey squirrels, hedgehogs, foxes and bats.

Shrews and voles are also likely, while badgers and deer may make an appearance if there's suitable habitat nearby. Rabbits and hares might occasionally turn up too. Only a lucky few will have stoats, weasels and moles (although you may not feel so lucky to have the last one). Rats could also enter your garden and, despite my plea for tolerance and understanding, shouldn't be encouraged (see page 169 for more on them).

Typically, mammals are less mobile than birds and are therefore less likely to be found in urban habitats. So the more rural your location, the more mammals you will attract. In this chapter I look at the mammals that may come into our gardens, how to make our gardens more attractive to them and what steps we can take to discourage less welcome visitors, or at least alleviate the damage they may cause. I also explain the impact cats have on garden wildlife.

▲ The brown long-eared bat (*Plecotus auritus*) is a regular garden visitor.

▼ Foxes (*Vulpes vulpes*) are common, especially in urban gardens.

▶ The wood mouse (*Apodemus sylvaticus*) is one of many small mammals likely to visit your garden.

▶▶ Beautiful but controversial, fallow deer (*Dama dama*) and their relatives will only enter rural gardens.

Small mammals

Small mammals range from Britain's smallest, the pygmy shrew, which we're unlikely to find in our gardens, to squirrels and rats, which often don't seem that small at all. Many are adaptable and are readily found in gardens. These include tiny species such as mice, voles, shrews and bats, and slightly bigger ones such as moles, hedgehogs and squirrels. Other small mammals, for example weasels and stoats, are less common but do turn up in rural gardens.

Gardening for these species involves creating habitats where they can feed and breed successfully. Let areas of grass grow long where mice, voles, shrews and hedgehogs can shelter. Dig a pond, and grow wildflowers to attract insects and caterpillars, which many small mammals eat. Avoid being so tidy and consider providing them with supplementary food – hedgehogs and red squirrels in particular will benefit from this. Some small mammals, such as rabbits and moles, are less welcome in gardens, so gardening for them might just include tolerating them rather than actively providing habitats for them.

Mice and voles

Mice and voles probably visit your garden without you knowing about it. Indeed, the first evidence of such are that your peas and broad beans have mysteriously not germinated, or you find a cache of plum stones with telltale wood mouse holes cut into them, or you lift your slow-worm refugium to find a little nest of squeaking pink blobs with their mother fretting over them until you return them to darkness (all of these things have happened to me).

The wood or field mouse is common in gardens and allotments – virtually anywhere it can carve out a living. Bank voles too. The common shrew, which is more closely related to moles and hedgehogs than mice, could turn up as well, although you'd be hard pressed to find it.

Of course, if you have a cat you may be very familiar with the types of small mammal that visit your garden (see page 178 for more on cats).

Gardening for mice, voles and shrews

Mostly this involves tolerating them, and recognising and respecting their role in the ecosystem; letting them get on with it and not worrying too much about your peas and broad beans. To help encourage their presence, see the table overleaf for suggestions.

Signs of mice and voles in gardens

- Teeth marks on stems, bulbs or corms, and fruit.
- Holes in the soil where mice or voles have dug down to eat bulbs, corms or seeds (peas or broad beans).
- Seedlings scattered on the soil surface.
- Voles sometimes eat the bark of woody plants, which can kill the plant. They may make a network of shallow tunnels in the soil, giving lawns an uneven appearance.
- Caches of seeds or nuts beneath amphibian refugia (see page 142) or in the corner of a shed.
- Seed packets with tell-tale chew marks.

Mice and voles can cause a bit of damage in the garden, but I wouldn't dream of harming them, and nothing they've done has warranted action other than going to the shop and buying another packet of peas. Mice and voles are a hugely important food source for a wide range of predators, particularly owls (and who doesn't love owls?). And did you know bumblebees like to nest in their burrows?

Quick ID tips

Mouse: Large eyes and ears, long tail, pointed snout

Vole: Small eyes and ears, short tail, rounded snout

Shrew: Small eyes and ears, short tail, pointed snout

▲ A bank vole peeping out from under a stone.

Ideas for attracting mice, voles and shrews

	Suitable for...				
	Small garden	Medium garden	Large garden	Allotment	Balcony/patio
Allow areas of grass to grow long.	✓	Consider a wildflower meadow	Consider a wildflower meadow	Consider a wildflower meadow	✗
Keep cats indoors at night.	✓	✓	✓	✓	✓
Plant known caterpillar food plants (see the Butterfly Conservation plant lists in Resources).	Room for a tree?	Trees and shrubs	Trees, shrubs, native hedge	Trees, shrubs, native hedge	Container pot of dandelions
Compost your waste.	Small bin	Large, open heap	Large, open heap	Large, open heap	Small bin or wormery
Make a log pile.	✓	✓	✓	✓	✗
Avoid using pesticides, including slug pellets.	✓	✓	✓	✓	✓
Dismantle and rebuild bonfires immediately before lighting them.	✓	✓	✓	✓	✗

ID parade

Bank vole *Myodes glareolus*
Description: The smallest vole in the British Isles at 8–12cm, it has a red-brown coat and a cream belly, a blunt snout, small eyes and ears, and a short tail. It may be confused with the field vole, which has more of a grey coat and is far less likely to come into gardens.
When to see it: March to November.
Nests: Underground, beneath sheds, in compost heaps.
Diet: Grass, roots, fruit, seeds and invertebrates.
Life cycle: Mating takes place throughout spring and summer, and females bear successive litters of three to five blind, hairless young. These become independent within nine weeks of birth.
Garden habitats: Mature gardens and allotments.
Distribution: Widespread throughout Britain but absent from Shetland, the Isle of Man, Isles of Scilly, Lundy and Ireland. Skomer island, off Pembrokeshire, has a subspecies that is twice the size of the mainland bank vole.

Common shrew *Sorex araneus*
Description: A small insectivore (5–8cm) with a velvety brown coat and whitish belly. It has a long, pointed nose, tiny eyes, small ears and red teeth. Its tail is half the length of its body.
When to see it: March to November.
Nests: Common shrews nest in burrows, often made by another animal.

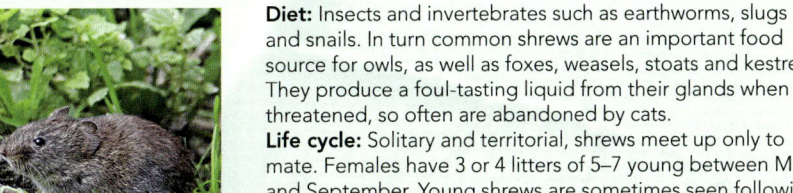

Diet: Insects and invertebrates such as earthworms, slugs and snails. In turn common shrews are an important food source for owls, as well as foxes, weasels, stoats and kestrels. They produce a foul-tasting liquid from their glands when threatened, so often are abandoned by cats.
Life cycle: Solitary and territorial, shrews meet up only to mate. Females have 3 or 4 litters of 5–7 young between May and September. Young shrews are sometimes seen following their mother in a 'caravan' – each baby grasps the base of the tail of the one in front. Shrews don't hibernate but become less active in winter – they can reduce their size so they require less food. They have a very short lifespan of up to 12 months.
Garden habitats: Mature gardens and allotments.
Distribution: Common and widespread but absent from Ireland, the Outer Hebrides and Shetland.

Wood mouse
Apodemus sylvaticus
Description: Our most common rodent, the wood or long-tailed field mouse is small (9–10cm) with light brown fur and a white/grey belly, large black eyes, large ears and long tail (up to 95mm). It is mostly nocturnal but may come out during the day.
When to see it: All year round.
Nests: Wood mice live in underground burrows made of leaves, moss and grass, often among the roots of plants. Communal living quarters are likely in winter. In spring, the females establish a 'home range' (similar to a territory) and nest independently.
Diet: A huge variety, including seeds, shoots, fruits, buds, invertebrates and fungi. Food is cached underground or in out-of-the-way places such as in the corner of your shed. In turn, wood mice are eaten by foxes, weasels, owls (particularly the tawny owl) and cats.
Life cycle: After mating, the female gives birth to between four and seven blind, hairless young. These are weaned within a couple of weeks and the female will breed again if conditions are right. She may continue breeding through winter if there is sufficient food. Their life expectancy is typically no longer than a year.
Garden habitats: Mature gardens and allotments.
Distribution: Widespread and common across the British Isles.

Bats

▲ Try to use less outdoor lighting in summer to encourage bats like the common pipistrelle (*Pipistrellus pipistrellus*), to visit your garden.

Bats are incredible. The world's only flying mammal, there are 17 species that breed in the British Isles, of which a surprising number may turn up in gardens. Sadly, bat populations have suffered severe declines during the last 100 years due to a combination of factors, including the loss of roosting sites and natural habitats such as hedgerows, woodland and ponds, and urbanisation. However, legal protection has enabled numbers of some species to recover slightly.

While bats may only fly above your garden rather than coming into it, there's plenty you can do to help them. Insect eaters, bats may use larger gardens for food, water or shelter, but they will benefit just as much from insect-friendly planting in small gardens, balconies and patios. Cram as many flowers and leaves into the space you have and you're essentially 'farming' insects for those species further up the food chain.

If you're lucky, bats may choose to roost in or around your home, typically beneath roof tiles or under the eaves, or among mature trees in your garden. The perfect house guests, they don't build nests or cause damage to your home, and their droppings are dry and odour-free.

Bats need a variety of habitats to enable them to feed and breed, including flowering plants, shrubs and trees, which provide a source of food as well as somewhere to roost; water to drink and feed from; and permanent structures such as cavities in house roofs, where they can set up maternity or winter roost sites.

Depending on the size of space you have, gardening for bats could range from growing a pot of ox-eye daisies on your doorstep, which will help insect populations, to digging a huge pond and hoping Daubenton's bats will use it to pick insects off the surface with their large, hairy feet. Growing as many flowering plants as we have space for is the most obvious way we can use our gardens to help bats. But it's also worth trying to lure them in by growing night-scented plants and pale flowers, which will bring moths (and hopefully their predators) right to the door.

If you have space, consider making a shelter belt. This is a sheltered spot, such as behind a hedge or the back of shrubs, where insects congregate in

▲ A wildlife pond will increase numbers of insects, which bats eat.

Bat-friendly flowers

- A variety of flower colours and shapes
- Plants with pale blooms that are more easily seen in poor light
- Single flowers, which insects can access more easily
- Night-scented flowers:
  - Dog rose (*Rosa canina*)
  - Bladder campion (*Silene vulgaris*)
  - Evening primrose (*Oenothera biennis*)
  - Honeysuckle (*Lonicera periclymenum*)
  - Ivy (*Hedera helix*)
  - Night-scented stock (*Matthiola longipetala* subsp. *bicornis*)
  - Sweet rocket (*Hesperis matronalis*)
  - Tobacco plants (*Nicotiana*)
  - White jasmine (*Jasminum officinale*)

swarms – typical of the woodland edge. By recreating this habitat in your garden, you're creating the perfect feeding site for bats.

Remember that most bats feed in the tree canopy, where there are far more insects than close to the ground. Trees also hide bats from predators such as birds of prey. If you have space for trees, they are much more likely to bring bats to your garden than any other habitat. You'll find further suggestions in the table overleaf.

Ideas for attracting bats

	Suitable for...				
	Small garden	Medium garden	Large garden	Allotment	Balcony/patio
Grow insect-friendly flowers (see box on page 153).	✓	✓	✓	✓	✓
Add water.	Dig a pond or make a container pond and birdbath.	Dig a pond and make a birdbath.	Dig a pond and make a birdbath.	Dig a pond and make a birdbath.	Make a container pond or birdbath.
Allow areas of grass to grow long to provide habitat for insect larvae.	✓	Consider a wildflower meadow.	Consider a wildflower meadow.	Consider a wildflower meadow.	✗
Put up a bat box (see pages 155-56).	✓	✓	✓	✓	✓
Join your local bat group.	✓	✓	✓	✓	✓
Create linear features, e.g. hedgerows/treelines.	✗	✓	✓	✓	✗
Plant a shelter belt.	✓	✓	✓	✓	✗
Reduce or remove artificial lighting, as this can disorientate bats.	✓	✓	✓	✓	✓
Keep cats indoors at night.	✓	✓	✓	✓	✓
Grow known caterpillar food plants (see the Butterfly Conservation lists in Resources).	Room for a tree?	Shrubs and trees	Shrubs, trees, native hedge	Shrubs, trees, native hedge	Container pot of dandelions
Compost your waste to attract bat prey.	Small bin	Large, open heap	Large, open heap	Large, open heap	Small bin or wormery
Make a log pile.	✓	✓	✓	✓	✗
Don't use pesticides.	✓	✓	✓	✓	✓
Use peat-free compost.	✓	✓	✓	✓	✓

Be careful...

- **If you have a cat.**
  Cats will readily take bats and can dramatically affect numbers, especially as they can sometimes wait at the entrance of roosting sites and pick off several each evening. If you own a cat, you can make a huge difference to bat populations by simply keeping your cat in at night or at least around dusk and dawn. It will allow bats to emerge from and return to their roosts undisturbed. This is especially important in summer, when bats are rearing their young. If you find a bat that appears to have been injured by a cat, call the Bat Conservation Trust (BCT) National Bat Helpline (see page 188) for advice and your nearest bat carer.

- **If you have outdoor lighting.**
  Since bats are nocturnal animals that have evolved to fly at night, most species don't respond well to artificial lighting (the exception being pipistrelle bats, which may be seen hunting insects attracted to lights). These include street lights, shop signs and outdoor lighting in gardens. If you have artificial lights in your garden, use them sparingly and consider not using them at all in summer.

Roosting

By day, bats shelter in locations such as hollow trees, loose bark on trees, roof spaces or beneath tiles on house roofs. They don't return to the same roost throughout the year but choose different roosts depending on their needs. The ideal hibernation roost remains cool and dry throughout winter, so a north-facing roof space is ideal. The summer maternity roost – where female bats congregate together to give birth and feed their young – needs to be warm, so they might choose a south- or west-facing space. Bats may also choose a variety of daytime roosts during the season.

Bats and the law

All bats in Britain are legally protected, and the shelter they use to roost or hibernate is protected too. This means it's illegal to interfere with their roost, and you must attain special permission to conduct works on buildings where bats are known to roost. For further information about this, visit the Bat Conservation Trust website (see page 188).

How to make your own bat box

What you need:
- Rough-cut, untreated timber. 25 mm
- Tape measure and pencil
- Saw
- Hammer and nails
- Rubber flap
- Odourless wood glue (optional)

Label panels: side 140 mm | side 200 mm | base 90 mm | roof 200 mm | front 150 mm | back 360 mm (height 150 mm)

angled cut at 22° / angled cut at 22°

Roughen back plate with 1mm deep cuts every 10mm.

22° cut

Seal gaps at edges with wood glue.

80 mm

IMPORTANT Do not use wood stain or preservative anywhere on the box

← Rubber hinge flap

10mm wide entrance slit between base and back plate

5m

Look for droppings below to check for occupancy

IT IS ILLEGAL TO DISTURB BATS WITHOUT A LICENCE – DO NOT INSPECT BOXES IF YOU THINK BATS ARE USING THEM

Bat boxes

Bat boxes are artificial roosts designed to replicate natural roosting sites, such as holes in trees. You can buy them or easily make your own. It's not clear how effective they are – research suggests woodcrete boxes are more likely to be used than wooden boxes, and those that have been up for a few years are more popular than recently erected ones. However, there's no harm in putting a box up, as long as you don't do it at the expense of creating other bat-friendly habitats.

A bat box checklist:

- Remember that bats don't like draughts, so ensure your box is well insulated and maintains a constant temperature.
- Use untreated, rough-textured wood so they have something to cling to.
- It's illegal to open or inspect a bat box without a licence.
- Bat boxes are more likely to be used if they are placed where bats are known to feed.
- Ideally, place several boxes facing in different directions to provide a range of conditions.
- Bat boxes should be positioned as high as possible in sheltered, sunny places. On buildings, boxes should be placed as close to the eaves as possible.
- A study of more than 3,000 boxes by the Vincent Wildlife Trust (see page 189) found that south-facing boxes were better than north-facing, and woodcrete was a better material to use than wood.

▲ A common noctule bat (*Nyctalus noctula*) clings to a woodcrete box.

What do bats eat?

Bats' diets vary, depending on the species. All British bats feed on insects, particularly those that are active at dusk and during the night. As well as moths, they feast on mosquitoes, midges and other flies, mayflies, some beetles, caddis flies, lacewings and other nocturnal insects. One pipistrelle bat (of which there are three closely related species) can eat around 3,000 tiny insects in a single night. Some European species eat fruit. Bats mostly catch insects on the wing, using echolocation (extremely high-frequency calls) to home in on their prey. Some bats will pick off insects that are resting on foliage.

City bats

Don't assume that bats are strictly rural animals. While more species are common in the countryside, you may be surprised how many bat species you can find in cities. Allotments, large gardens, canals, parks and disused buildings are the most likely urban locations for bats. If you have an allotment or large garden, then it's worth investing in a bat detector and keeping an eye on the sky at dusk in summer months. If not, you might want to join your local bat group to discover bats in your area (see Resources), and focus instead on ways you can help those populations by growing plants for the food they eat.

Both common and soprano pipistrelles roost in buildings in urban areas. You may spot them catching insects attracted to street lighting or even hunting over a garden pond. Larger species such as Leisler's and serotine bats sometimes breed in houses in urban areas, but typically travel to feed in more rural locations. However, both species can be seen hunting around white street lights, and Leisler's bats sometimes forage along urban canals.

Natterer's bats may roost in large old houses but forage in wooded parks and along canals and rivers. Daubenton's bats are closely associated with still or slow-moving water, such as rivers and canals, even in built-up areas.

The species most likely to use bat boxes is the brown long-eared bat. These bats have a slow, fluttering flight and they hover to pick insects off the leaves of garden trees. Occasionally you might see them outside windows, preying on insects attracted to light, and they may hang up in the porches of houses to eat, leaving a pile of discarded wings and faeces.

Bat-watching

Bats' echolocation calls are inaudible to most humans. The best way to experience bats is by using a bat detector, which enables us to listen to them. Once you've got your ear in, it's possible to learn the different calls of different bat species.

ID parade

Brown long-eared bat
Plecotus auritus
Description: The second most common bat in Britain, the brown long-eared bat has extremely long ears, which it tucks beneath its wings or curls back like ram's horns when at rest. Medium-sized (4–5cm long), it has long, grey-brown fur with a paler underside and broad wings.

As well as catching insects in flight, they pick them off leaves and bark – they are some of the most agile bats and can almost hover. Sometimes they land on the ground to catch insects, and can also take them from lighted windows. They fly very close to trees, making them difficult to spot.
When to see it: March to November.
Diet: Moths, beetles, flies, caddis flies, earwigs and spiders. Small prey is eaten on the wing but larger insects are taken to a 'perch', such as a porch, where you might find piles of discarded insect remains such as moth wings.
Life cycle: Mating takes place in autumn and maternity colonies are established in late spring, with young born in summer. These are breastfed by their mother until they are fully weaned at six weeks.
Echolocation: Known as 'whispering bats' because their calls are very quiet, they can be heard at 25–50kHz, most noticeably at 35kHz.
Garden habitats: Mature gardens with plenty of tree cover.
Distribution: Found throughout Britain, Ireland and the Isle of Man. Absent from Orkney and Shetland, and other exposed islands.

Common and soprano pipistrelles
Pipistrellus pipistrellus and *P. pygmaeus*
Description: Two closely related species, these are the most common British bats and those you're most likely to see, especially in urban areas. Only identified as separate species in the 1990s, the easiest way to tell them apart is by using a bat detector to determine the frequency of their echolocation calls. Pipistrelles are small (3.5-4.5cm long) and typically have dark brown fur with a paler underside and

blackish-brown ears and muzzle. They fly quickly and erratically (known as aerial hawking) as they pursue and catch insects, which they eat on the wing.
When to see them: March to November.
Diet: Small insects, including flies, aquatic midges and mosquitoes.
Life cycle: Mating takes place between July and November, but typically in autumn, with the young born the following summer. In summer, females form maternity colonies where they give birth to a single young in June or early July. For three or four weeks the young are fed solely on their mother's milk. After about four weeks the young are able to fly and at six weeks they are able to forage for themselves.
Echolocation: On a bat detector the common pip's calls range from 45 to 70kHz and the soprano pip's from 55 to 80kHz. The calls sound like a series of clicks and slaps.
Garden habitats: Mature gardens with plenty of tree cover.
Distribution: Widespread across the British Isles, apart from Shetland and parts of Orkney, although the distribution of the common pipistrelle appears to extend further north than that of the soprano pipistrelle. Populations have declined in the last few decades, but have recovered slightly in recent years.

Daubenton's bat
Myotis daubentonii
Description: Once known as water bats, Daubenton's are often seen flying low over large bodies of water, picking insects off the surface with their large, hairy feet or scooping them up with their tail.

They are medium-sized (5–6cm long) with red-brown fur, a pale underside and a pink, hairless patch around their eyes.
When to see it: March to November.
Diet: Small flies/midges, caddis flies, mayflies and pond skaters.
Life cycle: Mating takes place in autumn and maternity roosts are set up in late spring through to late summer. The females breastfeed their young until they are able to forage for themselves at six to eight weeks.
Echolocation: On a bat detector their calls range from range from 35 to 85kHz (loudest at 45–50kHz). The sounds are a series of regular clicks, similar to a machine gun.
Garden habitats: Large, mature gardens with a large pond.
Distribution: Widespread and common, apart from in the far north of Scotland. Populations may be increasing.

Squirrels

Most UK gardens are home to grey squirrels. Like some other mammals, opinion is divided as to whether they're welcome in our gardens. Known for their acrobatic antics at the bird table and feeders, they have a tendency to eat all the food we leave out for birds. Some of us leave separate food for squirrels instead, while others invest in so-called 'squirrel-proof' feeders to discourage them. Whatever your views, the grey squirrel is here to stay.

Red squirrels are far less common in gardens, and are mainly restricted to corners of coniferous woodland, where they're much more suited to the habitat than greys. They can be seen in Scotland, Anglesey, Formby near Liverpool, the Isle of Wight and parts of Northumberland and Northern Ireland. Numbers have steadily been declining for years. However, efforts to protect the species by controlling greys that stray into their areas have helped stabilise red populations in some regions. What's more, in recent years the increase in pine marten numbers has been shown to make a difference to squirrel populations. The pine marten is a predator of the native red, and because the grey has not evolved with this predator, it's thought that it's not as well equipped to escape the pine marten's attention, so the red suddenly has an advantage over the grey.

ID parade

Red squirrel *Sciurus vulgaris*
Grey squirrel *Sciurus carolinensis*

Description: Tree-dwelling mammals with a big bushy tail; the red is 18–24cm long, reddish brown with a white belly and furry ears, while the grey is bigger (24–28cm) and usually silver-grey. Both have similar habits. The red squirrel is native and the grey was introduced in the 19th century. Sadly, the grey has pushed the red to near extinction, by outcompeting it for food and spreading squirrel pox, which is deadly to reds.
When to see them: All year round.
Nests: Squirrels build their nest, or drey, by weaving a platform of twigs and leaves high up in a tree.
Diet: Tree seeds and nuts, berries, fungi, bark and tree sap tissue. In gardens grey squirrels may eat plant bulbs, flower buds, peanuts and birdseed. In the autumn they cache food below ground or in gaps in tree trunks.
Life cycle: Breeding starts in late winter and the females have up to two litters of around four kittens per year.
Garden habitats: The grey is more adaptable than the red, coming into a variety of different gardens, especially in urban areas. The red is closely associated with conifer and broadleaved woodland, and typically visits gardens close to that habitat.
Distribution: The grey is widespread and common across the British Isles. Away from its northern Scottish strongholds, the red is confined to a few sparse populations in specially managed areas.

Hedgehogs

Hedgehogs have suffered dramatic declines across Britain since the 1950s, although the 2022 State of British Hedgehogs Report suggests urban populations are showing signs of recovery. This could be due to people opening up their gardens and providing habitats that enable hogs to breed and feed – proof that wildlife gardening works!

As nocturnal, carnivorous mammals, hedgehogs need an undisturbed habitat, such as a compost heap, pile of leaves or logs to hibernate and breed in, nutritious food to eat and space to wander. They need to be able to travel between gardens, ideally without having to walk onto the road, and they need to be kept safe from danger within gardens. Meet these requirements and you'll give hedgehogs the best chance to live. See the table on the next page for further suggestions.

Ideas for attracting hedgehogs

	Suitable for...				
	Small garden	Medium garden	Large garden	Allotment	Balcony/patio
Cut or dig holes in fences to allow hedgehogs in and out.	✓	✓	✓	✓	✗
Leave supplementary food and water.	✓	✓	✓	✓	✗
Become a Hedgehog Champion (see overleaf)	✓	✓	✓	✓	✗
Take apart and rebuild bonfires immediately before lighting them, in case a hedgehog is sheltering within.	✓	✓	✓	✓	✗
Grow climbing plants to provide shelter and food for caterpillars and other hedgehog food.	✓	✓	✓	✓	✓
Plant known caterpillar food plants (see the Butterfly Conservation lists in Resources).	Room for a tree?	Shrubs and trees	Shrubs, trees, native hedge	Shrubs, trees, native hedge	Container pot of dandelions
Stop using slug pellets.	✓	✓	✓	✓	✓
Compost your waste.	Compost bin	Large, open heap	Large, open heap	Large, open heap	Compost bin or wormery
Make a leaf pile.	✓	✓	✓	✓	Allow leaves to build up in a corner or behind pots.
Make a log pile.	Small logs or twigs/prunings	Large, partially buried in the ground	Large, partially buried in the ground	Large, partially buried in the ground	✗
Mulch with compost, leaf mould or manure.	Small bin	Large, open heap	Large, open heap	Large, open heap	Small bin or wormery
Dig a pond.	Small	Medium	Large (make sure it has shallows)	Large	✗
Buy or make a hedgehog house (see page 163).	✓	✓	✓	✓	✗

Be careful...

- when strimming or mowing the lawn, as hedgehogs may rest here during the day.
- when netting plants, such as peas, as this can trap hedgehogs. Lift the netting 22–30cm off the ground to prevent any casualties – or better still don't use it.
- if your pond has steep sides. Hedgehogs like to drink from ponds and can swim, but quickly become exhausted and can drown. Add a plank or rope ladder to enable hedgehogs to climb out easily.
- when lighting a bonfire. If you build one, especially in autumn when hedgehogs are looking for space to hibernate, please dismantle and rebuild it immediately before lighting, as a hedgehog could be sheltering within.
- when fencing your garden. Make sure you're not cutting off hedgehog routes. Cut into or dig holes beneath the panels to create a 'hedgehog highway'.
- when dismantling your shed. Hedgehogs often nest or hibernate beneath sheds. Where possible, check beneath it before taking it down – or do so in April, when disturbance will be minimal.
- when cutting back large shrubs or ornamental grasses, such as pampas grass, as hedgehogs like to shelter beneath them.
- when you need to turn your compost heap or empty your compost bin. Observe it first, ideally by using a camera to see if a hog is using it.

 ## How to make a hedgehog highway

You will need:
- A fence panel
- Ruler
- Pencil
- Coping saw
- Sandpaper

1. If your neighbour is happy, remove your fence panel. 
2. Measure and mark a 13cm x 13cm hole at the bottom of the panel. 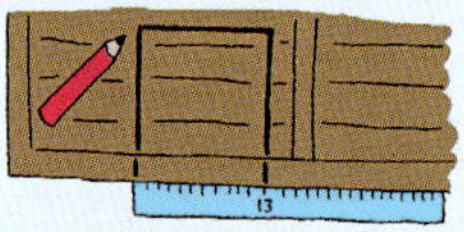
3. Cut the hole using the coping saw. 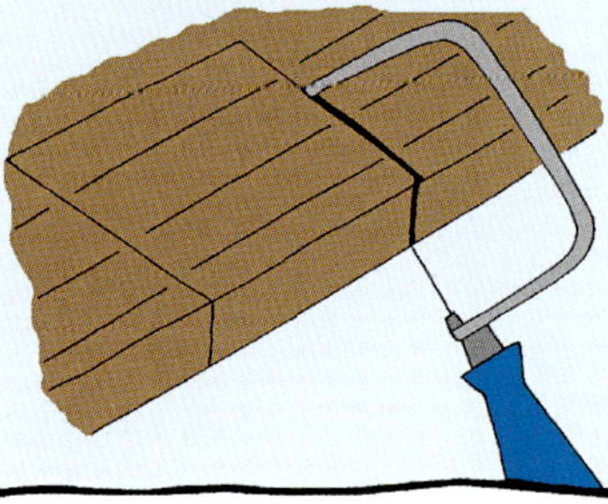
4. If there are any very rough edges, use the sandpaper to smooth them down. 
5. Put your fence panel back. Your hedgehog highway is now open for business!

Talk to your neighbour! It's important to get their consent to cut a hole in the fence – explain that hedgehogs need to move between gardens to access enough food.

You could set up your own trail cam to watch and see if any animals are using your highway.

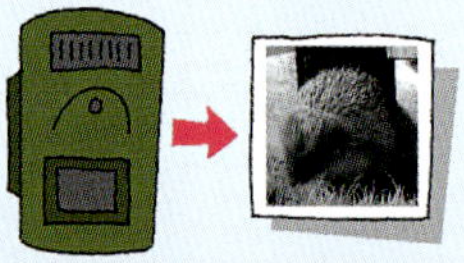

Hedgehog Street

The Hedgehog Street campaign is a fabulous initiative run by the British Hedgehog Preservation Society (BHPS) and the People's Trust for Endangered Species (PTES). It's designed to encourage neighbours to get together and help hedgehogs by enabling them to safely travel between gardens on a whole street of houses. To get involved and become a Hedgehog Champion in your neighbourhood, visit the Hedgehog Street website (see Resources, page 189).

Hedgehog boxes

A hedgehog box is designed to provide a safe, dry habitat in which hedgehogs can breed and hibernate. There are many designs available to buy or you could make your own (see below). The key things to ensure are that hedgehog boxes are weatherproof and sturdy. Place one in a corner of your garden, cover it with leaves and you might just attract a resident.

How to make a hedgehog house

You will need:
- 20mm FSC plywood boards cut to the sizes shown
- Hammer and nails
- 2 metal hinges
- Soil
- Dry leaves
- Straw
- Newspapers
- Polythene sheeting

Do not creosote or treat the wood

1. Construct the hedgehog house from the following diagram and dimensions.

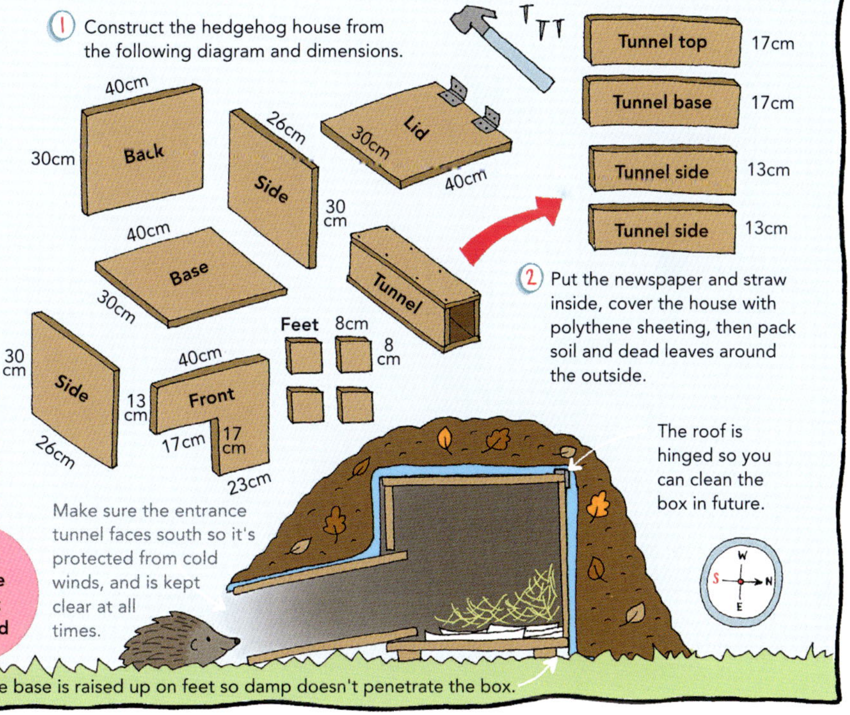

Back 40cm × 30cm
Side 26cm × 30cm
Lid 40cm × 30cm
Base 40cm × 30cm
Side 40cm × 26cm (30cm)
Front 40cm × 17cm, 13cm, 17cm, 23cm
Tunnel 30cm
Feet 8cm × 8cm

Tunnel top 17cm
Tunnel base 17cm
Tunnel side 13cm
Tunnel side 13cm

2. Put the newspaper and straw inside, cover the house with polythene sheeting, then pack soil and dead leaves around the outside.

Make sure the entrance tunnel faces south so it's protected from cold winds, and is kept clear at all times.

The roof is hinged so you can clean the box in future.

The base is raised up on feet so damp doesn't penetrate the box.

What do hedgehogs eat?

- Beetles
- Caterpillars
- Earthworms
- Ground-dwelling invertebrates such as centipedes and earwigs
- Slugs and snails (but far less than we gardeners would like to think)

You can also leave food out for them. Cat or dog food is best but particularly kitten biscuits which are designed for small mouths. Wet dog or cat food can be put out for hedgehogs but never leave it out during the day as flies may lay eggs in it. Bear in mind that wild animal food isn't regulated and therefore lots of food labelled 'hedgehog food' may contain ingredients that are harmful to hogs.

If you buy hedgehog food, always make sure the main ingredient listed is meat. Always leave food with a dish of clean water, as hedgehogs drink a lot.

Never give hedgehogs any of the following and check the list of ingredients in hedgehog food to make sure it doesn't contain them:

- bread and milk, which make them sick and dehydrates them
- mealworms, calciworms, sunflower seeds or peanuts, which have a poor phosphorous to calcium ratio and can lead to bone breakages in hogs
- raisins or other fruit – not only can hedgehogs not digest fruit, but it can get stuck in their teeth and prevent them from eating, leading to starvation

Hedgehog declines

The first State of Britain's Hedgehogs report, published in 2011, highlighted the findings of several surveys that pointed to a widespread loss of hedgehogs over the previous 10 years. In 2020, hedgehogs were put on the IUCN Red List as vulnerable to extinction in Great Britain. The last report, published in 2022, found stark differences across the country, with urban and suburban populations stable and showing signs of recovery, but rural populations still low and declining, with the biggest declines in the east of England.

Hedgehog declines are attributed to habitat loss and fragmentation caused by the loss of hedgerows and field margins in rural areas (leading to a lack of food and nesting/hibernation habitat), and the fragmentation and paving of gardens and other green spaces in towns and cities. However, the results appear to show that wildlife gardening works, and that the efforts of local communities in towns and cities to open up their gardens, create habitats and offer supplementary food, are enough to support urban and suburban hogs. This should spur us on to do even more for our hogs up and down the country, as there's proof that our efforts to help them work.

ID parade

Hedgehog *Erinaceus europaeus*
Description: A small, snuffling mammal up to 30cm long. Its upper body is covered with cream and brown spines (modified hairs), while the face, throat, chest, belly and legs are covered with dense, grey-brown fur. It has a long snout, small ears and small tail. When threatened, it rolls up into a protective ball.
When to see it: March to November.
Diet: Beetles, caterpillars, worms and other invertebrates.
Life cycle: Mostly solitary, hedgehogs come together to mate in late spring. The female makes a nest using grass, leaves, mosses and other garden debris, and gives birth to four or five young about six weeks later. She feeds the young milk for a month and then takes them on trips to look for other food. They are fully weaned at about two months. Sometimes hedgehogs have a second or even a third brood. Hibernation typically takes place between November and March, but hedgehogs may rise on warm days or if disturbed.
Garden habitats: Gardens with long grass, log and leaf piles and open compost heaps.
Distribution: Widespread. Rare in wet areas, mountain regions and pine forests. In decline.

Other small mammals

Only those with large, rural gardens or allotments will see these mammals in their gardens. While rabbits can eat vegetables and herbaceous plants, hares do very little damage. Stoats and weasels are important predators of mice, voles and some rabbits. Moles can be a nuisance but try to remember that they eat soil-borne pests, including carrot root fly. Also their molehills provide the perfect growing medium for those who make their own compost.

▸ If you live in a rural area, look out for stoats (*Mustela erminea*) in the garden.

Molehills

Moles are considered a pest by farmers and by some gardeners, due to their habit of tunnelling beneath the ground and creating molehills. While many mole tunnels are very deep underground, surface tunnelling is common and can disturb (and sometimes kill) plants. In farmland, molehills cause damage to machinery and can contaminate grass used to make silage.

However, moles play an important part in the aeration and drainage of the soil, as well as preying on insects that farmers and some gardeners regard as pests. In gardens, molehills offer the perfect sieved loam for making your own potting medium.

Trapping and killing moles is generally futile and extremely painful for the moles. Can you learn to live with them instead?

ID parade
Other small mammals

Brown hare *Lepus europaeus*

Description: Larger than the rabbit at 52–59cm long, the brown hare is sandy brown with long, black-tipped ears, a black-tipped tail and large, powerful hind legs. It was introduced from the Continent in the Iron Age and has recently been introduced to Northern Ireland, although populations have not spread far. Hares are solitary creatures but will sometimes come together in small groups to feed.
When to see it: All year round.
Nests: Unlike rabbits, hares don't live in burrows but make a small depression, called a form, in long grass.
Diet: Grass shoots, including cereal crops. In turn, the leverets are eaten by foxes.
Life cycle: Breeding takes place between February and September, and a female can rear three or four litters of two to four young a year. The young, called leverets, are born furred and with their eyes open, and are left by the female in their forms. For the first few weeks, the leverets join their mother at sunset to be fed by her, but otherwise receive no parental care. Adult hares normally live to three or four years but very rarely live much longer.
Garden habitats: Mature rural gardens.
Distribution: Common and widespread throughout Britain, largely absent from Ireland.

European mole *Talpa europaea*
Description: A small insectivore (11–16cm long) with a velvety blackish coat, spade-like forelimbs with large claws, a pink fleshy snout and tiny eyes.
When to see it: May and June.
Nests: Moles spend most of their lives underground in a system of tunnels. Solitary for most of the year, moles occupy exclusive territories.

Diet: Earthworms are the most important component of the mole's diet – an 80g mole needs 50g of earthworms per day. Moles also eat many insect larvae, particularly in the summer, though earthworms dominate the winter diet. Moles sometimes collect and store their food (earthworms) alive in special chambers. Moles' main predators are tawny owls and buzzards, stoats, cats and dogs, along with some vehicular casualties. Humans also kill many as agricultural or garden pests.
Life cycle: At the start of the breeding season, males enlarge their territories in search of females. Nests are made in spherical chambers, each lined with dry plant material. Females give birth to a litter of three or four naked babies in spring. These are weaned at four to five weeks. At this time, the young start to leave the nest, when you're most likely to see a mole above ground. They disperse to establish new territories and are sexually mature by the following spring. Moles can live up to six years but rarely live beyond three years.
Garden habitats: Rural gardens, where the soil is deep enough to allow tunnelling.
Distribution: Throughout Britain but not in Ireland.

Rabbit
Oryctolagus cuniculus
Description: Unmistakable, with long ears and hind legs, the rabbit is usually sandy brown with a white tail. Smaller than the hare at up to 40cm long, it moves in little jumps. It is native to the Mediterranean region but was introduced to Britain by the Normans in the 12th century.
When to see it: All year round.
Nests: Rabbits live in groups of up to 30, in a system of tunnels and chambers known

as a warren, which they burrow into the soil. They are normally nocturnal but will come out in daylight if undisturbed, especially during the long days of summer.
Diet: Grasses, cereal crops, root vegetables and young shoots of meadow plants. Rabbits will eat tree bark, especially when snow covers other food sources. In turn young rabbits are preyed on by badgers, buzzards and weasels. Rabbits of all ages are taken by cats, foxes, stoats and polecats.
Life cycle: Breeding takes place between January and August. Non-monogamous, females bear one litter of three to seven young per month. She makes her nest inside a burrow, using grass and soft fur from her chest and belly. The young are born blind, deaf and almost hairless, and are weaned after about four weeks. They are sexually mature at around four months of age. Rabbits don't often live for more than three years. Over 90 per cent die in the first year of life, mostly in the first three months.
Garden habitats: Typically larger rural gardens or gardens next to allotments.
Distribution: Rabbits are now widespread throughout Britain and Ireland, but are absent from the Isle of Rùm (Inner Hebrides), the Scilly Isles and a few smaller islands.

Stoat *Mustela erminea*

Description: The stoat is larger than the weasel (males are around 30cm long, females slightly smaller). It has gingery-red fur with a cream belly and a long tail with a black tip. Some individuals, especially in Scotland, turn white in winter. Stoats tend to hunt along ditches, hedgerows and walls or through meadows and marshes, often running in a zigzag pattern.
When to see it: March to November.
Nests: Stoats typically make their dens in the former nests of prey, of which there may be several within a stoat's territory. Male and female stoats live separately, marking their territories with scent. In spring, territories merge as individuals look for a mate.
Diet: Rabbits and small rodents.
Life cycle: Stoats use delayed implantation, so they mate in summer but don't give birth until the following spring. This includes the current year's young, which become sexually mature within a couple of weeks of birth. Females raise large litters of up to 12 blind, deaf and almost furless young. She feeds them for up to 12 weeks until they are ready to hunt alone. On average, stoats live for one to two years.
Garden habitats: Typically larger gardens in rural areas near farmland.
Distribution: Widespread and common throughout Britain and Ireland. They are legally protected in the Republic of Ireland but not in the UK.

Weasel *Mustela nivalis*

Description: The weasel is smaller than the stoat (males are about 20cm long, females shorter). It is gingery brown, with a cream belly and a short tail (with no black tip).
When to see it: March to November.
Nests: Weasel dens are usually nests of former prey and may contain the remains of food. There may be several such dens within a weasel's home range. Male and females live in separate territories. In spring, males extend their territories to look for a mate.
Diet: Small rodents, particularly field voles. A weasel's size enables it to search tunnels of mice and voles. It doesn't hibernate and even hunts in snow. Small birds, eggs and young rabbits may also be taken if rodents are scarce.
Life cycle: Females bear only one litter of four to six young per year. The young are weaned at four weeks and can kill at eight weeks; they disperse to set up their own home territories at 12 weeks. Few weasels live beyond the age of two.
Garden habitats: Mostly mature rural gardens.
Distribution: Widespread and common in Britain, apart from most offshore islands. Absent from Ireland.

Rats

▲ The brown rat is a common 'unwelcome visitor' to gardens.

As wildlife gardeners we provide food and shelter for a range of species, but are often too picky about who turns up as a result. We might create brilliant habitats for hedgehogs but be upset when foxes come along, or leave out food for birds but tut at the squirrels that learn to use the feeder, too. Perhaps the least popular are brown rats, which may be drawn to your garden by your bird feeding station, compost bins and pond, none of which you created for them.

Like all wildlife, rats will come into gardens if there is food, water and shelter available. They're known for setting up home in compost bins and will, if left undisturbed, quickly multiply. They will also burrow into buildings and are extremely adept at finding a way in – a rat once excavated a hole at the base of my gas meter and followed the pipe into my flat (luckily I noticed before it brought its friends). I know gardeners who tolerate and even encourage rats, and I think I would be more accepting of them if I lived in a more rural location (there are plenty on the allotment and they don't trouble me there). But I will always discourage them from setting up home in my small urban garden, as I'm mindful of them entering my house, as well as those of my neighbours.

But, while most of us wouldn't want rats in the garden, I'd like you to think about what it means to create habitats for one species over another, and the responsibilities involved in doing so with as little harm as possible. Would you leave food out for birds or hedgehogs and then poison for the rats that are attracted to it? Can you see why that might be problematic? Rat poison is often the first 'solution' for gardeners with a 'rat problem', but the problem often begins with the behaviour of the gardener. We leave poison out and have no real control over who eats it – rats are known to cache food and may take it out of the specially designed boxes and stash it elsewhere. Will it eventually be eaten by rats or will other species nibble at this 'food store'? And might it enter the food web if a dead or dying rat is unwittingly eaten by a barn owl or fox?

My point is, if our actions lead to a problem that we then have to 'fix', could we not simply change our behaviour to avoid creating a problem in the first place? Rats are grain eaters and are therefore instantly attracted to bird food. It's not too hard to discourage them – regularly sweep up any spilled seed or use a tray to stop seed spilling on the ground, and consider using more expensive food, which generates far less waste. But we could stop feeding birds altogether and focus on natural methods of feeding birds instead (see pages 123–24). This should stop the rats coming in, setting up home and causing problems. It would make our gardens safer for all as a result.

How to deter rats

Rats need access to food and water, so by cutting these off (such as taking down your bird feeders or blocking access to your shed), you will force them to set up home elsewhere. However, you may feel you need to take more direct action.

Electronic devices

These emit a high-pitched sound that rats can't stand but which is inaudible to humans. Worth trying if you have a lot of them.

Traps

Live traps are available. However, these must be checked at least every eight hours and there are potentially serious welfare issues because animals in the traps become stressed and can die. No studies have been conducted to assess the impact of releasing rats elsewhere and landowner's permission would be required to release them.

Poisoning

Poison can harm pets and other wildlife, and is ethically problematic to use, especially if the rats have been attracted to your garden because you feed the birds. Use this as an absolute last resort only. The safest method is to put the poison in bespoke rat boxes and place these along their run or near a source of water. Rats are clever and they may simply avoid the boxes.

Keeping rats out of your compost bin
- Rats like dry compost, so regularly watering it can put them off. However, only do this if you know a rat is living in the heap, as you could inadvertently be harming hedgehogs and bumblebees.
- Avoid adding cooked scraps and dairy or meat to the heap.
- Rebuild the heap, laying a wire mesh, such as fine chicken wire, beneath. This stops rats burrowing in from the bottom.
- Regularly turn the heap, but only if you know hedgehogs / slow-worms / bumblebees aren't nesting in it.

ID parade

Brown rat *Rattus norvegicus*
Description: The brown rat is fairly large (15–27cm long) with a long, scaly tail, pointed snout and short ears. It typically has brown to brownish-grey fur, but can vary in colour from white to almost black. Native to central Asia, the brown rat was introduced to the British Isles in the 18th century. Not territorial, it lives in hierarchical groups according to size and age. Rats are carriers of disease, including Weil's disease.
When to see it: All year round.
Nests: Rats dig burrows and runs, but also live in buildings and sewers.
Diet: Almost anything, including cereal, spilled seed from bird feeders, invertebrates and cooked foods. In turn, young rats are an important source of food for owls, polecats, stoats and foxes.
Life cycle: Breeding takes place all year round. Females are sexually mature at four months old and give birth to around five litters of 6–11 young each year. The young are born blind and hairless, but are weaned at three weeks.
Garden habitats: Virtually anywhere there is shelter and food.
Distribution: Widespread and common.

Large mammals

Large mammals are not always welcome in gardens. There's often the worry that they will wreak havoc or cause thousands of pounds' worth of damage; for example, badgers have a reputation for digging up lawns, while deer have a tendency to munch young plants. Foxes are considered to be an inconvenience by some: too brazen, a threat to pets and chickens. But others love them and welcome them with open arms.

Whatever your preference, there's probably not much you can do about these mammals coming into your gardens, so here we will look at ways to minimise damage as well as what to feed them, should you want to offer supplementary food.

Assuming you want to attract them, gardening for these mammals involves opening your garden to them and enabling them to feed (and even breed, if your garden is large enough). Many gardens are suitable for a fox den, but encouraging badgers and deer to set up home can be tricky – it's much easier to lure them in to feed. Why not set up a feeding station and watch them from the comfort of your home?

▲ A determined fox can get into just about any garden.

◀ Fox cubs are a joy to watch.

▶ Deer can browse and destroy many garden plants.

Badgers

▲ Badgers (*Meles meles*) are fascinating creatures and are wonderful to observe in the garden.

Many people welcome badgers to their gardens. They may visit at dusk in family groups and are a delight to watch. However, they can cause damage, particularly to lawns and plants, which they have a tendency to dig up in search of earthworms and larvae such as leatherjackets.

Regardless of how you feel about them, fencing them out is unlikely to stop them. Badgers are strong animals and will find a way in if they want to. It's worth remembering that badgers travel ancient routes long ago decided by their ancestors. Sometimes houses and even whole estates are built on top of these. You might look at your broken fence and wonder why badgers keep knocking it down – to the badger you have built a fence on a well-used walkway. Some estates are built on traditional feeding grounds and therefore badgers are forced to travel into gardens in search of food.

A little understanding goes a long way here. Perhaps make their life slightly easier by installing badger gates in your fence. You could even leave food such as apples scattered across your lawn. This will reduce damage to your garden and provide you with a fantastic opportunity to get close to these animals.

If badger activity in your garden is too much, it's worth asking your local badger group (see Resources, page 188) for advice, especially in the unlikely event that they start digging a sett.

Badgers and the law

Badgers are protected in accordance with the Protection of Badgers Act 1992 which makes it an offence to kill, injure, persecute or trap a badger, or to damage, destroy or obstruct a badger sett. However, in some areas, particularly in the South West, licences are obtained to cull badgers where they are thought to spread bovine tuberculosis (bTB) among cattle. At the time of writing, the debate on the role badgers play in the spread of bTB continues, with many conservation groups arguing that badgers are being blamed unfairly. For further information, visit The Wildlife Trusts website (see Resources, page 189).

Feeding badgers

If you want to lure badgers into your garden to feed, here's what to offer them:

- Dog or cat food
- Seedless grapes
- Apples
- Pears
- Plums
- Unsalted peanuts
- Peanut-butter sandwiches

ID parade

Badger *Meles meles*

Description: A nocturnal mammal with a long, black-and-white striped face, peppery-grey body, and black underside and legs. Low-set and stocky, it can reach up to 90cm long, including its tail.
When to see it: March to November.
Nests: It lives in a sett, a large system of underground tunnels and chambers where it nests, rests and spends winter. Each badger group typically has a main sett and several smaller, tributary setts dotted around the territory. Groups typically number around six, but can extend up to 23. Territories range from 30ha to 150ha, depending on the habitat, with boundaries marked by latrines in which they leave their droppings.
Diet: A variety of invertebrates, especially earthworms. They also may dig up bumblebee or wasp nests to feed on the larvae within. Badgers are predators of hedgehogs.
Life cycle: Mating takes place between February and May. Only one female badger per group normally breeds. Unusually, mated female badgers hold on to their fertilised eggs without implanting them in the womb until December (known as delayed implantation). Litters of up to three cubs are born in February, and are blind and hairless. They usually appear above ground after eight weeks and are fully weaned from three months. Badgers can live up to 14 years, although it's unlikely that they will reach this age – around one-fifth of adults die each year.
Garden habitats: Typically large, mature gardens or gardens near existing habitats.
Distribution: Widespread in Britain (south and east) and Ireland, but less common in Scotland and absent from offshore islands.

Foxes

Foxes can be found all over Britain, both in rural and more urban areas. While some gardeners are happy to welcome them, others would rather they stayed away. Fox dens are common in gardens, especially in urban areas. A house I lived in in London had a fox den beneath the decking. I loved to sit and watch them play but was less enthusiastic when they extended their den into my ornamental borders.

Foxes and the law
Foxes are not legally protected. Traditionally they were hunted for their fur, and fox-hunting remains today, although only 'without dogs'.

Feeding foxes
If you want to lure foxes into your garden to feed, here's what to offer them:

- Dog or cat food
- Cheese
- Scraps
- Fruit
- Cooked vegetables
- Chicken

Mange in foxes

Sarcoptic mange (also called canine mange) is a horrible condition that typically affects urban foxes and can kill them if left untreated. It's caused by a parasitic mite, *Sarcoptes scabiei*, which burrows into the skin and causes itching and irritation, eventually causing the fox's fur to fall out. As foxes become more preoccupied with scratching, they spend less time eating and ultimately waste away. Treatments are available to help wild foxes, and it's thought a protein-rich diet can help them build their strength up to fight infection. For more information, contact The Fox Project (see Resources, page 189).

ID parade

Red fox *Vulpes vulpes*

Description: A dog-like mammal around 70cm long (males are slightly bigger than females), with deep red-brown fur, a white belly and a white-tipped bushy tail.
When to see it: All year round.
Nests: Foxes live in small family groups, holding territories ranging from just $0.2km^2$ in urban areas to $40km^2$ in rural areas. They make burrows, or dens, within these territories.
Diet: Foxes are omnivores, which means they will eat virtually anything they come across. They are known for stealing chickens from hen houses, but will also eat invertebrates, rats, pigeons, slugs, fruit, berries, roots, dead animals and discarded human food.
Life cycle: Foxes mate in late December to January, and the female (vixen) gives birth to up to five cubs from March to May. The cubs venture from the nest after about four weeks. Between August and November, they are ready to leave the family to set up new territories of their own. Most foxes live for just two years.
Garden habitats: Large and small gardens, wherever they can find food and breed.
Distribution: Widespread and common, except on some Scottish islands.

Deer

There are six species of deer in the British Isles. Only two of these – red and roe deer – are native. Fallow deer were probably brought here by the Normans and are considered naturalised. The other three species – muntjac, Chinese water and sika deer – were introduced in the late 19th and early 20th centuries from Asia. The deer most likely to come into our gardens are fallow, muntjac and roe deer.

Although beautiful and majestic, deer can cause damage in gardens. And while it's usually hard to keep them out, you can take steps to reduce the amount they cause. If they're coming in, it's worth finding out which species you're dealing with, so you can take the most appropriate action to limit damage.

▲ Muntjac deer are the deer species most likely to visit gardens.

The three types of deer damage are:

- fraying – where males rub themselves against the bark of young trees
- thrashing – where males use their antlers to whip woody plants and low branches
- browsing – where deer eat the shoots and tips of plants

To completely keep deer out of your garden you need to erect a strong fence at least 1.8m tall with a mesh size of 7.5x7.5cm or less. Stake it to the ground or partially bury it to prevent deer from getting in from beneath. It's also important to create an exit for them, such as a self-closing gate or jump, in case they do manage to get in and then need to escape. Cattle grids or gates can also be fitted on driveways. Electric fencing can be effective against larger deer species, but this is not a good idea in urban areas.

Or you could accept that deer are in your garden and learn to live with, and love, them. Fit protective guards around the trunks and stems of broadleaved trees, use netting guards to shield conifers and shrubs. Growing deer-resistant plants and providing natural food alternatives (see box opposite) can also limit damage.

▲ Fraying damage caused to a tree by deer.

Planting schemes

Deer have preferences for different plants, so sowing plants they don't like to eat may reduce damage to your garden.

Vulnerable plants	Deer-resistant plants
Bluebell *Hyacinthoides non-scripta*	*Camellia*
Clematis	Hellebores *Helleborus*
Crocus	Herbaceous peonies *Paeonia*
Fuchsia	*Hosta*
Geranium	*Hydrangea*
Heather *Calluna vulgaris*	*Iris*
Holly *Ilex aquifolium*	Jasmines *Jasminum*
Honeysuckle *Lonicera*	Lavenders *Lavandula*
Lupinus	Poppies *Papaver*
Pansies *Viola*	Rhubarb *Rheum x hybridum*
Pines *Pinus*	Rock roses *Cistus*
Roses *Rosa*	Sedums *Sedum*
Rowan *Sorbus aucuparia*	
Sweet William *Dianthus barbatus*	

In large gardens, it's a good idea just to accept that deer may come in. By growing the plants they eat in the wild, you're less likely to suffer losses of your prized herbaceous plants if they do visit your garden.

The British Deer Society (see Resources on page 188) suggests allowing these plants to grow in the garden:

- Blackberry *Rubus fruticosus*
- Campions *Silene*
- Dandelion *Taraxacum officinale*
- Hoary cinquefoil *Potentilla argentea*
- Rosebay willowherb *Chamaenerion angustifolium*
- Rowan *Sorbus aucuparia*
- Sweet lupin *Lupinus polyphyllus*
- Redshank *Persicaria maculosa*
- Ribwort plantain *Plantago lanceolota*
- Yarrow *Achillea millefolium*

◂ Fallow deer typically reside in large open habitats, so don't expect them to visit if you have a small urban space.

ID parade
Deer

Fallow deer *Dama dama*

Description: A medium-sized deer up to 179 cm long and 120cm to the shoulder. It is variable in colour but is typically gingery brown with white spots on the back. Some are darker brown and others almost white. It has a long, twitching tail with a black stripe and white rump patch with black margins. Males have impressive broad, flat, palmate antlers. Fallow deer are native to south-west Asia, but were introduced to England by the Normans in around AD 1100. They live in small herds.
When to see it: All year round.
Diet: Grasses, herbs and young trees, plus autumn seeds such as acorns and beech mast.
Life cycle: The breeding season, or rut, takes place in autumn and the young (fawns) are born in summer. They can live to 16 years.
Garden habitats: Living in small herds, usually in open woodland and parkland, they may come into nearby gardens to feed.
Distribution: Now the most common deer in England, they are also widespread in Scotland, Wales and Ireland.

Muntjac deer
Muntiacus reevesi

Description: Our smallest deer, growing up to 91cm long and 52cm to the shoulder – slightly larger than a fox. It is red-brown in summer, turning grey-brown in winter, and has a ginger forehead marked with either black lines (males) or a dark diamond shape (females). It has a dark rump and a small tail with a white underside. Males have short, slightly hooked antlers and long, protruding teeth. Native to south-east China, muntjac were introduced to Britain in the early 20th century. They quickly became established in south-east England and are still spreading. Their small size helps them adapt to suburban habitats and they can do serious damage to important wild flowers – bluebell (*Hyacinthoides non-scripta*), honeysuckle (*Lonicera periclymenum*), orchids, oxlip (*Primula elatior*) and primrose (*Primula vulgaris*). Muntjac do not form herds but are seen either alone or in family groups of a doe with her kid.
When to see it: All year round.
Diet: Young shoots of shrubs, woodland herbs and garden plants, but blackberry (*Rubus fruticosus*) and raspberry (*Rubus idaeus*) are their most important foods.
Life cycle: Muntjac breed all year round, with the female giving birth to just one kid, although she typically mates soon afterwards and can bear three young every two years.
Garden habitats: Although most commonly found in woodland, they will use nearby gardens.
Distribution: Widespread and increasing in number and range.

Roe deer
Capreolus capreolus
Description: A small deer up to 135cm long and 75cm to the shoulder. It is red-brown in summer but turns grey or pale brown in winter, and has a short tail with a white rump patch. Males have rough or ridged short antlers, usually with three points on each. Roe deer are native to the UK, dating back to 10,000 BC. They are solitary, forming small groups in winter.
When to see it: All year round.
Diet: Herbs, tree shoots, blackberry (*Rubus fruticosus*), heather (*Calluna vulgaris*) and ivy (*Hedera helix*).
Life cycle: The rut takes place from mid-July to mid-August. Males mate with several females, and females mating with several males has also been observed. Like badgers, the females delay implantation until January, and the young are born in May to June.
Garden habitats: Living mainly in woodland and forest, they may come into nearby gardens when populations are at high densities.
Distribution: Common and widespread throughout Scotland and England, except for parts of Kent and the Midlands. They are spreading into Wales from England.

Cats

Some wildlife gardeners go out of their way to deter cats from their gardens; others are cat lovers themselves. Whatever your thoughts, it's worth brushing up on the facts and taking steps to give your garden wildlife the best chances possible when forced to live among cats.

According to the Mammal Society (see Resources), British cats catch up to 275 million prey animals per year, including snakes, slow-worms, small mammals, and an estimated 55 million birds. It's not known if cats affect wildlife populations specifically. The RSPB suggests they don't really affect bird numbers, as many birds die of natural causes each year and cats often take weak, sick and injured over healthy prey, but many people believe they do.

Research conducted by the University of Sheffield suggests that, as well as killing birds, cats affect their behaviour too, which exposes their nests to other predators. Researchers placed a stuffed cat close to a blackbird nest for 15 minutes before removing it (they did the same with a stuffed grey squirrel and a stuffed rabbit). The birds reacted with alarm calls as well as dive-bombing and sometimes striking the cat. Although it was in place for only for 15 minutes, the birds continued to be affected for an hour and a half after the stuffed cat had been taken away, most crucially by delivering a third less food to their chicks than before the cat was introduced. This suggests that the simple presence of cats in gardens could affect the survival rates of bird chicks in the nest, as potentially they could receive far less food than those reared without such pressures. (The squirrel and rabbit were paid a lot less attention.)

What's more, the researchers continued to check the nests for 24 hours after the experiment and found that a quarter of those exposed to the cat were predated by crows or magpies. This suggests that the alarm calls of the parent birds alerted predators to the presence of nests they might otherwise not have found. Or it could be that, in responding to the threat of cat predation, the parent birds were merely less able to defend the nest against other predators.

More research is needed, but it's clear that cats do affect the wildlife in our gardens.

How to keep wildlife safe from cats

There are various steps we wildlife gardeners can take to stop cats taking garden wildlife as prey. The most obvious is to keep them indoors, particularly at night and especially in late spring and early summer, when baby and fledgling birds may be taken, as well as baby bats, small mammals, amphibians and reptiles. Putting a bell on your cat could alert wildlife to the presence of the cat, but may only serve to generate those alarm calls more quickly, which could then alert different predators to the location of the nest. Some swear by applications of lion poo on the borders, the smell of which is thought to deter cats, and there are also ultrasonic devices that emit a high-frequency alarm inaudible to humans, or a jet of water, which cats don't like.

For amphibians and small mammals, hiding places are key to living with cats, although no research has been done on the stress levels induced from hiding from a cat (i.e. they might not be killed by the cat but could the fear of the cat kill them instead?). Piles of stones, open compost heaps, log and stick piles, and spiky or spiny plants can all provide shelter for amphibians, reptiles and small mammals.

Fungi

Search for advice on gardening for fungi and you will likely be presented with page after page on what to do with 'problem fungi', how to get rid of honey fungus or fairy rings, and other tips on removing mushrooms from your garden. Yet the vast majority of fungi are harmless, and actually form a vital part of a healthy garden ecosystem.

Technically neither plant nor animal, fungi sits in its own kingdom. There are around 144,000 known species, which includes yeasts, rusts, smuts, mildews, moulds and mushrooms. Fungi live almost everywhere on the planet, many in soil or water, while others form close relationships with plants or animals.

In gardens, fungi play an important role in the breakdown of plant and animal matter, in soil health and structure, and in plant health. What's more, fungi helps soil store more carbon, making it a huge win in the fight against climate change. We should therefore do everything we can to increase fungi in our gardens.

Much of the fungi in our gardens exists underground in networks of thread-like hyphae, known as mycelium. These spread underground, helping plant roots absorb nutrients and connecting plants to each other. Studies suggest that plants connected to each other by fungi via their roots can protect each other and even – in some cases – feed each other. Fungi can help plants warn each other of insect attack, produce natural remedies to injuries and even make them more resistant to drought. In return, the fungi feed from the sugars stored in the plant roots. This relationship is known as symbiotic, as the fungi and plants help each other.

Many fungi produce fruiting bodies, known as mushrooms, which produce reproductive spores.

> **Mycorrhizal fungi**
>
> Many gardeners are familiar with mycorrhizal fungi, which is often added to the planting hole when planting trees and shrubs. However, mycorrhizal fungi are already present in healthy soils. They attach to plant roots and makes them more able to absorb essential nutrients like phosphorus, calcium, magnesium, nitrogen, potassium, zinc, copper and iron, helping them to grow better.

This usually occurs in autumn, and provides a feast for us and wildlife (do always make sure you can correctly identify mushrooms if you are foraging, as many species are inedible and can be extremely poisonous).

How to increase fungi in your garden

Make compost

Fungi can break down all sorts of things, including food waste, plant material and woodier bits of compost. They work with bacteria and invertebrates,

transforming waste into humus-rich compost that you can use as a soil dressing. You can add uncooked kitchen waste such as vegetable peelings, chopped-up plant material, woody stems and pieces of wood, along with grass clippings and leaves (or make a separate pile of leaves to make 'leaf mould').

Add dead wood

Dead wood supports numerous invertebrates that use it as a breeding habitat and source of food, but it also attracts fungi, which help to break down and therefore return its nutrients to the soil. It's worth remembering that different types of wood can attract different species of fungi. For this reason, I 'collect' logs and branches from homeowners and tree surgeons (with permission) to bring home to my log pile. My log pile is currently a varied mix of ash, hazel, willow, hawthorn, walnut, birch and oak, which provides huge potential for different species of fungi to colonise.

Avoid using plant foods

Artificial plant foods give plants a quick boost but have shown to reduce soil fertility over time, resulting in plants more susceptible to diseases, including problem fungi. By avoiding using them in the garden, you will promote healthy, natural growth that works in harmony as part of a healthy ecosystem.

Reduce digging

Regular digging of soil destroys its structure and the complex fungal relationships with it. By using no-dig methods to grow food and digging much less often, you can preserve soil structure and its fungal networks. That's not to say all digging is bad – occasional 'disturbance' mimics the role of ancient herbivores such as wild boar, and increases opportunities for plants and wildlife.

Honey fungus

Honey fungus is one of the very few types of fungi that are dreaded in gardens. Named after its honey-coloured mushrooms, there are several species which spread underground and latch on to the roots of woody and perennial plants, often with devastating consequences.

Honey fungus usually causes few problems in the wild where other fungi are able to compete with it and keep its growth in check – indeed, I've been living with honey fungus on my allotment for years without any problems. However, in gardens where soil health may be compromised due to over-cultivation, use of pesticides and where fungi is not usually encouraged, honey fungus can take over. This is proof, if you still needed it, that we should do all we can to rewild our gardens and turn them into diverse sanctuaries, away from the lasting effects of insecticides, herbicides and fungicides. We should also do all we can to promote fungi in our gardens and allotments, so there's more of an equilibrium and no one species can take advantage over others.

Other 'bad' fungi

Other fungi gardeners are encouraged to deter include black spot, mildews, blight, rust, and clubroot. By keeping your soil and plants healthy you can keep some of these fungi at bay, but it also pays to make sure you always grow the right plant in the right place so it doesn't become stressed due to a lack of food or light, or too much water or sunshine. If your plot is susceptible to potato or tomato blight, grow resistant varieties. What's more, learning to tolerate small fungal outbreaks, such as black spot or pear rust, will make you and your garden healthier in the long term.

ID parade
Fungi

The fruiting bodies of fungi – sometimes known as mushrooms and toadstools – are usually found in autumn, although some species, such as jelly ear fungus, can be seen in winter. Fungi grow in all sorts of places, but keep an eye out on your log pile and other dead wood, in borders of undisturbed soil, around the base of trees, on tree bark, and on lawns. Never harvest mushrooms to eat without being certain what you're picking – many poisonous species look similar to edible ones.

Field mushroom
Agaricus campestris
Cap: Up to 10cm across. White when young, developing peeling scales with age.
Stem: Short and white, narrowing at the base.
Ring: Thin.
Gills: Pink, maturing to brown then black.
Edibility: Edible.

Shaggy ink cap
Coprinus comatus
Cap: Up to 15cm wide. Pale with scales. Develops a conical shape with age.
Stem: Tall (up to 20cm) and narrow.
Gills: White, then pink, then dissolving to drip black 'ink'.
Edibility: Edible but best consumed without alcohol.

Fairy ring
Marasmius oreades
Usually found in rings in lawns.
Cap: 2–5cm across, pale brown.
Stem: Narrow.
Gills: Whitish.
Edibility: Edible but can be easily confused with other, poisonous, species.

Sulphur tuft
Hypholoma fasciculare
Occurs in large numbers from tree stumps and logs.
Cap: Up to 8cm across, bright yellow with orange tints and a brown centre.
Gills: Yellow, aging to brown.
Stem: Long and fibrous.
Edibility: Inedible.

Jelly ears *Auricularia auricula-judae*
Ear-shaped bracket fungus found on logs and other dead wood.
Bracket: Cup-shaped, developing lobes that make them look like human ears. Purple brown. Individual lobes can grow to between 3 and 10cm across.
Edibility: Edible.

Climate change

Climate change poses a huge threat to wildlife, both at home and around the world. Extreme weather and rising temperatures will kill and displace wildlife, interfere with the availability of food and push some species northwards, while others are unable to move elsewhere due to loss of habitat. All of this interferes with ecosystems and threatens our own survival.

Already, climate change is responsible for changes in the behaviour, distribution and abundance of some species in the UK.

▲ Adapted to cooler montane habitats, mountain ringlet butterfly numbers are declining as the climate warms.

Amphibians are more active over winter, which reduces their likelihood of surviving, and are breeding earlier in the season, potentially putting their offspring at risk of frosts and lack of food.

Bumblebees may be flooded when nesting or hibernating, and their nests are also vulnerable to sudden cold snaps and lack of food caused by low temperatures or heavy rain. Some species are moving north while others are already at their northerly limit and have nowhere to go. Others are trapped in fragmented pockets of habitat due to insufficient habitat corridors. Many rare species are surviving on the Thames Estuary which is likely to be under water by the end of the century – where will they move to and how will they get there?

Butterflies are migrating, with heat-loving species, such as the red admiral and comma, expanding northwards but cool-weather specialists, like the mountain ringlet, declining in areas where they used to thrive. Droughts can stop nectar production of flowers, preventing butterflies from feeding and finding a mate, while heavy rain can wash caterpillars off leaves.

Birds are, in some cases, nesting earlier, and then struggling to feed their chicks due to a lack of caterpillars. Extreme wind, rain and heat also affect survival and breeding success. Some migratory species are arriving earlier or leaving later, and a few – such as the chiffchaff – are overwintering in some parts of the country rather than migrating south in winter.

Hedgehogs are less likely to hibernate in milder winters, or will have a disturbed hibernation. This reduces their chances of survival as there is less food available in winter. Food availability in summer may be compromised due to earthworms retreating far into the soil in times of drought. Heavy rain may flood and destroy hedgehog nests.

Dragonflies are increasing in abundance and diversity, with most species moving northwards and expanding their ranges. Whether they continue to benefit from climate change remains to be seen.

Bats are likely to be disturbed during hibernation, which studies suggest may shorten their lives.

What can we do about it?

We need to drastically reduce emissions. At the time of writing global emissions are still increasing despite promises from governments around the world to reduce emissions in line with the 2016 Paris Agreement. We have already breached the 1.5°C agreed 'safe' limit of average global warming since industrialisation, and are on track to reach 2°C of average warming by 2045. This will put more people and wildlife at risk of extreme weather and temperatures, and lead to significant food and water shortages.

While collective action is key to pushing governments to make the right climate decisions, there's a lot we can do in our gardens. Many of these actions will not only help fight climate change but can also mitigate against some of the extremes of temperature, helping us and wildlife to cope better. All of this can be done while creating habitats for wildlife to breed, feed and and rest. Providing habitats and other opportunities for wildlife will also absorb carbon and draw it down into the soil.

Save water – the more water that our gardens can hold on to, the less flows into drains and overwhelms sewers (usually leading to the release of sewage into rivers and the sea). Capturing more water also prevents flooding and, conversely, fire. Dig a pond or swale to store water, and a land drain to divert water from your house gutters into. Using water butts lets you store water to use in dry weather. Fit as many as you have space for. Using less water also puts less pressure on mains water, which is reduced in times of drought.

Plant hedges – a hedge or other dense planting scheme will filter wind and slow it down, so can help reduce the velocity of wind in your garden

(as opposed to fences which cause turbulence on the leeward side that can damage plants. Because of this, hedges and dense plantings can also provide a sheltered spot (called a shelter belt) that will protect other plants and enable insects to feed without being blown about. Bats will also use the shelter belt, feeding on the insects accumulated there.

Grow more plants – studies have shown that plants help increase humidity and decrease temperatures, particularly in urban areas. They also trap polluting particles, helping to clean the air we all breathe, and absorb water, further preventing flooding and fire. Grow more shrubs and permanent planting, including evergreens that trap pollution all year round, and grow climbers up fences and walls to maximise your growing space.

Reduce hard surfaces – hard surfaces like patios and paved areas trap heat, increase risk of flooding and don't absorb CO_2. Dig a pond or grow more plants instead.

Plant trees – every garden has space for at least one tree, even if it's only a dwarf tree or a tree you can grow in a pot. Choose a native tree to maximise the opportunities for wildlife, especially one that provides berries, seeds or nuts in autumn. Trees provide habitat, absorb water, stabilise temperatures and soil structure, and create cooling shade for you and wildlife.

Build a compost heap – by composting your kitchen and garden waste you are reducing the amount sent to landfill, which releases greenhouse gasses – such as methane – as it breaks down anaerobically (without oxygen) underground. Composting also helps return nutrients to the soil, aiding soil structure and supporting fungal relationships that aid plant growth.

Wildlife gardening in a changing climate

The more habitats we create, the better for wildlife, but there are lots of other things we can do to use our outdoor spaces to help wildlife cope with the effects of climate change (see page 189).

Create habitat piles on slightly raised ground to prevent any hedgehog and bumblebee nests from being flooded in heavy rain.

Grow flowers for as long as possible to help pollinators on the wing in colder months. Early spring flowers include mahonia, winter honeysuckle, winter heather and winter clematis, and late summer/autumn flowers include *Verbena bonariensis*, rudbeckias, asters and Japanese anemones. If grown in a sheltered spot, perennial wallflowers can flower all year round in southern regions.

Grow flowers under cover to provide emerging queen bumblebees with a reliable and quick source of nectar and pollen. Choose a porch, greenhouse (with doors and windows open), conservatory or other sheltered space that provides full access but protects the flowers from rain. Also grow more robust flowers, like winter heather, which survive better in a downpour.

Make a hibernaculum for amphibians which, sited in a shady spot, will remain moist and cool even in times of extreme heat (see page 142).

Leave supplementary food (such as kitten biscuits) for hedgehogs to make up for natural food shortages (see page 164).

Top up your pond with stored rainwater to save tadpoles and other aquatic invertebrates during times of drought. This will also provide drinking and bathing opportunities for other species when sources in the wild dry up.

Make a hoverfly lagoon (see page 96) to mitigate against the drying out of 'rot holes' in woodland.

Water plants in dry weather (using stored rainwater) to keep nectar flowing for pollinators.

Identifying and recording wildlife

We all know the potential gardens have to support wildlife. But, as well as creating habitats for wildlife in our gardens, it's a good idea to keep biological records of the species that visit. This helps us understand what's using the habitats we create, and can also help naturalists build a bigger picture of how species are doing.

The process of making biological records involves recording observations from a known location, by a known person, on a known date, and it's important for four reasons:

1. It helps to influence the conservation of species. If we don't know what's living in our gardens and green spaces, how do we know what's missing or needs help?
2. It helps to influence planning decisions. Every planning decision depends on accessible wildlife information. The more you contribute, the more planning can be arranged around existing species.
3. It helps track species population changes, and the spread of invasive species such as the Asian hornet.
4. It helps measure uplift – if you dig a pond you can then track all of the species that arrive to your pond, so you can measure the positive effect this has had on your garden.

I like to think of recording as following on from wildlife gardening. If you're already gardening for wildlife, creating habitats and providing food, then recording is the logical next step. It's not only nice for you to see which species have found homes in your garden, but recording also contributes to wider ecological knowledge. With climate change, species are expanding and contracting their ranges, arriving in places they've previously not been recorded and even turning up to our shores from the continent. Gathering data from our gardens contributes to wider scientific knowledge around increases and decreases in populations.

Biological recording has been taking place for years. There are, nationally, excellent records of butterflies, birds and hoverflies, for example. But, in gardens, data is extremely lacking. And yet gardens can be incredibly rich habitats for a huge range of species. The zoologist Jennifer Owen recorded wildlife in her suburban Leicester garden over a 30-year period, from 1972 to 2002. Over the course of her study she found 1,997 insect species, of which 533 were parasitic wasps, 138 other invertebrates and 64 vertebrates. Imagine how many discoveries we would make, and how much we would contribute to the national picture of invertebrate declines and movements, if we all recorded what's going on in our gardens.

▲ A selection of moths in a moth trap.

How you can record wildlife

Build a species list – you can do this by simply photographing and recording species when you see them. Take a photo and upload it (see 'Where to add your records', overleaf). It helps if you can identify species before you upload photos to the site where they will be recorded but you don't have to.

Carrying out a regular count at a particular time – for example, spend one hour a week at the kitchen window, counting the birds you see.

Conduct regular surveys in the same areas – to record the variety and abundance of specific species in an area. You can do this once a month or at certain times of year, which helps track climate-related changes, and you can count everything or concentrate on particular groups.

> **Useful kit for recording**
> - Phone or a camera
> - Binoculars
> - Sweep nets
> - Pots
> - Notepad
> - Soil sieve

How to identify wildlife
There are many books, leaflets and websites to help you ID the species you find, along with Facebook groups and apps – like ObsIdentify – dedicated to the identification of certain species groups.

Where to find wildlife
There are loads of ways to find wildlife in your garden, from setting traps and cameras to looking in particular habitats to find certain species. As a general rule we know we'll find pollinators (bees, flies and butterflies) on flowers and sunny places

▲ Camera traps are a brilliant tool for discovering nocturnal visitors to your garden, such as hedgehogs.

such as a stone, amphibians in damp spots (in a pond in spring), invertebrates in compost heaps and beneath stones and logs. But there are other habitats to check out too.

You can also set a moth trap, trail camera, pitfall trap or malaise trap to record species. Malaise traps kill the insects they catch, so it's worth deciding how much you want to record. Jennifer Owen used malaise traps among other types and recorded huge amounts of species but this isn't something I'm comfortable doing – I like my wildlife alive.

> **Garden hotspots to find wildlife**
> - Garden border (pollinating insects)
> - Walls or fences (basking insects)
> - Areas of long grass/wildflowers (pollinators, caterpillars and other invertebrates)
> - Beneath stones and logs (detritivores, amphibians and invertebrates)
> - Compost heaps (detritivores/invertebrates)
> - Pond (aquatic invertebrates)

Start small

You may find that starting with a particular group can really help, rather than recording all things at once. When I started learning how to identify wildlife I started with bumblebees, using a small field guide to bumblebees of Britain and Ireland. I then moved on to solitary bees (many of which I still struggle with) and then butterflies and moths. I don't know every species, but I do know that if I take a photo of it, someone will be able to identify it for me and then I can add it to my record.

Tips on photographing insects

If you cast a shadow over an insect it will usually fly off. Approach very slowly and take photos as you go along, so at least you can bank a bad photo before (hopefully) getting a good one. If you approach slowly and then the insect flies off at the last minute, you will have no photo to even attempt a record with. Always step softly as many animals (including aquatic species) can detect ground vibrations.

▲ Garden butterflies, like this red admiral, are some of the easiest species to identify and record.

Where to add your records

In the UK there are a number of tools available to record wildlife. Two of the most popular for recording across all wildlife groups are iNaturalistUK and iRecord. Records added to these systems are available to national recording schemes, local environmental record centres and can be shared with the NBN Atlas, the UK's largest collection of biodiversity data.

iRecord App

Once you have identified the species you have seen, you can submit details to the iRecord online platform, which receives and verifies more than one million wildlife sightings in the UK each year.

iNaturalistUK

Best for beginners as there are experts on hand to help you with identification before you submit a record. Feeds back to iRecord.

Specific group surveys

You can also contribute to the species recordings of specific conservation groups including:

- Nature's Calendar (by the Woodland Trust)
- National Plant Species Monitoring Scheme
- UK Pollinator Monitoring Scheme (Flower-Insect Timed Count) between April and September
- Butterfly Conservation's Big Butterfly Count (July)
- Moths – what's flying tonight?
- European Ladybird app
- Birdtrack (with British Trust for Ornithology)
- Bat Conservation Trust's National Bat Monitoring Programme
- Badger Trust's Reporting Centre

Glossary

Arachnid Joint-legged invertebrate with eight legs and a two-segmented body.

Blowfly A large and typically metallic blue or green fly that lays its eggs on meat and carcasses.

Brood parasite Insect that steals food from other insects. Typically, those that lay their eggs in the nests of other insects and their young consume the eggs/larvae of the host wasp.

Chelsea chop A pruning method that enables you to limit the size and delay the flowering season of some herbaceous plants. So-called because this is usually carried out at the end of May, the time of the RHS Chelsea Flower Show.

Elytra The hardened forewings of beetles.

Ericaceous (of compost) Suitable for heathers and other lime-hating plants.

Exoskeleton An external outer skeleton that covers and protects the body of an inverte-brate.

Halteres Balancing organs of a fly, taking the place of the rear wings – tiny, club-shaped balancers vibrate during flight and detect when the fly veers off course.

Honeydew As aphids and other sap-sucking insects feed on sap they take in more sugar than they need and eject it as honeydew.

Instar (of insect larva) A stage between two moults.

Invertebrates Animals without a backbone.

Larva/e Immature offstage of an insect that goes through complete metamorphosis.

Mandibles The jaws of an insect.

Metamorphosis The stages of change that occur before an animal reaches its adult form.

Parasitoid Insects that lay eggs on or near the larvae of other insects; the larvae develop on or in the host and kill it.

Parthenogenesis Asexual reproduction without the need of a male, mating or pollination. Common in lower plants and some invertebrates.

Proboscis The elongated, flexible mouthpart of an insect.

Pupa/e The stage of insects between larvae and adult of those insects that undergo complete metamorphosis.

Rot hole Cavities in which water accumulates, usually within the main trunk but they can also occur at root bases or at branch forks.

Sooty mould A black velvety mould that grows on the surfaces of leaves and stems affected by honeydew.

Thorax The middle section of the insect body.

Resources

Amphibian and Reptile Conservation Trust
arc-trust.org/

Amphibian and Reptile Groups of the UK (ARG UK)
arguk.org

Badger Trust
badger.org.uk

Bat Conservation Ireland
batconservationireland.org

Bat Conservation Trust (BCT)
bats.org.uk
National Bat Helpline: 0345 1300 228

BeeBase
nationalbeeunit.com
Please visit for information on how to report Asian hornet sightings to the NNSS.

Bees, Wasps and Ants Recording Society (BWARS)
bwars.com/content/atlases-and-maps
Online distribution maps from NBN data.

British Beekeepers Association
bbka.org.uk
Includes list of local beekeeping associations for England only.

The British Deer Society
bds.org.uk

British Dragonfly Society
british-dragonflies.org.uk

British Hedgehog Preservation Society (BHPS)
britishhedgehogs.org.uk
Helpline: 01584 890 801

British Trust for Ornithology (BTO)
bto.org

Buglife
buglife.org.uk
The only organisation in Europe devoted to the conservation of all invertebrates.

Bumblebee Conservation Trust (BBCT)
bumblebeeconservation.org

Butterfly Conservation caterpillar food plant lists
Butterflies
butterfly-conservation.org/sites/default/files/butterflyfoodplants.pdf

Moths
butterfly-conservation.org/sites/default/files/moth-foodplant.pdf

The Fox Project
foxproject.org.uk

Freshwater Habitats Trust
freshwaterhabitats.org.uk

Froglife
froglife.org

Garden Wildlife Health
gardenwildlifehealth.org
Aims to monitor the health of, and identify the threats to, British wildlife. Those with no internet access are asked to call the GWH vets on 0207 449 6285.

Great British Non Native Species Secretariat (NNSS)
nonnativespecies.org

Hedgehog Street
hedgehogstreet.org

The Mammal Society
mammal.org.uk

National Moth Recording Scheme (NMRS)
mothrecording.org

People's Trust for Endangered Species (PTES)
https://ptes.org/britains-first-national-hedgehog-conservation-strategy

RHS – Get Involved
rhs.org.uk/get-involved

RHS Plants for Bugs
rhs.org.uk/plants-for-bugs

RHS Plants for Pollinators
rhs.org.uk/science/research/plants-for-pollinators

RSPB Big Garden Birdwatch
rspb.org.uk/whats-happening/big-garden-birdwatch

Scottish Badgers
scottishbadgers.org.uk

UK Beetle Recording
coleoptera.org.uk

UK Butterflies
ukbutterflies.co.uk/index.php

UK Moths
ukmoths.org.uk

Vincent Wildlife Trust (VWT)
vwt.org.uk

Wildlife Gardening Forum
wlgf.org

Wildlife Insight: illustrated guide to British caterpillars
wildlifeinsight.com/guide-to-british-caterpillars

The Wildlife Trusts
wildlifetrusts.org

Actions
wildlifetrusts.org/actions

Climate change
wildlifetrusts.org/things-you-can-do-climate-change

Gardening
wildlifetrusts.org/gardening

Species information
wildlifetrusts.org/wildlife-explorer

Acknowledgements

I couldn't have written this book without the patient help of Emma Pritchard and Julie Bailey at Bloomsbury, copy-editor Marianne Taylor, designer Rod Teasdale, and everyone else at Bloomsbury who has helped make this book possible. At the RHS, thanks to Helen Griffin, Simon Maughan and Helen Bostock, and thanks to Joanna Richards, Jamey Douglas and Thomas Hibbert at the Wildlife Trusts. I'm also grateful to Becki Lawson for help with the Garden Health pages, Judith Conroy for her tips on Blooms for Bees and John Little for his advice on using sand to make solitary bee habitats. Thanks to Helen Ginn for kindly letting us use her garden and Sarah Cuttle for photographing it. Thanks, as ever, to my brilliant agent Jane Turnbull, who always has my back.

Index

Bold type indicates main ID entry for species.

Acanthosoma haemorrhoidale **106–07**
adder 144
Aegithalos caudatus **133**
Agaricus campestris **181**
Aglais urticae **73**
amphibian spawn failure 144
amphibians
    attracting 135, 138
    climate change 182, 184
    declines 143–44
    diet 143
    diseases and health 144
    garden habitat 136, 137, 143
    hibernaculum 142
    pond creation 12, 136, 138, 139–40, 143
    shelter spots 14, 178, 186
    see also frog; newt; toad
Andrena fulva **50**
Andrena nigroaenea **50**
Anguis fragilis 14, 137, 142, **146**
ant, black/garden 104, **112**
Anthidium manicatum **49**
Anthocharis cardamines **72**
Anthophora plumipes see bee species, solitary: hairy-footed flower
aphid-hunting wasps **82**
aphids 100, **103–04**
    predators 19, 27, 33, 75, 77, 94, 95, **105**, 123
    relationship with ants 104
Apis mellifera see honeybee
Apodemus sylvaticus see wood mouse
Araneus diadematus **115**
Arctia caja 70, **74**
Arion hortensis **114–15**
    see also slugs and snails
Asian hornet 83
Auricularia auricula-judae **181**
avian pox 122, 128

badger 171, 172, **173**
    gates 172
    legal protection 173
bats
    boxes and roosts 155–56
    cats 154
    climate change 182
    declines 152
    diet 156
    garden habitats and planting 153, 154
    hedges (bat corridors) 13, 183
    legal protection 155, 156

    lighting 130, 154
    monitoring 157
    urban habitats 157
bat species
    brown long-eared 157, **158**
    Daubenton's 153, 157, **158**
    Leisler's 157
    Natterer's 157
    pipistrelle, common and soprano 154, 156, 157, **158**
    serotine 157
bee habitats 37, 65
    bumblebee 39–40
    honeybee 12, 39
    leafcutter bees 46–47
    solitary bees 44, 52–53
bee health
    bumblebee lifecycle 35, 36
    pesticide effects 18
    solitary bee lifecycle 43
    see also Asian hornet; bee hotels, parasites/disease
bee homes, natural 27, 36, 38, 39, 184
    bee bank 51
    compost heaps 14, 39
bee hotels 54–55, 56, 61
    best buys 59
    bird-proofing 60
    bumblebee nester, making 40
    cleaning and managing 60–61
    making your own 58
    parasites/disease 55, 60
    solitary bees 43–45
    tips on materials and size 56–57
    use by wasps 57, 59, 75, 77, 78
bee species, honeybee 35, 36, 38, 41, **42**, 83
    see also honeybee
bee species, social
    buff-tailed bumblebee 28, 39, **41**
    common carder bumblebee 39, 40, **41**
    garden bumblebee **42**
    red-tailed bumblee **42**
    tree bumblebee 38, 40
    white-tailed bumblebee 39
bee species, solitary
    ashy mining **50**
    brown-footed leafcutter 45
    buffish mining 50
    hairy-footed flower 36, 37, 44, **48**, 57
    ivy 36, **50**, 51
    patchwork leafcutter 45, **48**
    plasterer **51**
    red mason 37, 41, 44, **49**, 55, 61
    specialist feeders 52–53
    tawny mining **50**
    Willughby's leafcutter 45
    wool carder 44, **49**
bee-fly, large **98**
beetles
    attracting 85–87

    declines 84, 88
    dung beetles 85, 86, 88
    ground beetles 84, 85, 88
    ladybirds and aphid control 19, 33, 85, 105
    pollinators 87, 90
    rove beetles 84, 85
beetle species
    cockchafer **89**
    great diving **89**
    minotaur 88
    pollen **90**
    red soldier 85, 87, **90**
    seven-spot ladybird **90**
    stag 84, 88, **90**
    thick-legged flower 87, **91**
    violet ground **91**
    wasp 15, 86, **91**
birds
    cats 178
    climate change 182
    declines 69, 129, 133, 134
    effects of lighting 130
    garden habitat/planting 116–17, 118, 120–21
    health risks 125–26, 128–29
    making nest boxes 119
    pesticide effects 20–21
    providing cover/shelter 13, 16
birds and feeding 122
    commercial food 125–26
    making a feeder 127
    natural sources 11, 13, 16, 105, 123–24
    rats 169
    risks (feeders) 128, 129
    risks (foodstuffs) 125, 126
birds and water
    birdbaths 12, 39
    pond access 12, 124, 140
    winter (heated) birdbath 117
bird species
    blackbird **131**, 178
    blue tit 21, 68, **131**
    chiffchaff 182
    coal tit **131–32**
    goldfinch 116, 123, 125, **132**
    great tit 21, 119, 122, 128, **132**
    greenfinch 122, 125, 128, 129, **132–33**
    house sparrow 119, 122, 123, 125, 126, 128, **133**
    long-tailed tit **133–34**
    robin 19, **134**
    starling 119, 122, 123, 126, 128, **134**
blue tit 21, 68, **131**
bluebottle **97**
Bombus lapidarius **42**
Bombus lucorum 39
Bombus pascuorum 39, 40, **41**
Bombus hortorum **42**
Bombus hypnorum 38, 40
Bombus terrestris 28, 39, **41**

Bombylius major **98**
bonfires, best practice for 150, 161
bovine tuberculosis 173
braconid wasps 81
Breeding Bird Survey 129
brimstone butterfly **72**
Bufo bufo **145**
    see also amphibians; toad, common
bug species
    common green shield **106**
    froghopper **106**
    hawthorn shield **106–07**
    pond skater **107**
    water boatman **107**
    see also aphids
bugs, true 100, 103–04, 106–07
    attracting 101, 102
bulb fly, large 94, **99**
bumblebee
    see bee garden habitats; bee species, social
bumblebee nester 40
    see also bee hotels
butterflies
    attracting 27, 62–63, 65–66
    declines 26, 69
    indicator species 69
    life cycle 68
    nectar plants 64
    overwintering habitat 16, 64
    pollinators 31, 34
butterfly species
    brimstone **72**
    comma 182
    meadow brown **72**
    mountain ringlet 182
    orange-tip **72**
    red admiral **73**, 182
    small tortoiseshell **73**

Calliphora vomitoria **97**
Capreolus capreolus see deer, roe
Carabus arvensis 88
Carabus violaceus **91**
Carduelis carduelis see goldfinch
cat food 126, 164, 173, 174
caterpillar
    food plants 72–74, 124
    life cycle 68
cats and risks to wildlife
    bats 154
    medication risk 20–21, 93
    mitigation 137, 150, 178
centipedes 108, 111, **114**
Cepaea nemoralis **113**
    see also slugs and snails
chalcid wasps **79**
Chloris chloris see greenfinch
Chloromyia formosa **97**
Chorthippus brunneus see grasshopper
Chrysis ignita **82**
chytridiomycosis 144
climate change

    addressing 183–84
    effects on wildlife 182
    wildlife gardening 184
Clytus arietis 15, **91**
coal tit **131–32**
Coccinella septempunctata **90**
    see also ladybirds and aphid control
cockchafer **89**
Colletes daviesanus **51**
Colletes hederae see ivy bee
compost heaps and wildlife 14, 108, 124, 178, 179–80, 186
    beetles 85
    bumblebees 38, 39, 40
    climate change 184
    hedgehogs 160
    rats 169, 170
    reptiles 137
Coprinus comatus **181**
cricket, speckled bush 108, **113**
Cyanistes caeruleus see blue tit

dairy products, risks of
    birds 126
    compost 170
    hedgehogs 164
Dama dama see deer, fallow
damselfly, common blue **112**
damselfly habitat 108, 124
dead wood habitat 5, 15, 36, 38, 85, 86, 180
deer 175–76
Deilephila elpenor (elephant hawk-moth) 70, **73–74**
detritivores 14, 85, 110, 186
Dipogon variegatus **81**
diseased material, disposal of 19
dog food 126, 164, 173, 174
dogs
    dangers of dried fruit 126
    pesticide risk to wildlife 20–21, 93
dragonflies
    climate change 182
    habitat 12, 108, 124
dragonfly, common darter **112**
Dytiscus marginalis **89**

earthworm 19, 108, 110, **114**
earwig 105, **113**, 158, 164
Ectemnius spp. **80**
Enallagma cyathigerum **112**
Episyrphus balteatus **98–99**
Erinaceus europaeus see hedgehog
Erithacus rubecula (robin) 119, **134**

fairy ring mushroom **181**
fallow deer 175, **177**
    see also deer
field mushroom **181**
flies
    garden habitat for true flies 92–93

hoverflies 94–96
fly species
　Batman hoverfly 92, **98**
　bluebottle **97**
　broad centurion **97**
　crane 93, **97**
　golden dung **97**
　hornet hoverfly **98**
　large bee-fly **98**
　large bulb hoverfly 94, **99**
　marmalade hoverfly 98–99
　owl midge (moth fly) **99**
　thick-headed **99**
Forficula auricularia see earwig, common
fox, red 171, **174**
frog 145
　dangers to 137, 139, 140
　see also amphibians
froghopper **106**
fungi
　encouraging good fungi 179–80
　honey fungus and 'bad' fungi 180
　mycorrhizal 179, 181
fungi species **181**

Gerris lacustris **107**
glyphosate, effects of 18–19
goldfinch 116, **132**
　diet 123, 125
Gonepteryx rhamni 72
grass snake 137, 143, 144, **146**
　attracting 12, 14
　refugium 142
grass, importance of long 16, 64, 123
　see also meadow planting
grasshopper 108, **113**, 123
great tit 21, **122**, **132**
　avian pox 128
　nest box dimensions 119
greenfinch **132–33**
　diet 125, 133
　disease and declines 122, 128, 129

hare, brown 166, **167**
harvestmen 115
hawk-moths 70, **73–74**
hedgehog **165**
　access to/from ponds and drains 12, 137, 140, 161
　attracting 13, 14, 15, 149, 160–61
　box/house 163
　climate change 182, 184
　dangers to 7, 161, 164, 170, 182
　declines 69, 160, 165
　diet 7, 111, 164, 165, 184
　hibernation 161, 165, 182
　highway 17, 162
　predators 173
　societies and campaigns 162
hedges 13, 16, 23, 123, 183

Helix aspersa **115**
　see also slugs and snails
honey fungus 180
honeybee 35, 36, 37, 38, 41, **42**
　access to water 12, 39
　Asian hornet 83
　pesticide effects 18
hornet, Asian 83
hornet, European **79**
hoverfly
　declines 26
　garden habitat 94–95
　hoverfly (silage) lagoon 96, 184
　larvae and aphids 105
hoverfly species
　Batman hoverfly 92, **98**
　bumblebee 94
　hornet 94, **98**
　large bulb 94, **99**
　marmalade **98–99**
hunting wasps 80
Hypholoma fasciculare **181**

ichneumon wasps 81
identifying wildlife 186
indicator species 69
ivy bee 36, **50**, 51

lacewings and aphid control 19, 105
ladybird, seven-spot 90
ladybirds and aphid control 19, 33, 85, 105
lagoon, hoverfly/silage 96, 184
Lasius niger see ant, black
leaf litter 15, 124
　beetles 85
　bumblebees 37, 38
　butterflies and moths 64, 70
　hedgehogs 13, 160, 161
　wasps 78
Leisler's bat 157
Leptophyes punctatissima see cricket, speckled bush
Lepus europaeus see hare, brown
lighting, outdoor 130, 154
Limacus maculatus **115**
Lissotriton vulgaris see newt, smooth
Little, John 51
lizard, common 137, **146**
lizard, diet 143
lizard, sand 137
log/twig pile 15, 109, 118, 124, 154, 180
　amphibian shelter 136, 178
　beetles (see also dead wood habitat) 86
　bumblebees and wasps 37, 78
　mammal shelter 150, 160, 161, 178
long-tailed tit **133**
Lucanus cervus see beetle species, stag

Lumbricus terrestris see earthworm

Macroglossum stellatarum 74
mammals, gardening for 147, 149
　see entries for each species
Maniola jurtina 72
Marasmius oreades **181**
meadow planting 16, 53
　annual meadow 65, 66
　mini meadow 66, 67
　perennial ('hay' meadow) 65, 66, 67
mealworms 126
　risk to hedgehogs 7, 164
Megachile centuncularis 45, **48**
Megachile versicolor 45
Megachile willughbiella 45
Meles meles see badger
Meligethes spp. **90**
Melitta tricincta 53
Mellinus arvensis **80–81**
Melolontha melolontha **89**
Merodon equestris see bulb fly, large
mice 11, 149–50
　see also wood mouse
millipedes 14, 108, **114**
mole, European **167**
molehills 166
moths
　attracting/planting for 27, 62–63, 65–66
　declines 4, 26, 69
　indicator species 69
　life cycle 68
　nectar plants 64
　pollinators 31, 34
　role and range 70
　trapping and identifying 71
moth species
　angle shades 73
　elephant hawk-moth 70, **73–74**
　five-spot burnet **74**
　garden tiger 70, **74**
　hummingbird hawk-moth 74
mulch, benefits of 19, 22, 108, 124, 136
muntjac deer 175, **177**
　see also deer
Mustela erminea 166, **168**
Mustela nivalis **168**
Myathyropa florea 92, **98**
Myodes glareolus see vole, bank
Myotis daubentonii (Daubenton's bat) 153, 157, **158**
Natrix helvetica see grass snake
Natterer's bat 157
nematodes 19, 111
neonicotinoid, effects of 18, 20
newt, smooth 135, **145–46**
newts 135, 139, 140
　diet 139, 143
　see also amphibians
niger seeds 125

Notonecta glauca **107**
nuts (native plants) 11

Ocypus olens **89**
Oedemera nobilis see thick-legged flower beetle
Oniscus asellus **114**
Opiliones **115**
Oryctolagus cuniculus **167–68**
Osmia bicornis see red mason bee
overwintering care
　food 11, 28, 62
　shelter 16, 61, 64, 87, 137

Palomena prasina **106**
parasitoid
　flies 19, 60, 93, 98, 99
　wasps 19, 56, 60, 75, 79, 82, 105, 185
Parus major see great tit
Passaloecus spp. **82**
Passer domesticus see sparrow, house
paving
　detrimental effects and mitigation 23, 69, 165
　risk to young amphibians 137, 140
peanuts 125
　attracting badgers 172, 173
　risk to hedgehogs 7, 164
peat use 22
Periparus ater **131–32**
pesticides 18–21
　agricultural/commercial use 26, 122, 125
　livestock medications 20, 88
　natural alternatives 19
　neonics and glyphosate studies 18–19
　pet treatments/medications 20–21, 93
　slug pellets 110
Philaenus spumarius **106**
Philanthus triangulum 80
Phlogophora meticulosa 73
pipistrelle bat, common and soprano 154, 156, 157, **158**
plant lists
　bats 153
　birds 120–21, 123, 124
　bumblebees 39
　caterpillar 72–74, 124
　deer 176
　hoverflies 95
　leafcutter bees 47
　nectar plants 64
　pollinators 29
　see also entries for particular species
plasterer bee 51
Plecotus auritus (brown long-eared bat) 157, **158**
pollinators, planting for 30–32, 34
　breeding habitats 33–34

container planting 28
planting basics/timing 27, 28–29
pollinator study 39–40
principles 25–26
pond skater **107**
ponds 149, 153
　amphibians 12, 138, 139–40, 143
　birds 12, 118, 124, 140
　child safety 141
　drought 184
　hedgehogs 12, 137, 140, 161
　hoverfly (silage) lagoon 96, 184
　invertebrates 37, 78, 93, 102, 108
　maintenance 140
　making a pond 139
　types 12
principles, wildlife gardening
　food 10–11
　peat use 22
　pesticides and alternatives 18–21
　plants and planting 23
　shelter 13–16
　water 12
　see also wildlife corridors
Psychodidae family 99

rabbit **167–68**
Rana temporaria see frog, common
ranavirus 140
rat, brown 169, **170**
recording wildlife 185–87
red admiral butterfly 73, **182**
red mason bee 37, 41, 44, **49**, 55, 61
red soldier beetle 85, 87, **90**
reptile
　declines 137, 143
　diet 143
　garden habitat 15, 137–38
　hibernaculum 142
　refugium 142
reptile species
　adder 144
　common lizard 137, **146**
　grass snake 12, 14, 137, 142, 143, 144, **146**
　sand lizard 137
　slow-worm 14, 137, 142, **146**
resistant cultivars 19
rewilding gardens 5
robin **134**
　nest box dimensions 119
roe deer 175, **177**
　see also deer

scabious mining bees 53
Scathophaga stercoraria **97**
Sciurus carolinensis **159**
Sciurus vulgaris 149, **159**
seedheads 11, 14, 124, 129
serotine bat 157

191

shaggy ink cap fungus 181
shelter belt 13, 23, 153, 183
  see also hedges
shrew, common 151
shrews, attracting 149–50
Sicus ferrugineus 99
slow-worm 137, **146**
  shelter spots 14, 142
slugs and snails 19, 108, 110–11
  homing range 111
  predators 85, 110, 123, 143, 164
slug species
  garden 114–15
  green cellar 115
snail species
  brown-lipped 113
  garden 115
soldier beetle, red 85, 87, **90**
Sorex araneus 151
sparrow, house 133
  avian pox 128
  nest box dimensions 119
sparrow (house and tree), feeding 122, 123, 125, 126
spider, garden 115

squirrel, grey 159
squirrel, red 149, **159**
stag beetle 84, 88, **90**
starling 128, **134**
  diet 122, 123, 126
  nest box dimensions 119
stoat 166, **168**
  bat boxes 156
  bee hotels and parasites/disease 55
  bee pollination rates 41
  beetle declines 88
  bird nesting behaviour and cats 178
  bumblebee behaviour 18
  fungi support network 179
  garden invertebrates 185
  glyphosate (fungi, crop disease and soil quality) 18–19
  neonicotinoids 18, 20
  pesticides in pot soil 19
  pet treatments/medications 20–21
  plants improving air quality/temperature 183

pollination planting 39–40
slug and snail homing range 111
Sturnus vulgaris see starling
suet products 126
sulphur tuft mushroom 181
sunflower hearts/seeds 125
  risks to hedgehogs 7, 164
Symmorphus bifasciatus **82**
Sympetrum striolatum 112

Talpa europaea **167**
Tipula paludosa (crane fly) 93, **97**
toad, common **145**
  dangers to 140, 143
  see also amphibians
trichomonosis (*Trichomonas gallinae*) 122, 128
Turdus merula (blackbird) 131, **178**
Typhaeus typhoeus 88

Vanessa atalanta see red admiral butterfly
Vespa crabro **79**
Vespa velutina 83

Vespula vulgaris **79**
vole, bank **151**
  attracting 11, 13, 14, 149, 150
Volucella bombylans 94
Volucella zonaria 94, **98**
Vulpes vulpes **174**

wasps 75
  attracting 78
  social wasps 76–77, **79**
wasps, solitary 77, 79–81
  using bee hotels 82
wasp species, parasitoid
  chalcid **79**
  ichneumon and braconid wasps 81
wasp species, social
  common **79**
  European hornet **79**
wasp species, solitary
  aphid-hunting **82**
  European beewolf **80**
  field digger 80–81
  hunting **80**
  ruby-tailed **82**

spider-hunting **81**
willow mason **82**
water *see* ponds
water boatman **107**
weasel **168**
wildflower meadows *see* meadow planting
wildlife corridors (highways) 17, 62, 162, 182
wood mouse 149, **151**
woodlouse 114
worms *see* earthworm

Zootoca vivipara see lizard, common lizard
Zygaena trifolii **74**

Photograph credits

Bloomsbury Publishing would like to thank the following for providing photographs and for permission to reproduce copyright material within this book. While every effort has been made to trace and acknowledge all copyright holders, we would like to apologise for any errors or omissions, and invite readers to inform us so that corrections can be made to future editions.

With the exception of the photographs listed on the page numbers below, all photographs in this book remain © Sarah Cuttle.

Key to page positions t = top; l = left; r = right; b = bottom; tl = top left; tr = top right; cl = centre left; c = centre; cr = centre right; bl = bottom left; br = bottom right.

Abbreviated photo agency names: AL = Alamy; G = Getty Images; iS = iStock; MP = Minden Pictures; NP = Nature Picture Library; RS = RSPB Images; SS = Shutterstock.

1 Paul Sawer/RS; **2** Harry Wedzinga/iS; **10** b Amy Lewis; **11** t Thijs de Graaf/SS, cl VIDOK/G, cr Margaret Holland **12** tr RHS/Carol Sheppard, bl Amy Lewis; **13** Jake Stephen/Getty; **14** RHS/Tim Sandall; **15** RHS/Tim Sandall; **16** RHS/Neil Hepworth; **17** blickwinkel/AL; **18** RHS/Tim Sandall; **19** Christian Mueller/SS; **20** tl Wirestock Creators/SS, tr Shaplov Evgeny/SS; **21** Steve Midgely/SS; **23** Oxford Media Library/SS; **24** RHS/Neil Hepworth; **26** RHS/Carol Sheppard; **27** Photofusion/G; **30** RHS/Joanna Kossak; **31** t Chris Lloyd/RS, **bl** Richard Becker/AL, **br** Phil Savoie/NP; **32** tl Phil Savoie/NP, tr RHS/Andrew Halstead, cl Thomas Delahaye/AL, cml Peter Entwistle/AL, cmr RHS/Andrew Halsead, cr RHS/Leigh Hunt, **b** RHS/Carol Sheppard, bcl RHS/Carol Sheppard, bcr SS, br SS; **33** Kim Taylor/NP; **34** Alex Hyde/NP; **35** Chris Gomersall/SS; **38** t Alan Wright, c RHS/Julian Weigall, b SS; **39** Peter Wilson/RP; **41** tl Anna Guthrie, tr Rachel Scopes, b SS; **42** t RHS/Helen Bostock, c WT Richard Burkmar, b LightShaper/iS; **43** Kate Bradbury; **44** Kate Bradbury; **45** l SS, c Premaphotos/AL, r RHS/Jason Ingram; **46** Richard Becker/MP; **48** t Kate Bradbury/SS; **49** t Penny Frith, b SS; **50** tl Keith Hider/SS, bl HWall/SS, br Gucio_55/SS; **51** bl bearacreative/SS, br Charlie Harpur; **52** cl HWall/SS, bl Wirestock Creators/SS, br HWall/SS, br Wirestock Creators/SS; **53** tl Henri Koskinen/SS, cl Steven Falk, bl Steven Falk, br HWall/SS; **54** RHS/Jason Ingram; **55** Helen Bostock; **59** t nurturing-nature.co.uk, b SS; **62** RHS/Mark Bolton; **64** tl RHS/Tim Sandall, tr RHS/Tim Sandall, cl RHS/Tim Sandall, cr RHS/Mark Bolton, b RHS/Mark Bolton; **60** RHS/Jason Ingram; **66** RHS/Jason Ingram; **70** tl Denis Jackson, tr SS, b SS; **72** t Heidi Morris, c Chris Lawrence, b Scott Petrek; **73** t Richard Burkmar, tr GaryBP/SS, bl Gabrielle Horup, br Donald Sutherland; **74** tl John Bridges, bl Margaret Holland, br Alex Cooper/SS; **75** Nick Upton/RS; **77** SS; **78** RHS/Andrew Halstead; **79** tl SS, tr RHS/Malcom Storey, b Hugh Lansdown/MP; **80** t Kate Bradbury, c Margaret Holland, b Jon Hawkins; **81** l Penny Frith, r Richard Becker/MP; **82** t Jeremy Early, c Richard Becker/AL, b Andy Sands/NPL; **83** t Damien Meyer/G, b RHS/Andrew Halstead; **84** RHS/Tim Sandall; **85** Jon Hawkins; **87** tr Jon Hawkins, bl RHS/Carol Sheppard; **88** RHS/P. Becker; **89** tl Viktor_Kitaykin/iS, bl SS, br Viktor_Kitaykin/iS; **90** tl Bob Coyle, tr Alex Hyde/NPL, bl Rod Williams/NPL, br David Longshaw; **91** tl SS, bl Goldfinch4ever/iS, br SS; **94** tl RHS/Andrew Halstead; **95** t RHS/Rachel Tanner, b RHS/Paul Debois; **97** tl Bob Coyle, tr Alex Hyde/NPL, bl Rod Williams/NPL, br David Longshaw; **98** tl Nick Upton/NPL, tr Chris Lawrence, br Richard Burkmar; **99** t Nick Upton/NPL, c RHS/Andrew Halstead, b Rod Williams/NPL; **100** RHS/Entomology; **101** Rachel Scopes; **103** Paul Maguire/SS; **104** RHS/Entomology; **105** t HHelene/G, c SS, b SS; **106** l RHS/Andrew Halstead, r RHS/P. Becker; **107** t Richard Burkmar, bl Chris Lawrence, br Picavet/G; **108** t RHS/Paul Debois, b Richard Burkmar; **110** l RHS/Georgi Mabee, r Amy Lewis; **111** t SS, b RHS/Neil Hepworth; **112** t Don Sutherland, c Les Binns, b RHS/Andrew Halstead; **113** tl Chris Lawrence, tr RHS/Katie Prentice, bl Philip Precey, br SS; **114** tl Alex Hyde/NPL, tr Chris Lawrence, c Joy Russell, b RHS/Andrew Halstead; **115** tl Tom Marshall, c Paul Richards, b Austin Morley; **116** Kevin Sawford/RS; **117** Margaret Holland; **119** SS; **120** SS; **121** SS; **122** RHS/Paul Debois; **123** Ray Kennedy/RS; **124** t Ian_Redding/iS, b Ballygally View Images/SS; **125** Amy Lewis; **126** Gillian Day; **127** David Chapman/AL; **128** DKeith/SS; **129** tl czjonyyy/SS; br SS; **130** georgeclerk/iS; **131** t Richard Burkmar, bl Amy Lewis, br Gillian Day; **132** l Margaret Holland, r Amy Lewis; b Derek Moore; **133** l SS, r Gillian Day; **134** Jon Hawkins; **135** Richard Burkmar; **136** t Peter Cairns/NPL, b waeske/iS; **137** RHS/Andrew Halstead; **140** l Roger Tidman/RS, r RHS/Andrew Halstead; **141** t RHS/Paul Debois, m Misty Hutton, b Emma Websdale; **142** David Tipling/NPL; **143** l Sue Kennedy/RS, r imageBROKER.com/AL; **144** RHS/Andrew Halstead; **145** t SS, bl Dawn Monrose, br Margaret Holland; **146** t David Chamberlain, c James Rogerson, b Bruce Shortland; **147** Gillian Day; **148** tl Roger Tidman/MP, tr Jon Hawkins, bl Margaret Holland, br Steve Waterhouse; **150** Donald Sutherland; **151** tl David Hosking/MP, bl Menno Schaefer/SS, br MikeLane45/G; **152** SS; **153** RHS/Jason Ingram; **155** Amy Lewis; **156** Tom Marshall; **157** l PeterPaunchev/iS, r Emma Bradshaw **158** t Tom Marshall, c Fenlanddavid/iS, **b Tom Marshall; 159** l, c Gillian Day, r RHS/Tim Sandall; **160** t myartoym/SS, b cath5/SS; **162** RHS/Lee Beel; **163** RHS/Julian Weigall; **164** David Tipling/RS; **165** Tom Marshall; **166** r Linda Lyon/G, b RHS/Entomology; **167** tl Damian Waters, tr Steve Bottom, b Jon Hawkins; **168** l Margaret Holland, r John Hawkins/MP; **169** SS; **170** Margaret Holland; **171** t SS, b Jon Hawkins, r Rob Sutherland/AL; **172** SS; **173** t Jon Bowen, b Don Sutherland; **174** l Paul Williams/NPL, r Don Sutherland; **175** t Don Sutherland, b RHS/Andrew Halstead; **176** RHS/Andrew Halstead; **177** t Don Sutherland, c Jon Hawkins, b Amy Lewis; **179** Reflexpixel/SS; **180** DigitalPearls/SS; **181** cl Kabar/SS, bl Gonzalo Jara/SS, tr Oli S photography/SS, cr kristof lauwers/SS, br godi photo/SS; **182** M G East/SS; **183** Kristine Rad/SS; **184** Evan Lorne/SS; **185** Alex Hyde/MP; **186** WildMedia/SS; **187** Kevin Sawford/RS.